'In *World Factory*, the audience becomes
around factory desks playing out a carefu
requires you to run a clothing factory in China. How to deal with a
troublemaker? How to dupe the buyers from ethical retail brands?
What to do about the ever-present problem of clients that do not
pay? Because the choices are binary they are rarely palatable. But
what shocked me – and has surprised the theatre – is the capacity of
perfectly decent, liberal hipsters on London's South Bank to become
ruthless capitalists when seated at the boardroom table… Capitalism
subjects us to economic rationality. It forces us to see ourselves as
cashflow generators, profit centres or interest-bearing assets. But that
idea is always in conflict with something else: the non-economic
priorities of human beings, and the need to sustain the environment.
Though *World Factory*, as a play, is designed to show us the parallels
between nineteenth-century Manchester and twenty-first-century
China, it subtly illustrates what has changed.'

Paul Mason, *Guardian*

'A smart, complex and genuinely thought-provoking exercise in game
theatre: this ingenious thought experiment from Zoë Svendsen and
Simon Daw [is] an ambitious, provocative and intricate piece of
game-making, evading easy answers and polemic while succeeding
in making us think – and think hard – about the cost of our clothing.'

Natasha Tripney, *The Stage*

'This is a show that tests the relationship between our competitive
impulses and other factors. How far will ethical and environmental
considerations impinge on commercial ones? Wrestling with this
question, against the clock, makes for a richly absorbing experience.'

Henry Hitchings, *Evening Standard*

'We know that the ultra-competitive fashion industry is engaged in a constant cost-cutting battle. We know that the price war starts on our high streets. We know that results in poor working conditions, even sweat-shops and child labour. However, *World Factory* lets you live those ideas as an embodied experience. It's one thing to be told about low rates of pay, another to be the person implementing those rates. Responsible capitalism isn't easy. You've little control. Consequences are unforeseeable, not least the invisible environmental impact, and decisions must be made, sometimes arbitrarily and often without any real alternative. The sense of competition carries you away, and the game is great fun as a result, but there are no prizes for principles. Only your numbers count. It's your conscience that has to cope.'

Matt Trueman, *What'sOnStage*

'Many of us like to think of ourselves as ethical shoppers, but *World Factory* brings the murky economic realities of the globalised textile industry uncomfortably close to home. This clever and entertaining show... is part documentary drama, part game – and the result is smart, mischievous and genuinely thought-provoking.'

Sarah Hemmings, *Financial Times*

'This lively and ambitious show from the directors and designers Zoë Svendsen and Simon Daw amuses, involves and unnerves us throughout its 100 minutes... How neatly *World Factory* makes us complicit in the process of exploitation before pulling us back to see a bigger picture that ain't so pretty.'

Dominic Maxwell, *The Times*

'An innovative and thoroughly well-researched exploration of the global textile industry, which remains not only comprehensive and coherent, but genuinely enthralling from start to finish.'

Bob Trafford, *City A.M.*

WORLD FACTORY
THE GAME

NICK HERN BOOKS

London
www.nickhernbooks.co.uk

A Nick Hern Book

World Factory: The Game first published as a paperback original in Great Britain in 2017 by Nick Hern Books Limited, The Glasshouse, 49a Goldhawk Road, London W12 8QP, in association with METIS Arts

Cover image: Zoë Svendsen
Back cover image: David Sandison

Designed and typeset by Nick Hern Books, London
Printed in the UK by Mimeo Ltd, Huntingdon, Cambridgeshire PE29 6XX

A CIP catalogue record for this book is available from the British Library

ISBN   978 1 84842 633 7

CONTENTS

"The bulk of the inhabitants of a great city, such as London, have very indistinct notions of the means whereby the necessaries, the comforts or the luxuries of life are furnished.

[Money is a] veil which hides the producer from the consumer."

George Dodd
Days at the Factories
1843

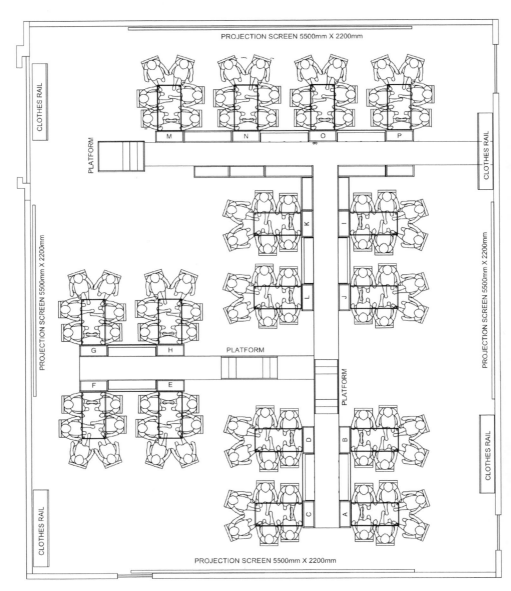

Plan of *World Factory* layout, Young Vic production
© Simon Daw

INTRODUCTION

Made more than 150 years ago, journalist George Dodd's observation that money is 'a veil that hides the producer from the consumer' still rings uncannily true. It is also a reminder that there is nothing new about global trade. Globalised consumer capitalism has simply made the patterns of production and consumption incredibly complex, such that no process of research can easily lift the 'veil'. We can rarely see the extent to which the things we take for granted in our everyday lives connect us to the lives of so many others across the world, and we struggle to see the relations that drive the larger mechanism. *World Factory* is a project that explores how we might render visible – and historicise – such interconnectedness. It thus exists in a variety of media: as an exchange of ideas between China and the UK; as a research project; as a digitally enhanced cotton shirt; as an app; as a series of public conversations; as a theatre performance; and now it is the book you are about to read. Each of these elements intersect with one another – and none would have been possible without those that preceded it. Through its various components, the project explores ways of representing and asking questions of global consumer capitalism, using the textile industry as both a lens and a case study. In doing so, *World Factory* takes us from the heart of the Industrial Revolution in nineteenth-century Manchester to the world behind the 'Made in China' labels on our clothes today.

The performances of *World Factory* first played at the New Wolsey Theatre, Ipswich, and the Young Vic Theatre, London, in May and June 2015, where it sold out; it subsequently toured to Cambridge Junction, ACCA in Brighton and HOME, Manchester in 2016; and was then performed at Brierfield Mill, a former textile mill, at the Fabrications Festival in 2017. At the heart of the performance is a scenario-based card game that invites audiences to make decisions as though they were running a small Chinese clothing factory. METIS worked with Shanghai-based Chinese theatre director Zhao Chuan and his company Grass Stage to undertake the research and development for the project. From the pooled research, Grass Stage and METIS each produced a theatre production germane to their own social and political contexts in China and the UK respectively.

This book reproduces the card game at the heart of the UK theatre performances. Audiences who experience the game in the context of the performance trace a single story route through the 'pathways' of the *World Factory* game, playing in groups of up to six over the course of an hour: 'a year in the life of a Chinese clothing factory'. Casino-style, audiences trade in workers and money, replicating the capitalist system of production and consumption explored – but whilst *World Factory* represents the values of capitalism through the structure of a game, implying there are 'winners' and 'losers', it is nevertheless a game in which players have to decide what it means to win. In performances, most 'factories' play between 18 and 24 cards over the course of an hour, interlinking questions of ethics, fashion, environmental impacts, working conditions, migration and globalisation. Almost every card offers a binary decision between two incompatible alternatives, presented as a kind of ethical conundrum. Indeed, frustration with having to decide between two un-ideal options in fact catalyses what is often a utopian discussion of ethics between audience members. In the performance, a bespoke computer system ran the card system. For the book, we have devised an analogue system for reading/playing the cards, which sometimes involves following a short decision tree to identify which card to go to next, depending on earlier decisions made.

Every story on the cards is based on extensive research conducted over several years in the UK and China; and therefore, as well as the entire card game, this book includes a series of essays that continue to explore the wider geopolitical context of the textile industry and of contemporary capitalism. Jenny Chan's essay is essential reading to understand the Chinese context more specifically, in relation to migrant workers, and the contradictions inherent in the state-sanctioned, manager-controlled trade union. Brendan

Burchell and Alex Wood's piece on precarious work in the UK makes clear the impacts of uncertainty on workers in the UK. Orsola Da Castro, founder of the campaigning organisation Fashion Revolution, sets the scene for understanding the mind-blowing scale of overconsumption of resources inherent in fast fashion, whilst Joe Smith and Renata Tzsyck demonstrate that there are other ways of operating, historically and into the future, focusing on the idea of quality. Mark Sumner's essay on the complexities of farming organic cotton goes to the heart of the issues at the very start of the supply chain, whilst Lucy Norris explores what happens to our discarded garments – and how they enter a new round of capitalist circulation. Norris opens up some wider questions around sustainability and capitalism which are taken up in Ha-Joon Chang's contribution, inviting us to think about the relationship between contemporary financial structures and the social dangers of short-termism.

Overall, *World Factory* requires a different kind of reading from a standard play script – or even a choose-your-own-adventure book. For the stories on the cards are shaped by the conditions under which decisions are being made, conditions which are not directly visible when reading – that is, in particular, the size of your workforce and the amount of money you have. In the performances, audiences were provided with *World Factory* money and folders of Worker ID Cards, but for ease of reading we have created a chart to help readers keep track of those elements (page 267) that are external to the cards, but integral to the story. It is therefore not just a question of turning the pages, but of keeping note of your factory's size and financial situation – as decision-making is always conditioned by circumstance.

What follows is a description of the wider context for the game, and its relationship to the theatre performance. If you want to encounter the game directly first (which we would recommend), please turn to page 13 for instructions of how to read/play.

Origins

In October 2010, in a bar in Shanghai, I had the conversation that catalysed *World Factory*. I had just been introduced to theatre director Zhao Chuan, who runs an independent performance company in Shanghai, by Rachel Parslew, a British arts consultant with long-term links to the Chinese cultural scene. Zhao Chuan was talking to me about communism, capitalism, textiles and factories – and the idea of the 'world factory' (a direct rendition of the phrase in Chinese that is more commonly translated into English as 'workshop of the world'). I sat there, uncomfortable in my skin, wondering which of my clothes had 'Made in China' on the label, feeling awkward that I did not know. But Zhao Chuan was not talking about the conditions in contemporary Chinese clothing factories, but about the social and political situation of nineteenth-century Manchester. As the site of the first global cotton exchange, the industrialisation of Manchester in the eighteenth and nineteenth centuries was globally connected. As well as being the epicentre of the invention of the factory system, Manchester also played an important role in the lives of those who sought to critique the social ravages of industrial capitalism; Marx's reading of British economic theorists in the Manchester library would change the course of history.

In that one conversation, my perception of myself as simply a privileged consumer with a vague sense of guilt was upended. Suddenly there was a historical as well as a global connection to the question of the making and wearing of garments – and a sense that any given relationship to consumption involved participation in a system much bigger and more complex than any myth of 'consumer choice' would allow. With artist and designer Simon Daw, we started to explore the potential for collaboration. In 2012, 2013 and 2014, Zhao Chuan visited the UK to undertake research with us, and for his own performances in China, whilst in 2013 and 2014, Simon and I spent time in Shanghai and Beijing.

On the UK side we decided to focus specifically on the production of clothing for our investigations, given our British history as originators of the factory system in the Industrial Revolution, and its connection with textile production. We then discovered clothing to be the ideal territory for an investigation of contemporary consumer capitalism, thanks to the invention of 'fast fashion' in the mid-2000s. Fast fashion is produced by a management system that exponentially increases customer footfall in shops, the number of garments sold, and the speed of design and production. It is often considered to be led by 'consumer choice', but the reality is that the system is driven by the maximisation of profit. Shortening the amount of time garments are on the shop floor has proved spectacularly successful in driving up sales, but produces proportionately more waste. Clothing itself is generally more poorly produced, and is designed not to last, with prices often no indicator of quality. This has led to a situation described by designers we interviewed in both the UK and China, in which even 'design' itself becomes extremely fast, and entirely sales-driven, rather than a creative act.

Early on, it had become clear that standard methods of research were not bringing us tangibly closer to understanding this global system – so we decided to attempt to have a shirt manufactured in a Chinese clothing factory. To our surprise, our investigations proved successful. After being turned down by a number of factories once it became clear we wanted to interview workers, we found several factories willing to engage with the project. As well as visiting a button factory and a fabric factory, we were able to have a shirt manufactured, whilst watching every stage of its production in the garment factory – from pattern-cutting to button-holing to final packing – as well as interviewing the workers involved. As the minimum order was for two hundred shirts, the *World Factory* shirt is for sale online – and it is digitally enhanced (with barcodes that unlock stories of its production) to enable wearers to explore all the people and processes behind its making. It later turned out that factory owner Madame Wang had herself once been a textile worker, from farmland then just outside Shanghai that is now a factory district. Being too sickly as a child to work in the fields, she was assigned to a clothing factory. After borrowing money from friends and families, she then opened her own factory – which folded under the pressures of business after just a few years. Being aware that she would never be able to repay her debts from a worker's wage, after a few years she took on further debt to start up again. Her factory is now a long-established, successful business producing workwear for all over China, the USA and beyond, specialising in using fabrics designed to withstand extreme temperatures.

The process of having to engage with the realities of manufacture provided a very different insight into the way this world works, particularly in terms of our recognition of the degree of day-to-day uncertainty, and the way that negotiation is everything when it comes to price and timescale. Madame Wang's biography further profoundly affected our perspective, justifying our decision to focus on the position of the managers of small factories, under pressure from all sides. By coincidence, we were in the midst of research and development at the National Theatre Studio when the Rena Plaza garment factory complex in Bangladesh collapsed in April 2013, killing over a thousand people and injuring many more. It was the response to this disaster that turned our attention to the way that the position of factory manager encapsulates the relationship between individual decision-making and systemic pressure, and shone a light on how we find it easier to blame individuals than change systems. The dramaturgical aim of creating a game structure was to explore this world, and then to offer an immersion in the conundrums faced by those at the sharper end of those global pressures brought to bear by consumer capitalism. Therefore, rather than the traditional relation between audience and characters, where we judge or empathise with them from a position external to the world represented, we invite our audiences to take up a position *within* it.

The Performance Structure

In both the performances and the book, it might appear that *World Factory* is fundamentally structured as a game – but this is not so. It deliberately lacks the key to any game: what the objective is, and therefore how to win. Indeed, our theatrical provocation consists of inviting audiences to reflect critically on what constitutes success in this system. There is a clear divergence between the values, on the one hand of profit and moneymaking (which involves speed, lack of care, and concentration of power in the hands of the bosses), and the values on the other, of people's rights (including children's) and care for the environment. In this, the game is mimetic of the system as it currently operates, with a disabling lack of transparency and little incentive or reward for ethical practice. Yet it is rarely a case of active amorality; the conditions in which most factories produce the goods for consumer capitalism do not allow for long-term, considered strategies that are run on ethical principles. It is often simply a case of sink or swim. Ethical practice takes time: real-life situations are complex, and the 'right' course of action is rarely evident. But taking time to make decisions flies in the face of the breakneck speed of contemporary business practice. What audiences have discovered in playing the game is that very Brechtian thing: if you are going to play, you are going to get your hands dirty. When it comes to survival, it is often a case of 'eat first, think later'.

The 'game' that is reproduced here was originally designed to be played in the context of the environmentally immersive performance. Audiences of up to 96 at a time were seated around 16 tables within a design that mixed a catwalk with a factory floor (see page viii for the original ground plan). The performance opened with Lady Gaga's pop classic 'Fashion!', complete with quick-fire quotations from three of the architects of contemporary consumer capitalism: Ronald Reagan, Margaret Thatcher and Deng Xiaoping. You will find some of these statements reproduced amongst the cards. This deliberately theatrical opening was followed by verbatim stories from the front lines of the 'world factory' phenomenon, spanning the UK's history of garment craft to the production of fast fashion in present-day China. In every performance, each 'factory' (up to 6 audience members grouped around a table) then received a red box from their 'dealer' (a member of the cast). The box contained instructions for how to play the game, with the idea being to evoke the culture of the family board game and the tangible pleasures of unpacking stuff from a box. It was a reminder that this game is less one of role-play than of decision-making – a bit like a cross between Monopoly and Poker.

Further cards were dealt by a 'dealer', each one managing 4 teams, with the stories on these cards unfolding to a backdrop of video footage of Chinese garment factories at work. As well as the general soundscape characteristic of a garment factory, a localised, desk-mounted sound system also played to each 'factory' a unique soundtrack that was specific to their chosen path through the game. For example, when the factory had 'completed' an item of clothing, the audience received an actual example of it from their dealer, to the accompaniment of an audio advertising jingle from the garment's brand. Over the course of the performance, each factory's clothes rail gradually filled with a variety of garments, the style and number of which was determined by the decisions taken. This tangibility of garment production is not easily replicable in the context of reading the book, but we have suggested keeping track of manufactured garments as a way of gaining a more specific sense of your factory's productivity.

In the book, you simply turn to the page with the card on it corresponding to the option you have chosen. In the performance, a barcode scanner was provided to each factory. When a decision over which option to take had been reached by the group, the barcode on the card was scanned corresponding to the option that had been chosen – with a satisfying beep that recalled a shop assistant scanning your latest purchase. The beeps slowly started to punctuate the soundscape of sewing-factory machinery and mixed with the live chatter of discussion – soon everyone was busy playing to a subliminally effective juxtaposition of production and consumption. Added to this was the increasingly sinister power dynamic between each factory and their 'dealer'. The dealer's role involved dealing the cards, and handling money, workers and garments. What might initially appear to audiences as simple service changed into something rather darker, for the dealers mediated the relationship between audiences and the game through giving encouragement, making threats and offering gnomic pieces of wisdom: like latter-day capricious Greek gods. Pages 253–60 details some of the ways in which the dealer interacted with the audience throughout the game.

Overall, the challenge that we set ourselves in creating the game – with the awareness that the original audience would only ever experience one route through – was to ensure that every individual route touched on a range of issues. The result is an overall structure that is best described as a story jigsaw. If you read multiple routes, you will re-encounter pieces of that jigsaw, but in different combinations, with different implications for the decisions that you are making. Demonstrated in grey on the Map of Card Routes (page 263) are the cards at which decisions occur in relation to stories that happen in almost all routes; these do not necessarily immediately alter the direction generally of your story pathway, but will have implications for the stories on later cards. There are 416 cards in total – with a significant number sharing similar segments of story occurring in different routes – but the structure of the relationship between these cards overall, the different implications for the numbers of workers, and the amount of money you have at any given point, means that there are more than 100,000,00 mathematically different routes through the game.

Despite mimicking a game, the atmosphere at a performance of *World Factory* was only tacitly competitive – at no point were the 'factories' in actual competition with one another. However, the effect of modelling the factory system, with 16 separate routes being taken through the *World Factory* cards in every performance, was to simulate a feeling of needing to fight to survive. Decision-making was also driven by an increasing sense of time pressure, partly generated by the show's immersive, multi-sensory design, and partly by the attitudes of the dealers. The slogans interspersed between the cards are a selection of those used by the dealers in conversation with their factories. Indeed, at the time of writing, no factory in the performance has ever gone 'bankrupt', although this possibility is built into the way the card system works in performance, demonstrating perhaps the power of survivalism.

Once the hour of playing the game was over, the performance offered back to its the audience the aggregate of their decisions in the form of data, displayed on vast graphs. Entitled 'The Reckoning', this theatrical finale was played out as a merging of game-show, award-ceremony, and political-news broadcasting – and it was performed with presentational flair, mixed with some ambivalence, by the performers/dealers. The script for this section of the performance is reproduced here (pages 285–302); although the data was different every night, here we include as an example the data from one night's performance, 6 June 2015 at the Young Vic. As a finale, at the end of every performance, each member of the audience received a printed till-roll receipt. This snake-like curl of paper – sometimes as much as a metre long – showed every decision their factory had made that night, and also gave links to the real-world situations on which the stories were based.

Further Explorations

This book makes it possible to explore the stories of *World Factory* beyond taking a single route (ways of doing so are detailed at the end of the cards, starting on page 247). Where necessary, the sources for our stories remain anonymous, but each card is linked to a URL on the *World Factory* online 'digital quilt', which maps the research that can be held in the public domain. You can explore the digital quilt at digitalquilt.info, or see the direct links between the cards and research at **www.nickhernbooks.co.uk/worldfactory**. Here you will also find further samples of materials for playing a game as a group, as well as some recommendations for using the game in a workshop context. As well as linking to the digital quilt, the database allows you to explore the number and type of garments made throughout the game.

The barcode system that underpinned the multiple routes allowed us an unusual degree of complexity in the structure of the game; but it also enabled us to capture the data of decision-making from every route taken, thus yielding some fascinating insights – and ones which corroborate our impressions from hearing audiences talk themselves about playing the game. As Lucy points out in The Reckoning (page 288), generally two-thirds of audiences opt to lower wages rather than sack workers at the first card – and this does indeed mimic the different directions in which labour markets in Europe and the UK have gone since the financial crash. However, analysis of the routes taken through the cards cannot yield insight into motivation, and this has been one of the fascinating discoveries of the *World Factory* performances. It often turns out to be impossible to tell the difference between prudence and profiteering when margins are so low, and the very survival of a factory is at stake. Further, it seems, it is easier to remember what we would like to happen (as revealed in the highly sophisticated and detailed discussions around ethics undertaken by our audiences) than the final decision that we make, which is often based on more pragmatic considerations. Indeed, much of the pleasure – and the humour – of playing *World Factory* lies in the revelation of this gap between (ethical) intention and (pragmatic) action.

What *World Factory* has thus revealed to us, and hopefully to our audiences, is not only a glimpse of the complex web that binds us to the lives – and fates – of so many others; that transparency is immensely valuable in bringing face to face the producer and consumer (as embedded in the hopeful gesture of our *World Factory* shirt). Nevertheless, such transparency simply does not enable a rebalancing of the uneven power relations embedded in consumer capitalism. The way that the game invites us to 'play' demonstrates how *knowing* is not enough on its own to change a system. Within the machinations of capitalism there is no 'right' answer, and whether the reasoning is profit-motive, expediency or sheer survivalism, the same kinds of decisions are made which privilege the well-being of those in power. Working as a small factory owner at the bottom end of the mass-production supply chain is full of risk; and such precariousness means that it is often the workers who are forced to absorb the shocks on behalf of their bosses. In staging this dynamic – and offering audiences the chance to pass the risk on (often taken up with pleasurable alacrity), the game lifts the 'veil' on the very nature of the transactions that underpin contemporary life.

Zoë Svendsen
September 2017

WORLD FACTORY: THE GAME CARDS

HOW TO ENTER
THE WORLD FACTORY

World Factory is a game in which *you* must decide what it means to win.

You have been chosen to run a clothing factory in China.

You will need:

- This book.
- Paper.
- A pen.
- A timer.

You start with:

- 100,000 in capital.
- 24 Worker ID Cards.

Your capital is the money that you have once the factory has dealt with day-to-day running costs, including workers' pay. At the start of the game your workers earn a monthly wage of 3,000, which is just below living wage, but commonplace for the industry. The game uses its own *World Factory* money (see page 269).

How to Play

Every route through *World Factory* starts at CARD 1. On each card, there is a scenario, and a conundrum. Each conundrum is based on a real-world situation discovered through our research. When making your decision, consider how many workers and how much capital you have gained or lost so far. Occasionally there will be a card that only offers one pathway. The cards are placed in numerical order in the book for ease of reference, so you will be constantly moving back and forth through the book as you follow your story. There are no right or wrong decisions, just different paths through the game. If you encounter a worker on the cards who is named, and want to find out a little more about them, you can turn to page 277, where you will find biography cards (ordered alphabetically).

You can run your factory as an individual, or play as a group. If playing in a group, between 3 and 6 players is optimal. If there are more than 6 of you, you can split to play the game separately. Each factory will need their own book. If you are playing in a group, you must make decisions collectively. If you cannot agree, you must devise a way of coming to a decision.

Before you start, create a chart to keep track of your capital and your workers. A sample chart can be found on page 267 and downloaded/printed from: **www.nickhernbooks.co.uk/worldfactory**. Each time you make a decision, before moving on to the next card, make a note of:

► The next card number.

► The running total of your capital.

► How many workers you currently have.

► The current wage level of your workers.

► Anything else of interest, e.g. the garment orders you receive.

You may either play to the end of a route (as indicated on the cards), or play for a set time, as in the performances of *World Factory*.

If you are reading solo, set the timer to 30 minutes.

If you are reading as a group, set the timer to 50 minutes.

Remember: this is a game in which *you* must decide what it means to win.

To start, turn to CARD 1.

Read the card, and then the two options offered on the card next to it. Select one of the options, and turn to the card that has the number indicated by that option.

Continue until you reach the one of the final cards or your time is up – then turn to page 247.

WORLD FACTORY

You have taken over a clothing factory; you have to cut the wage bill.

Keep the workers' wages at their current level, but sack half your workers.

Lose 12 workers.

 2

Keep all your workers and lower their wages by a third.

 3

WORLD FACTORY

You are currently in the middle of a large order for mining jackets for miners in Northern China. Your factory is visited by an Australian buyer who is in China for the first time. As a result of the meeting, and your hospitality, you receive a small order from Sydney Workwear for red lab coats.

You complete the mining jackets and are paid the balance, which enables you to cover your bills and make a profit.

Receive 30,000.

 4

You are in the midst of a medium order for mining jackets for miners in Northern China, which is currently occupying your whole workforce. Your factory is visited by an Australian buyer who is in China for the first time. As a result of the meeting, and your hospitality, you receive an order for hi-vis vests that Sydney Workwear supply to the largest construction firm in Australia. Although vests are not complicated, it is a large order and they want it turned around quickly.

Take the order and hire 5 workers to manage it. This will increase your monthly wage bill by 10,000 in future.

Gain 5 workers.

 5

Tell your workers you will pay them a one-off bonus on completion (costing half your expected profit), if they do overtime to finish the vests on time.

 6

Your accountant, Wang Lin, informs you that you need to increase your turnover to enable the factory to survive. Other factories she works for make garments for high-street chains in the fast-fashion market. You will need to make a wider range of garments to a tighter timeframe, but if you are successful you will be inundated with orders: the appetite for new clothes is insatiable, globally.

Advertise online your specialism in workwear; workwear is more predictable, and allows a more stable financial return for you and your employees.

 300

Market your factory to fast-fashion brands by hiring an English-speaking salesperson to negotiate on price.

Spend 10,000.

 254

5 WORLD FACTORY

Your accountant, Wang Lin, informs you that you need to increase your turnover to enable the factory to survive. Other factories she works for make garments for high-street chains in the fast-fashion market. You will need to make a wider range of garments to a tighter timeframe, but if you are successful you will be inundated with orders: the appetite for new clothes is insatiable, globally. You complete the mining jackets and are paid the balance, which brings in a good profit.

Market your factory to fast-fashion brands by using half your profit to hire an English-speaking salesperson to negotiate on price.

Receive 15,000.

▶ **255**

Advertise online your specialism in workwear; workwear is more predictable and allows a more stable financial return for you and your employees.

Receive 30,000.

▶ **257**

---

6 WORLD FACTORY

Your accountant, Wang Lin, informs you that you need to increase your turnover to enable the factory to survive. Other factories she works for make garments for high-street chains in the fast-fashion market. You will need to make a wider range of garments to a tighter timeframe, but if you are successful you will be inundated with orders: the appetite for new clothes is insatiable, globally.

Market your factory to fast-fashion brands by hiring an English-speaking salesperson to negotiate on price.

Spend 5,000.

▶ **256**

Advertise online your specialism in workwear; workwear is more predictable and allows a more stable financial return for you and your employees.

▶ **260**

7

Liu Huiquan from the factory on the other side of the complex gives you a call. Her factory escaped the fire, and she wonders whether you could handle some jeans? They need to be sandblasted to make them look preworn. She has the equipment, but not enough workers to get the order completed in time. If you provide 7 workers, you will make a very large profit: much more than your usual profit from a single order.

Ask to see the sandblasting equipment before agreeing to provide workers: you have heard it can be dangerous.

 296

Provide the workers. It is better not to know; you need the income, and they will not be exposed to the sandblasting particles for long, as it is only a temporary arrangement.

 301

8

You complete the hi-vis vests for Sydney Workwear, and also the blue vest tops for Zina. You check your accounts and discover that after running costs of buying fabric, utility bills, and rent for the factory and the migrant workers' dormitories, you have made a profit again. You let your new workers (Hou Yu, He Na, Yang Weina, Qian Yufen and Liu Fang) go again as you are concerned that your income will not cover the wage bill next month.

Next morning you receive a letter from Hou Yu, who, in despair at the hiring and firing, asks you to appreciate his skills and consider him if you are ever re-recruiting.

Receive 23,000. Lose 5 workers.

 14

9

Sydney Workwear are surprised by your honesty and accept the discount. You persuade them to give you another chance, saying you will waive the deposit so they can check the quality before payment. They place an order for waterproof trousers. After paying bills for fabric, dormitories, rent and electricity, your accountant, Wang Lin, tells you that you have made a very small profit. You now need to rebuild your workforce.

Seek out the workers you sacked previously with the aim of giving them their job back: they were highly skilled and loyal.

Receive 3,000.

 271

Hire Tian Jianying's contacts from Sichuan. They are all trained in tailoring, and looking for work in the city.

Receive 3,000. Gain 10 workers.

 272

10

You complete the order for the hi-vis vests on time, and are paid the balance. You check your accounts and discover that after running costs of utility bills, rent for the factory and the workers' dormitories, and fabric costs, you have made a very small profit. You let your new workers (Hou Yu, He Na, Yang Weina, Qian Yufen and Liu Fang) go again as you have no more work for them.

Next morning you receive a letter from Hou Yu, who, in despair at the hiring and firing, asks you to appreciate his skills and consider him if you are ever re-recruiting.

Receive 3,000. Lose 5 workers.

 19

11 ◀ WORLD FACTORY

You get the red lab coats and the blue vests finished, and start on an order for Christmas jumpers for the UK market. Payment comes in for several orders; although you have had to pay running costs of buying fabric, utility bills, and rent for the factory and the migrant workers' dormitories, you have made some profit. However, to meet Zina's deadline, your workers have been doing 16-hour days. They are exhausted and are starting to make mistakes. You now need to rebuild your workforce as a matter of urgency.

Try to find the workers you previously had to sack when you took over the factory to give them their jobs back.

Receive 30,000.

 42

Hire Tian Jianying's contacts from Sichuan. They are all trained in tailoring and looking for work in the city. They could start tomorrow.

Receive 30,000. Gain 10 workers.

 99

12 ◀ WORLD FACTORY

Zina are impressed by the speed at which you complete the trial order for the tops and say they will order again soon. You complete the hi-vis vest tops on time, but your workers are exhausted from the amount of overtime required. Liang Qiang comes to see you to ask that you now pay their overtime: they each want an extra week's wages; equivalent to paying double time for the extra hours worked. You do not currently have enough cash to pay out of your running costs, so you will have to use your capital.

Pay the workers the rate that they ask for; after all their wages are already low.

Spend 10,000.

 120

Pay the workers for all the additional hours worked at their normal rate. You cannot afford more at the moment and they know this.

 14

Your twelve workers are working very long hours, resulting in the red lab coats being shoddily sewn: a good number of the seams are not straight and they are not finished well. You do not have enough fabric or time to redo them. The workers claim there are too few workers to manage the workload.

Offer Sydney Workwear a discounted price in recompense for the uneven seams.

 9

Iron and pack the lab coats really neatly, and cross your fingers and hope that Sydney Workwear do not notice.

270

You get an order for men's checked shirts from Zina at the cheaper end of the market. Machinist Liang Qiang catches you as you leave the factory office: the workers understood the low pay level while you were starting up. But they would now like the wages to be returned to 3,000 a month. Currently, Liang Qiang points out, they have barely enough to cover food bills, and certainly can't save anything to send home.

Tell the workers you cannot put up the pay; workwear pays a deposit upfront, but fashion brands do not, and therefore your income is not yet stable enough to raise pay.

273

Put the wages back up. Source cheap fabric so that you can afford it.

 275

15

You have dinner with Madame Wang from ZhengXing Clothing Co. and your friend, the merchandiser Gloria Yeung. The conversation turns to rumours of strikes in other provinces, although there is no information in the official news. The following day, machinist Liang Qiang accosts you as you leave the office to ask how you plan to move forward with enabling workers' rights.

Suggest your workers set up a legal Union under government auspices, linked to the All-China Federation of Trade Unions.

 306

Agree to their request for regular consultation, although it will be unofficial as independent unionisation is illegal.

412

16

You complete the hi-vis vests on time, but your workers are exhausted from the amount of overtime required. Liang Qiang comes to see you to ask that you now pay their overtime: they each want an extra week's wages; equivalent to paying double time for the extra hours worked. You do not currently have enough cash to pay out of your running costs, so you will have to use your capital.

Pay the workers the rate that they ask for; after all their wages are already low.

Spend 10,000.

 121

Pay the workers for all the additional hours worked at their normal rate, which you can do without having to touch your capital.

407

You get a rush order for dresses with a frill skirt from Zina. You make a reasonable profit this month. You receive an email from Run Rabbit saying they cannot raise the price for the organic-cotton sports T-shirt as their research shows that people will not pay more. You find a company in Vietnam who have half the labour costs you do, and produce very high-quality work.

Outsource to Vietnam in order to cover the cost of the organic cotton. Your pattern-cutter cuts and bundles the fabric, which is then sent to Vietnam for sewing.

Receive 30,000.

 17a

Take the hit yourself on the organic cotton: you want to use it for environmental reasons, but decide outsourcing is not for you.

Receive 8,000.

▶ **49**

MAXIMUM DESIGN WOW AT MINIMUM COST

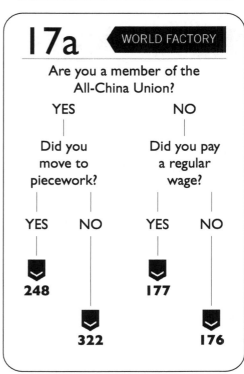

17a WORLD FACTORY

Are you a member of the All-China Union?

YES		NO	
Did you move to piecework?		Did you pay a regular wage?	
YES	NO	YES	NO
248		177	
	322		176

18

The search for your old workers takes longer than planned. 6 have new jobs and can't be lured back; Wang Haiyan has moved city; Sang Hong's mobile number doesn't work; and Xu Daiqun had a heart attack and is unfit to work. In the end you can only reinstate Xie Qingfang, Liu Lequn and Cao Tao. Due to the delay in rebuilding your workforce, you must turn down an order for waterproof jackets from one of your regular clients.

Hire 7 new people in addition to your 3 former workers.

Gain 10 workers.

▶ **410**

19

Machinist Liang Qiang comes to see you: they were willing to put up with the low pay level while you were starting up. But he and the other workers would now like the wages to be put back up to 3,000 a month. Currently, Liang Qiang points out, they have barely enough to cover food bills, and certainly can't save anything to send home.

Put the wages back up. Source cheaper fabric to balance the books.

▶ **274**

Do not put up the wages as you cannot afford it.

 276

Rob Baxter, Zina's international compliance inspector, suddenly appears one morning, asking questions. You realise that he has been staying in the hotel opposite the factory and spying on you. He is keen to see ID showing age for all your workers. It occurs to you that you do not have a record for Lu Qingmin, who looks very young.

Ask Lu Qingmin to take 'unpaid holiday' for the foreseeable future, and tell Rob Baxter she has left the company.

Lose 1 worker.

▶ **284**

Ask Lu Qingmin to bring ID; you do not care if it is fake. She is a good worker and you would like to keep her.

▶ **286**

You receive an order of grey polo shirts from Sydney Workwear. The workers are glad of the wage increase; all the younger ones have taken up the offer of English lessons. Liang Qiang mentions you to a local NGO he is involved with. They put your name on a list of 'ethical' factories. You hear from fashion line Garb, who are bringing out an 'ethical' range. They will place a large order of blue stripe skirts if you comply with a number of international directives, including providing air conditioning.

Install air conditioning and make a thorough check to ensure you comply with international standards for working conditions. Take the order.

Spend 15,000.

▶ **337**

Ask Li Pengjian to find out, subtly, whether the workers are likely to appreciate the installation of air conditioning.

▶ **252**

22

When you come in the next day, the workers are sitting silently at their machines. They are exhausted by you enforcing what Li Pengjian describes as inhumane working hours. Production stops for 3 days. Word gets out about the strike and you have to handle anxious phone calls from clients. As a result, Marvellous and Workers Comfort cancel their orders.

Incurring building/rental costs without generating income to match means you have to pay your bills from your capital.

Spend 20,000.

▶ 132

23

You get an order for skirts with zip details from British brand Marvellous. You have dinner with a client, Gloria Yeung, and neighbouring factory owner, Madame Wang. The conversation turns to rumours of strikes in other provinces: there is nothing in the official news. Madame Wang is providing her workers with free tuition in computing and English. Gloria talks about the night school she went to, to learn English, which helped her fulfil her dream of a desk job.

Invest in training workers in skills that are useful to the factory.
It is not your role to direct the education of the workers.

Spend 3,000.

▶ 58   IF accepted heating grant
▶ 59   IF declined heating grant

Offer free extra tuition to your workers at the end of their working day, as well as improving their sewing skills.

Spend 6,000.

▶ 47   IF accepted heating grant
▶ 40   IF declined heating grant

You complete the Christmas jumpers and get an order for men's checked shirts from Zina at the cheaper end of the market. Xie Qingfang, Liu Lequn and Cao Tao are glad to be back. The new workers settle in quickly; like all your workers, they do not have hukou (city residency) and therefore have no rights in the city. Like most other factories, you rent dormitories for them. Your workers' dormitories are on site, but no additional rooms are currently available for the new workers.

Provide additional beds for the current dormitories; there is space and 5 to a room is not unusual.

 32

Take out an annual lease on new dormitories; it cannot be covered by your running costs so will have to come from your capital.

Spend 12,000.

 109

"Let our banner proclaim our belief in a free market as the greatest provider for the people. Let us also call for an end to the nit-picking, the harassment and over-regulation of business and industry which restricts expansion and our ability to compete in world markets."

Ronald Reagan, President of the United States of America 1981–1989, 1975

You get an order for dresses with a frill skirt from Zina. You make a reasonable profit this month. You also receive an order from Hong Kong-based ethical sportswear company Run Rabbit for organic-cotton T-shirts. When you query the price point, which will be hard for you to achieve given the cost of organic cotton, they say they cannot raise it as their research shows that people will not pay more. You find a company in Vietnam who have half the labour costs you do, and produce very high-quality work.

Outsource to Vietnam in order to cover the cost of the organic cotton. Your pattern-cutter cuts and bundles the fabric, which is then sent to Vietnam for sewing.

Receive 30,000.

》25a

Take the hit yourself on the organic cotton: you want to use it for environmental reasons, but decide outsourcing is not for you.

Receive 8,000.

》49

UNCERTAINTY MEANS PROGRESS

25a   WORLD FACTORY

Are you a member of the All-China Union?

YES	NO
Did you move to piecework?	Did you pay a regular wage?
YES NO	YES NO

248		**177**	
	322		**176**

You get a rush order from Zina for dresses with a frill skirt. You receive an email from Run Rabbit saying they cannot raise the price for the organic-cotton sports T-shirt as their research shows that people will not pay more. Your vanished Vietnamese workers left a business card for a factory in Vietnam. On checking them out you discover they produce very high-quality work at a much lower price point than you, due to lower labour costs.

Outsource to Vietnam in order to cover the cost of the organic cotton. Your pattern-cutter cuts and bundles the fabric, which is then sent to Vietnam for sewing.

Receive 30,000.

 26a

Take the hit yourself on the organic cotton: you want to use it for environmental reasons, but decide outsourcing is not for you.

Receive 8,000.

▶ **49**

KEEP GOING FORWARD

Are you a member of the All-China Union?

YES		NO	
Did you move to piecework?		Did you pay a regular wage?	
YES	NO	YES	NO
248		**177**	
	322		**176**

27

WORLD FACTORY

Your Vietnamese workers are quickly back at work once the official is gone, and promise you they will stay late to finish. You have dinner with Madame Wang from ZhengXing Clothing Co., Ltd and your friend, the merchandiser Gloria Yeung. The major topic of conversation is a new police crackdown on illegal immigrants. The conversation later turns to rumours of strikes in other provinces, although there is no information in the official news.

Arriving at your factory mid-morning the next day, there is no sign of your Vietnamese workers. They have simply vanished: you never find out what happened to them.

Lose 5 workers.

▶ **35**

28

WORLD FACTORY

You complete the waterproof trousers and receive new orders: organic-cotton T-shirts from Run Rabbit and orange gilets from Sportex. You are again in danger of missing your deadlines. You have dinner with Madame Wang from the neighbouring factory. The conversation turns to rumours of major strikes in other provinces. Madame Wang tells you that Qiu Lian, a former worker, has set up her own small factory in a makeshift extension on the roof of a nearby building and needs orders.

Outsource to Qiu Lian; you admire her entrepreneurial spirit. Furthermore you can pay for the work she does from your running costs, without touching your capital.

▶ **106** IF accepted heating grant
▶ **98** IF declined heating grant

Hire 2 new workers, which means having to dig into your capital this month. Outsourcing is out of the question.

Spend 6,000. Gain 2 workers.

▶ **405**

You do the accounts and have made back some profit. Plantlife say they will pay you 1.5 times the going rate for an order for women's vest tops if you commit to raising the pay level of your workers to a decent living wage. Wang Lin raises the question of how this will be paid for in the longer term.

Raise the pay level, paid this month from your capital; you will worry about the future later.

Receive 15,000.

▶ **104** IF accepted heating grant
▶ **105** IF declined heating grant

Tell Plantlife you will raise pay but instead spend part of your recent profit on improving dormitories and providing wifi.

Receive 30,000.

▶ **200** IF accepted heating grant
▶ **201** IF declined heating grant

"We've looked at the facts about equality. We've looked about whether the people want it – and they are more interested in growth and the creation of wealth. The pursuit of equality itself is a mirage. And opportunity means nothing unless it includes the right to be unequal."

Margaret Thatcher, Prime Minister of the UK 1979–1990, 1975

You complete the faux-fur jackets for SexiBabi. Zina call to thank you for getting the clothing out of customs and pay the balance; you make a small profit. You need to get more orders in to increase production and your profit; setting up a sales office in another city will make you stand out from the competition and lead to orders in new markets. Carol Zhang, your most successful salesperson, will run the new office.

Set up a sales office in Milan; rental costs are on a par with Beijing. You'll benefit from the city's association with high-quality clothing in attracting European clients.

Receive 15,000.

 30a

Set up a sales office in Beijing to focus on the Chinese fashion market and lucrative government orders; relocation costs are less than moving abroad.

Receive 20,000.

 144

BITTER FIRST SWEET LATER

30a

WORLD FACTORY

Did a compliance inspector ask to see ID for all your workers?

YES   NO

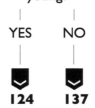
135

Did you allow Lu Qingmin to keep working despite her looking very young?

YES   NO

124   137

It turns out to be much harder than you thought to source organic cotton for the Plantlife order: it is expensive, as it has to be stored separately from normal cotton, and there is not much of a market for it. Plantlife explain they cannot improve on their offer, as they have set the retail target price, and their research shows that people will not pay more. You also receive an order from Marvellous, a British brand, for suit jackets.

Decline the Plantlife order: you cannot afford to take the financial risk on it given your commitment to paying your workers at this level.

>> 43

Take the Plantlife order and try to make it work; organic cotton does not use pesticides which damage the health of cotton pickers.

>> 379

You hear rumours of discontent regarding the cramped dormitory conditions, but no one addresses you directly about it. Carol Zhang is finding it hard to get orders for you in the fast-fashion world, as your labour costs are too high for you to be competitive in this market. She strongly recommends lowering the workers' pay in line with industry standards.

Implement lower wages.

>> 273

Source cheaper, low-quality cloth to enable you to keep workers' wages up.

 275

WORLD FACTORY

You complete the faux-fur jacket order. Setting up an office in Beijing was an excellent idea; the internal market is on the up due to the rapid expansion of the Chinese consumer base. You are inundated with orders including one from a Chinese high-street brand, Peace&Love, for skinny jeans.

Expand your workforce to cope with demand.

Gain 8 workers.

▶ **33a**

SURVIVAL IS WINNING

33a WORLD FACTORY

Are you a member of the All-China Union?

YES	NO
Did you move to piecework?	Did you pay a regular wage?
YES NO	YES NO

YES → **242**

NO → **267**

YES → **182**

NO → **181**

34

WORLD FACTORY

The municipal authorities are clamping down on the unbearable smog; you are fined for using the city incinerators, reducing this month's profit by 5,000. Paying the workers per piece of garment has however increased productivity. Li Pengjian reports that Yan Rong and Yao Lin, who are older, are earning less despite the high quality of their work, as they work more slowly. He would like to see a pay increase: would you be willing to meet with them informally to discuss an idea for changing how the pay is structured?

Meet Li Pengjian and other workers to negotiate the pay structure; you offer them tea.

Receive 25,000.

▶ 385

Put pay up a little: you know that is what they want.

Receive 25,000.

▶ 406

35

WORLD FACTORY

You complete the waterproof trousers and receive new orders: organic-cotton sports T-shirts from Run Rabbit and gilets from Sportex. Without the Vietnamese workers you are again in danger of missing your deadlines. You hear that Qiu Lian, a former worker, has set up her own small factory in a makeshift extension on the roof of a nearby building and needs orders. You admire her entrepreneurial spirit, and you know her work is of a high quality.

Outsource to Qiu Lian; you can pay for the work she does from your running costs, without touching your capital.

▶ 106 IF accepted heating grant
▶ 98 IF declined heating grant

Hire 2 new workers, which will mean having to dig into your capital this month to pay them. Outsourcing is out of the question.

Spend 6,000. Gain 2 workers.

▶ 216 IF accepted heating grant
▶ 405 IF declined heating grant

36 WORLD FACTORY

In the end you have to outsource to Liu Huiquan as well as Qiu Lian, as the latter cannot manage the volume required. It is a properly collective effort. The dresses are sent out as completed and are flying off the shelves. No one seems to notice that each factory has different ways of making them and that the fabric differs significantly in quality. You make a massive profit. However, you had to let down other clients to get the order done, and will soon be in need of new orders.

Bank your profit first, and drink a toast to Kate Middleton for wearing your dress and bringing you good fortune.

Receive 90,000.

▶ **223**

37 WORLD FACTORY

You are unsettled; a clique of workers seem unhappy that you changed the payment method without discussion. Your supervisor, Li Pengjian, is working long hours to keep track of the different work rates. You ask him about their attitudes but he says it is difficult to get an overview because some talk in dialect or use their mobiles to share information. He suggests you hear their demands directly. Mud recommend you to fashion brand Garb who place a large order for distressed T-shirts.

Adopt a policy of lowering the pay of the troublemakers until they find work elsewhere.

Lose 5 workers.

▶ **173**

Agree to meet Yan Rong, Yao Lin and Zhu Qing informally.

 165

You start several orders, including orders for fashion T-shirts and gold-printed leggings from SexiBabi. Carol Zhang's efforts in the Milan office are already paying off in the increase of international orders you are receiving. You will need to keep expanding and recruit more workers if you are to deliver your orders on time.

Hire 10 new workers to manage the workload.

Gain 10 workers.

》44

Force all workers to increase their standard working hours from 12 to 16 hours per day for the foreseeable future.

》56

You complete and ship the Run Rabbit T-shirts and the orange gilets, although payment has not yet come through. Run Rabbit's buyer emails to discuss a new order; he attaches a photo of David Beckham modelling the T-shirt. A man turns up at your office looking for his 15-year-old daughter, Yang Lin, who he says works in your factory. He lost contact with her when she left their village to find work in the city 8 months ago. He has travelled for 26 hours.

Usher Yang Lin's father quickly out of the door, telling him to return at the end of the shift and you will see what you can do.

》404

Tell Yang Lin's father that you have a fast turnover of staff and that you do not recognise his daughter: you worry he might be a compliance inspector.

220

WORLD FACTORY

Most of the younger workers take up the offer of English lessons with alacrity. Yang Lin tells you it makes her feel valued as an individual: she is glad to be working for you. Zina call you: they have not received their shirts. Your shipping company tell you the order has got stuck at the port and that customs report that it is in a queue for checking, and it could take months. You ring Ku Fang in the municipal authorities business department to see if he can help but he is somewhat cool with you on the phone.

Ku Fang is clear that if he is to help, you must use a local cotton mill he recommends, and make a significant contribution to his Factory Development Fund.

Spend 30,000.

▶ **30**

WORLD FACTORY

You receive more orders for organic items, including baby clothes from Plantlife. You hear a report on the radio about major fabric dyeing factories (including the one recommended by Ku Fang) using cotton mills in Bangladesh that employ and house homeless children, who they have rescued from the streets.

Do nothing: the order is underway now, and anyway you applaud attempts to improve children's lives.

▶ **100**

Remake the order with non-organic cotton; they will not be able to tell. You cannot deal with a factory employing young children under any circumstances.

 68

The search for your old workers takes longer than you thought. 6 have new jobs and can't be lured back; Wang Haiyan has moved city; Sang Hong's mobile number does not work; Xu Daiqun has had a heart attack and is unfit to work. You do find Xie Qingfang, Liu Lequn and Cao Tao. Due to the delay in rebuilding your workforce you have to turn down an order from Chinese fast-fashion chain, Peace&Love.

Hire 7 new people in addition to your 3 former workers.

Gain 10 workers.

▶ 24

You complete the suit jackets. Word has spread about your pay-level rise. In addition to a steady stream of workers seeking employment with you, one morning Tony Nie, the factory boss downstairs, turns up. There has been a strike in his factory because his workers want the same wages as yours, but he cannot afford it. He does not have the relationship with ethical brands you do.

Tell him: tough, he should raise his game; the workers have rights and their labour should be rewarded.

▶ 112

Share your ethical contacts despite the intense competition for orders, by putting him in touch with the NGO who recommended you to Plantlife.

 214

44

You quickly complete the SexiBabi order for fashion T-shirts. You are in profit on the orders and can bank a good profit. A worker, Deng Weiqing, visits you. She describes her family's difficulties: her mother has died so she needs to pay for her children to come to live with her as there is no one to look after them now back home. She hopes you can help.

Give Deng Weiqing a week off work and a loan of 5,000, to be repaid when she returns with her children and starts work for you again.

Receive 35,000.

 63

Let Deng Weiqing go. Migrant workers have many problems: if you help her everyone will expect it. You are sorry to see her go as she was a good worker.

Receive 40,000. Lose 1 worker.

 294

45

Mick Fletcher from Run Rabbit offers you a new large order for 100% organic-cotton hoodies on the understanding that you will adhere to their ethical guidelines and allow your factory to be inspected. Ku Fang's mill cannot supply this quantity so you will have to use another mill as well.

Take the order from Run Rabbit and allow your factory to be inspected; tell Yang Lin that she will have to hide if there is an inspection.

> 64

Decline the order from Run Rabbit to avoid being inspected, which you have heard from other factory owners always ends up costing money.

 208

You have dinner with Madame Wang from ZhengXing Clothing Co., Ltd and your friend, the merchandiser Gloria Yeung. The major topic of conversation is a new police crackdown on illegal immigrants. The conversation later turns to rumours of strikes in other provinces, although there is no information in the official news.

Arriving at your factory mid-morning the next day, there is no sign of your Vietnamese workers. They have simply vanished: you never find out what happened to them.

Lose 5 workers.

▶ **35**

The younger workers sign up for English lessons with alacrity. Yang Lin says it makes her feel valued as an individual. She is glad to be working for you. Zina call: they have not received their shirts. Your shipping company tells you they are stuck in customs and could take months to clear. You ring Ku Fang in the municipal authorities business department. He says he'll see what he can do and gives you a strong recommendation for a local fabric factory: if you mention his name, they will give you a good price.

You place an order with the fabric factory immediately; by the end of the day you get a call from customs to say the clothes have been cleared for shipping.

 30

You complete the Run Rabbit T-shirts. Thanks to the efforts of Carol Zhang in the Milan office, Marvellous, a classic brand from the UK, give you a medium order for women's suit jackets. Workers Comfort return with a very large repeat order of workshirts. They want the order completed very quickly in response to their rival's collection so you name a high price – which they accept. You do not have enough workers to complete the orders.

Hire 10 workers: you have made profits of 15,000.

Gain 10 workers.

▶ **48a**

Tell your workers they will have to take on overnight shifts in order to finish the order. Keep the profit.

▶ **22**

MONEY IS POWER

Are you a member of the
All-China Union?

YES   NO

Did you move to piecework?   Did you pay a regular wage?

YES   NO   YES   NO

250   **180**

323   **179**

49

WORLD FACTORY

You complete the dresses with frill skirts on time. You are introduced to Jenny Rivers from Knitdare, a Manchester-based knitwear supplier, by Wu Fenfang, who owns a knitwear factory downstairs. Kanye West has been seen wearing a mock-collar sewn into a jumper, and they wonder whether you would be able to do some collar inserts for a run of jumpers they are looking at doing? There isn't much profit in it, but you are happy to oblige.

Despite producing several samples, the order never materialises; you later find out that the knitwear factory has gone bust.

> 401

50

WORLD FACTORY

Paying the workers per piece of garment rather than a wage has significantly increased productivity, and your profits. Zhu Qing has taken on the leadership of the Union: you are surprised Li Pengjian is not involved, as he has always taken an interest in workers' rights. Zhu Qing reports that Yan Rong and Yao Lin, who are older, are earning less due to their slower working speeds, despite the quality of their work.

Do nothing about the workers' concerns. The Union is controlled centrally and therefore workers' demands are managed by protocol.

Receive 30,000.

> 51 IF taught workers English
> 38 IF did not teach English

Agree to a request from Li Pengjian for a meeting external to the Union, to explore an idea the workers would like to put to you regarding how the pay is calculated. You offer them tea.

Receive 30,000.

> 346

51

Learning English and computing is popular with the workers, but it is a mixed blessing: you have been able to promote one worker to a sales position as a result, but there is frustration among the others about a lack of opportunity. Carol Zhang's efforts in the Milan office are already paying off: you get a number of new orders, including orders for fashion T-shirts and gold-printed leggings from SexiBabi. You will need to keep expanding and recruit more workers to deliver the orders on time.

Hire 10 new workers to manage the workload.

Gain 10 workers.

▶ **44**

Force all workers to increase their standard working hours from 12 to 16 hours per day for the foreseeable future.

▶ **56**

52

You are relieved to discover that Zina do not seem concerned; they are very surprised by your honesty, saying it is not a concern for their target market, as it is unlikely that the shirts will be worn many times. They place an order for American flag vest tops. Meanwhile, after many cold calls to ethical retailers, Plantlife call you back. They visit the factory and you send everyone home early that day.

Plantlife place an order for organic-cotton long-sleeved T-shirts. Unlike in fast fashion, they give a deposit upfront which you plan to use for the fabric.

▶ **290**

53 ◀ WORLD FACTORY

Despite Carol Zhang bringing in plenty of orders, you struggle to cover the newly increased wage bill via your fast-fashion income. You start to research ethical retailers who might pay a fairer price. In the meantime you let 4 workers go. The cheaper fabric you bought for the checked shirts frays easily and proves difficult to sew; about half the order (around 3,000 shirts) turn out shoddy, with misaligned buttons.

Get Lu Qingmin to iron and pack the shirts really neatly and cross your fingers that Zina do not notice.

Lose 4 workers.

 III

Confess the error to Zina, and offer a discounted price.

Lose 4 workers.

▶ 52

54 ◀ WORLD FACTORY

A compliance inspector, sent by Run Rabbit, turns up unexpectedly and stays 3 days; he is checking that the working conditions comply with their customer promise. You haven't told them you've outsourced to Vietnam, in breach of contract. Luckily you have some spare fabric, and quickly switch your workers to making the T-shirts for Run Rabbit. You will now have far too many Run Rabbit T-shirts and will have to decide what to do with the excess.

Have the extra T-shirts incinerated: this is standard for unwanted branded goods.

▶ 67

Sell the garments on to a textile reseller who has outlets in inland China.

Receive 15,000.

▶ 70

WORLD FACTORY

You receive an order for women's suit jackets from British brand Marvellous. Zina call: the dresses have not arrived. Your shipping company tells you they are stuck in customs and could take months to clear. You ring Ku Fang in the municipal authorities business department to see if he can help. He says he'll see what he can do and recommends a local fabric factory: if you mention his name, they will give you a good price.

You place an order with the fabric factory immediately; by the end of the day you get a call from customs to say the clothes have been cleared for shipping.

 **55a**

EQUALITY IS A MIRAGE

55a

WORLD FACTORY

Did a compliance inspector ask to see ID for all your workers?

YES   NO

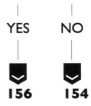
54

Did you allow Lu Qingmin to keep working despite her looking very young?

YES   NO

156   154

You complete the fashion T-shirts. You come in one day to find the workers are sitting silently at their machines. Even those who usually choose to do additional hours whenever possible have joined the protest at the enforced increase in working hours, as well as low pay levels and poor working conditions. Production stops for 3 days. Word gets out about the strike and you have to handle anxious phone calls from clients.

Incurring building/rental costs without generating income to match means you have to pay your bills from your capital.

Spend 10,000.

 132

"Revolutionary spirit is a treasure beyond price. But revolution takes place on the basis of the need for material benefit. We are in favour of allowing a part of the population to become rich first. [...] The superiority of the socialist system over the capitalist system should manifest itself first and foremost in the rate of economic growth and in economic efficiency."

Deng Xiaoping, Paramount Leader of the People's Republic of China 1978–1989, 1980

British brand Marvellous place an order for women's suit jackets. Zina call you: they have not received the dresses. Your shipping company tell you the order has got stuck at the port and that customs report that it is in a queue for checking, and it could take months. You ring Ku Fang in the municipal authorities business department to see if he can help but he is somewhat cool with you on the phone.

Ku Fang is clear that if he is to help, you must use a local cotton mill he recommends, and make a significant contribution to his Factory Development Fund.

Spend 30,000.

 57a

BIGGER FASTER CHEAPER MORE

Did a compliance inspector ask to see ID for all your workers?

YES   NO

54

Did you allow Lu Qingmin to keep working despite her looking very young?

YES   NO

156   154

58

2 of your more skilled workers, fed up with the low pay and lack of opportunity for self-improvement, jump to another factory. Zina call you: they never received their checked shirts. Your shipping company tells you the order has got stuck in customs at the port; it could take months to clear. You ring Ku Fang in the municipal authorities business department to see if he can help. Ku Fang says he will see what he can do, and gives you a strong recommendation for a local fabric factory.

You place an order with the fabric factory immediately; by the end of the day you get a call from customs to say the clothes have been cleared for shipping.

Lose 2 workers.

▶ **30**

59

2 of your more skilled workers, fed up with the low pay and lack of opportunity for self-improvement, jump to another factory. Zina call you: they never received their checked shirts. Your shipping company tell you the order has got stuck at the port and that customs report that it is in a queue for checking, and it could take months. You ring Ku Fang in the municipal authorities business department to see if he can help but he is somewhat cool with you on the phone.

Ku Fang is clear that if he is to help, you must use a local cotton mill he recommends, and make a significant contribution to his Factory Development Fund.

Spend 30,000. Lose 2 workers.

▶ **30**

60 ◀ WORLD FACTORY

You complete the waterproof trousers. Tian Jianying comes to see you. She tells you that, cut adrift from their families, the child workers you refused to employ have ended up trapped in unpaid bonded labour in Shenzhen, in an electronics factory. More generally, unrest in the factory is palpable; the workers are angry that you sacked Liang Qiang, and do not believe your promise of increasing pay. You come in the next day to find them sitting silently at their machines, not working.

Give in to your workers and put the pay up, despite the hit to your profits both this month and in the longer term.

Receive 10,000.

>> **236**

Negotiate a one-off bonus if they return to work immediately.

Receive 30,000.

>> **216** IF accepted heating grant
>> **80** IF declined heating grant

---

61 ◀ WORLD FACTORY

Once in Hanoi, you visit a few factories. The working conditions shown to you by the owners do not look unreasonable. However, as you turn the corner after leaving one factory, a child runs up to you. Your interpreter translates: she is saying her family cannot live on the wage, that all the children have to work, usually at home, sewing on sequins or other adornments.

Decide not to do business in a country where the employment conditions are so much worse than your own in China. Bring production home.

Receive 30,000.

>> **240**

Outsourcing is the only way you can make garments for the price your clients demand. Select a factory that is also used by European brands.

 110

WORLD FACTORY

Your workers are struggling to complete the military order, as it is on such a large scale. You need to work fast, especially as Marvellous want a quick turnaround on the denim-detail shirts. Your factory-floor supervisor, Li Pengjian, says the workers say they are happy to work longer hours to earn more money to send home to their families.

Recruit 20 extra workers and increase shifts from 12 hours to 15 hours per day for the foreseeable future.

Gain 20 workers.

▶ **269**

Recruit 40 extra workers.

Gain 40 workers.

▶ **65**

WORLD FACTORY

You complete the gold-printed leggings and get a substantial new order for bibs from Savaday, a multinational supermarket chain whose profit margins are minimal, but could be a long-term source of income. On the way out of the meeting the salesperson mentions that their goods aren't intended for long-term use. Deng Weiqing is back; you now notice she is highly skilled. You make her workshop supervisor, and ask her to identify who the weakest workers are.

Sack the 3 weakest workers, identified by Den Weiqing, and replace them with faster workers.

Lose 3 workers. Gain 3 workers.

▶ **69**

Ask Deng Weiqing to train the weakest 3 workers. Over the next few weeks, this slows production by 2 days.

 211

64 ◄ WORLD FACTORY

Your workers are struggling to manage the workload. Grateful for being reunited with his daughter, Yang Lin's father offers to help; a trained tailor and pattern-cutter, his input doubles the speed at which you can prepare garments. He recommends further contacts from Teke Village in the rural Sichuan province.

Hire Yang Lin's father's contacts.

Gain 14 workers.

▶ 170

Outsource to your former worker, Qiu Lian; you do not want to increase your own workforce; the more you expand, the more remote you become from your workers.

▶ 402

---

65 ◄ WORLD FACTORY

Recruiting workers with sewing skills is not easy but Li Pengjian has a chat with an associate in rural Sichuan and arranges the recruitment of new workers. You complete the order for military uniforms on time and make a large profit. As your workforce grows it is harder to keep track of who should be doing what, so you introduce a colour-coded uniform to help keep control. You are offered a long-term (1-year) contract for the supply of UN peacekeeping uniforms.

Continue to supply military uniforms. This will bring a stable income, with an upfront deposit paid on signing the contract.

Receive 80,000.

▶ 75

Refuse the contract; you would rather focus on other orders. You bank this profit and move on.

Receive 60,000.

▶ 103 IF sacked young worker
▶ 157 IF kept young worker

You have dinner with Madame Wang from ZhengXing Clothing Co., Ltd and your friend, the merchandiser Gloria Yeung. The major topic of conversation is a new police crackdown on illegal immigrants. The conversation later turns to rumours of strikes in other provinces, although there is no information in the official news. You ask their advice about training your new workers: their opinions are divided.

Get the more experienced workers to show your new workers what to do as and when it is needed.

 96

Take a hit of 5,000 in lost productivity to pay your best machinists to teach the new workers how to use a sewing machine properly.

Spend 5,000.

 185

It is not a good day. The municipal authorities are cutting down on the increasingly unbearable smog in the city. They issue fines to everyone using the many illegal city incinerators. Although you were not aware of their illegality, you must pay the fine. And then your pattern-cutter Liu Chengtian slices a finger off, ruining a stack of fabric. As a migrant worker, he does not have any access to health care.

Pay your pattern-cutter's medical bills and compensation, as well as the fine for pollution; you have to dig into your capital to cover the costs.

Spend 15,000.

 89

Sack Liu Chengtian for negligence; you have to dig into your capital to cover the cost of the ruined fabric and the fine for pollution.

Spend 8,000. Lose 1 worker.

102

68

You complete the baby clothes and Plantlife accept your faked organic-cotton certification without question. You do not feel good about this. Plantlife would like to place another order, also for garments made with organic cotton. An environmental NGO you contacted keep sending you reports. One reveals that the fabric factory you bought the non-organic cotton from source it from Uzbekistan, where child labour is state-sanctioned.

Keep exploring the options for organic cotton. You are determined to find a clean source, even though it will cost you time and money.

Receive 8,000.

 151

Decline the Plantlife order. The issues with sourcing organic cotton are too time-consuming: you cannot be held responsible for the whole supply chain.

Receive 15,000.

 139

69

New orders are coming thick and fast, your turnover is higher, and you are making regular profits. You start to notice that everyone is more deferential; they seem to be scared that they might be sacked, too. The other workers do not speak to Deng Weiqing.

You come in the next day to discover Deng Weiqing has jumped to another factory: she was angry that you didn't tell her why you wanted her to identify the weaker workers.

Receive 60,000. Lose I worker.

 210

It is not a good day: Run Rabbit send you photos of a fake 'Run Rabbie' shop in Chongqing selling their garments you made. They set legal proceedings in motion for breach of contract and your lawyer charges 3,000 for an initial consultation. And then your pattern-cutter Liu Chengtian slices a finger off, ruining a stack of fabric worth 5,000. As a migrant worker, he does not have any access to health care.

Pay his medical bills and compensation; you have to dig into your capital to cover the costs.

Spend 25,000.

 162

Sack Liu Chengtian for negligence; you have to dig into your capital to cover the cost of the ruined fabric.

Spend 5,000. Lose 1 worker.

 102

Marvellous call you. They have changed their minds about their order. A fashionista has been seen wearing a similar shirt, but with short sleeves. Can you make it with short sleeves? You have made a lot already, but you agree to adapt them. Later that day they call again and pull the order altogether. To afford the fabric you had to buy in bulk and Marvellous had indicated they would want 5,000, so although they only contracted you for 1,000, you risked buying enough fabric for the full order.

Have the shirts incinerated on the insistence of Marvellous. This is the standard way of protecting the identity of a global brand.

212 IF accepted heating grant
207 IF declined heating grant

Finish the shirts and sell them on to a textile reseller who has outlets in inland China.

Receive 15,000.

 229

72

WORLD FACTORY

You complete the denim shirts for Marvellous and are about to ship them. Yuan Bao comes to see you, upset; she tells you that after you sacked her, Lu Qingmin ended up in unpaid bonded labour in an electronics factory in Shenzhen. For 3 days now she has not turned up to work or answered her phone; all Yuan Bao's efforts to locate her have come to nothing. And then you get a call from Marvellous: they want to cancel the shirts.

Have the clothes incinerated on the insistence of Marvellous. This is the standard way of protecting the identity of a global brand.

▶ 212 IF accepted heating grant
▶ 207 IF declined heating grant

Sell the shirts on to a textile reseller who has outlets in inland China.

Receive 15,000.

▶ 229

73

WORLD FACTORY

Despite the turmoil, you receive a small order from Plantlife, for men's T-shirts. The neighbouring factory goes bankrupt due to the strikes and all the workers lose their jobs. The space is now on offer at half-price rent. It is a rare opportunity to expand and develop the company.

Talk to Plantlife to see if you can get a larger order before deciding whether to take over the neighbouring factory.

▶ 79

Take over the neighbouring factory and hire its workers.

Gain 15 workers.

▶ 213

You complete the order for hoodies. A compliance company arrive without warning to inspect your factory on behalf of Run Rabbit. Their report lists key points that require immediate action. They note that Yang Lin looks very young and ask for proof of age by their next visit. You must pay for fire extinguishers, ventilation fans, the compliance inspection fee – and the cook wants some extra for the new spicy menu. But you do get another order from Run Rabbit: this time, for organic-cotton shorts.

Arrange for a fake ID card to be made for Yang Lin; she has only recently been reunited with her father and her links to Teke Village are providing skilled workers.

Spend 25,000.

 268

Ask Yang Lin to take an 'unpaid holiday' for the foreseeable future, at least until the Run Rabbit order is complete.

Spend 25,000. Lose 1 worker.

 374

You need to make sure you hold on to your workforce and cover your costs of recruiting them. You receive several orders, as well as the continued military uniforms. Business is booming.

Inform the workforce they must work for 6 months before they can leave your factory or else they will forfeit pay.

 103 IF sacked young worker
 157 IF kept young worker

Form a workers' folk band and hold a social evening to encourage integration amongst the workforce.

 223

You immediately start to get more orders thanks to Carol Zhang's efforts. But today the phone will not stop ringing for another reason. Your clients have heard a BBC World Service programme about Chinese factories. You listen to the interview online, and realise that Lu Qingmin has given an interview about being a child worker. You go onto the factory floor to talk to her, and find she did not turn up to work today. Marvellous cancel their order for denim shirts.

Have the clothes incinerated on the insistence of Marvellous. This is the standard way of protecting the identity of a global brand.

》 212 IF accepted heating grant
》 207 IF declined heating grant

Sell the garments on to a textile reseller who has outlets in inland China.

Receive 15,000.

》 229

It was a good decision: Zina put a steady stream of orders your way. Peace&Love call you: they have not received their order of skinny jeans. Your shipping company tells you it has got stuck in customs at the port; it could take months to clear. You ring Ku Fang in the municipal authorities business department to see if he can help. Ku Fang says he will see what he can do, and gives you a strong recommendation for a local fabric factory.

You place an order with the fabric factory immediately; by the end of the day you get a call from customs to say the clothes have been cleared for shipping.

》 139

WORLD FACTORY

It was a good decision: Zina send more orders your way. Peace&Love call: they have not received the skinny jeans. Your shipping company tell you the order is stuck in customs; it could take months to clear. You ring Ku Fang in the municipal authorities business department to see if he can help but he is somewhat cool with you on the phone.

Ku Fang is clear that if he is to help, you must use a local cotton mill he recommends, and make a significant contribution to his Factory Development Fund.

Spend 20,000.

▶ 139

WORLD FACTORY

Plantlife are not keen to place a larger order yet. Geosync have come back with an order of skirts but it only covers paying the workers at your previous rate, just below the living wage; like Plantlife, they claim they can't raise the end price. How do you fulfil your obligation to the new pay levels for the workers?

Dig into your capital to enable you to market yourself as an ethical brand online called Greenlee.

Spend 20,000.

▶ 87

Reduce the number of workers you have, and partially outsource any large orders somewhere cheaper.

Lose 6 workers.

 134

80

2 skilled machinists jump to another factory, but the other workers accept the bonus and return to work, completing the Run Rabbit T-shirts. Classic brand Marvellous place an order for zip-detail skirts. Sydney Workwear call you: they haven't received the waterproof trousers. Your shipping company tell you the order is stuck in customs and could take months to clear. You ring Ku Fang in the municipal authorities business department to see if he can help but he is somewhat cool with you on the phone.

Ku Fang is clear that if he is to help, you must use a local cotton mill he recommends, and make a significant contribution to his Factory Development Fund.

Spend 30,000. Lose 2 workers.

▶ **409**

81

International brand Mud call you. A celebrity has been seen wearing one of the workshirts that you made for Workers Comfort. They want to place a huge order (for 10,000) with their brand label, immediately, which means prioritising them ahead of other orders. They give you a good price, although as a fashion brand they do not pay a deposit. You need to hire new workers to manage. Your best machinist, Tian Jianying, suggests hiring contacts of hers from home, all trained in tailoring.

Refuse to hire Tian Jiangying's contacts when you meet them. They have arrived from Sichuan after travelling all night; but they look very young and do not have ID.

▶ **292**

Tell Tian Jianying she must provide ID for them; you don't mind how. You have tested their skills, and are impressed; they must have been working for several years.

Gain 10 workers.

▶ **158**

You complete the vest tops for Plantlife and they give you another order for organic baby clothes. But it's not a good day: Marvellous send you photos of a fake 'Marbleous' shop in Chongqing selling the garments you made for them. They set legal proceedings in motion for breach of contract: they are protective of their brand. And then you hear a report on the radio about Ku Fang's fabric-dyeing factory using cotton mills in Bangladesh that employ and house homeless children they have rescued from the streets.

Do nothing. The order is underway now, and anyway you applaud attempts to improve children's lives.

Spend 5,000.

 141

Cancel the order for the fabric and to meet the deadline make the clothes from non-organic cotton; Plantlife will not be able to tell.

Spend 5,000.

 68

Peace&Love call you: they have not received their order of skinny jeans. Your shipping company tell you the order has got stuck at the port and that customs report that it is in a queue for checking, and it could take months. You ring Ku Fang in the municipal authorities business department to see if he can help but he is somewhat cool with you on the phone.

Ku Fang is clear that if he is to help, you must use a local cotton mill he recommends, and make a significant contribution to his Factory Development Fund.

Spend 20,000.

 139

84 WORLD FACTORY

Paying wages, guaranteeing workers a stable income, rather than paying per piece is manageable at this wage level: you have been able to cover the wage bill this month through your income. However, the workers want to return the wages to their previous levels. Zhu Qing has taken on the leadership of the Union: you are surprised Li Pengjian is not involved, as he has always taken an interest in workers' rights. Zhu Qing tells you the faster workers would rather be paid by piece so they can earn more to send home.

Continue paying wages. You do not trust how Zhu Qing is trying to ingratiate herself with you as management.

》51 IF taught workers English
》38 IF did not teach English

Reconsider your decision and move to piecework, which will increase your productivity, which you desperately need, and satisfy your more ambitious workers.

》383

85 WORLD FACTORY

That very evening, perhaps as a result of the electrics being handled by the inspector, a fire starts that damages your factory and spreads to several buildings in the complex. 3 workers, who worked in the next-door factory, and were sleeping overnight there, are killed.

Move fast to repair your factory to a higher safety standard before starting work again. Give your workers a week's paid holiday to ensure they do not jump to another factory. **Spend 30,000.**

》148

Set up the machines that are still working, and bring in builders to do repairs around the workers while they work: you cannot afford to stop production. **Spend 5,000.**

》241

86 WORLD FACTORY

Yan Rong is waiting for you as you leave the office. He wants you to know that the dormitories are now overcrowded, causing altercations between the workers, as well as general discomfort. He points out that another toilet is needed and that workers have been cooking in their dorm rooms instead of the designated kitchen area, as it is too small. An estimate for installing a new toilet is 7,000.

Install a new toilet to calm the situation and research the cost of an onsite canteen.

Spend 7,000.

 291

Fine the workers eating in their rooms; tell Yan Rong that the toilet will have to wait and reduce his pay to encourage him to find work elsewhere.

 223

87 WORLD FACTORY

You complete the skirts for Geosync. You get your first order from a British ethical retailer site, as Greenlee, for patterned tops: you now have to design and make them. The work goes well and it is satisfying to see your own brand developing. Tian Jianying, 1 of your most skilled machinists who makes her own clothes, turns out to have a great eye for design.

Break out the champagne: you are featured in a British ethical magazine, with Cara Delevingne wearing your dress; you are inundated with orders.

Receive 60,000.

 215

88

When you come in the next day, the workers are sitting silently at their machines. Upset by the accident, despite your generous handling of it, and determined to fight for their own rights, they are refusing to work. They are protesting at the increasingly cramped conditions, which was partly a cause of the accident, as well as the continued low pay. Production stops for 3 days. Word gets out about the strike and you have to handle anxious phone calls from clients.

Incurring building/rental costs without generating income to match means you have to pay your bills from your capital.

Spend 20,000.

▶ 132

89

You place more orders from Garb and Zina with the Vietnamese factory. When you put the phone down, you hear a radio report that most factories in Vietnam pay well under a living wage, with labour conditions more precarious than those in China. A compliance inspector from Marvellous visits. She does not enquire as to whether you outsource orders but notes that your electrics are out of date and you should get them checked. You complete and ship the women's suit jackets.

Get the electrics checked immediately.

Spend 3,000.

▶ 149

Leave the electrics for now: there have never been any problems before, and you do not want to disrupt the work.

 239

Paying the workers per piece of garment rather than a wage has significantly increased productivity, and your profits. Li Pengjian reports that Yan Rong and Yao Lin, who are older, are earning less due to their slower working speeds, despite the quality of their work. He would like to see a pay increase: would you be willing to meet with them informally to discuss an idea for changing how the pay is structured?

Meet Li Pengjian and other workers to negotiate the payment structure; you offer them tea.

Receive 30,000.

▶ **385**

Put pay up a little: you know that is what they want.

Receive 30,000.

▶ **406**

The municipal authorities are clamping down on the increasingly unbearable smog; you are fined for using the city incinerators. You get an order for bibs from supermarket Savaday. Peace&Love call you: the skinny jeans you shipped for their export market have disappeared. Your shipping company tell you the order has got stuck in customs; it could take months to clear. You steel yourself to ring Ku Fang in the municipal authorities business department to ask for help. He is rather cool with you on the phone.

Ku Fang is clear that if he is to help, you must use a local fabric factory as your main supplier for organic cotton and contribute to his Factory Development Fund.

Spend 30,000.

▶ **211**

92

WORLD FACTORY

The municipal authorities are clamping down on the increasingly unbearable smog; you are fined for using the city incinerators. Zina call you: they have not received the dresses. Your shipping company tell you they are stuck at the port and that customs report that it is in a queue for checking; it could take months. You ring Ku Fang in the municipal authorities business department; he says he will see what he can do, and recommends a local fabric factory.

Place an order with the fabric factory immediately: and by the end of the day you get a call from customs to say the clothes have been cleared for shipping.

▶ 41

93

WORLD FACTORY

Peace&Love call you: they have not received their order of skinny jeans. Your shipping company tells you it has got stuck in customs at the port; it could take months to clear. You ring Ku Fang in the municipal authorities business department to see if he can help. Ku Fang says he will see what he can do, and gives you a strong recommendation for a local fabric factory: if you mention his name, they will give you an excellent price.

You place an order with the fabric factory immediately; by the end of the day you get a call from customs to say the clothes have been cleared for shipping.

▶ 139

WORLD FACTORY

The kaftan order is completed and shipped. The workers tell you that more than half of them would prefer to keep to a monthly wage, as then they are able to rely on a stable income; and it will not discriminate against those who are highly skilled but older and therefore a little slower. Your workshop supervisor Li Pengjian also tells you that 1 of your most adept machinists, Huang Jiao, wants to move to piecework.

Decide to stick with paying wages and to investigate how to move forward with consultation in future. Your accountant is not impressed.

 15

Move to piecework and now you know the attitude of your workers plan to replace some of those who wanted wages with more ambitious ones hungry to work hard and earn more. **Lose 5 workers.**

 304

WORLD FACTORY

The municipal authorities are clamping down on the increasingly unbearable smog; you are fined for using the city incinerators. You get an order for bibs from supermarket Savaday. Peace&Love call you: the skinny jeans you shipped for their export market never reached their destination. Your shipping company tells you they are stuck in customs and could take months to clear. You ring Ku Fang to see if he can help. He says he will see what he can do, and recommends a local fabric factory you should use.

Place an order with the fabric factory immediately: and by the end of the day you get a call from customs to say the clothes have been cleared for shipping.

⟩ 211

WORLD FACTORY

You complete the waterproof trousers. Watching the new workers struggle to use a sewing machine makes you realise how undervalued sewing is. A man turns up at your office looking for his 15-year-old daughter, Yang Lin, who he says works in your factory. He lost contact with her when she left their village to find work in the city 8 months ago. He has travelled for 26 hours.

Usher Yang Lin's father quickly out of the door, telling him to return at the end of the shift and you will see what you can do.

Receive 30,000.

 404

Tell Yang Lin's father that you have a fast turnover of staff and that you do not recognise his daughter: you worry he might be a compliance inspector.

Receive 30,000.

 220

WORLD FACTORY

The kaftan order is completed and shipped. You have dinner with client Gloria Yeung and neighbouring factory owner, Madame Wang. The conversation turns to rumours of strikes in other provinces: there is no information in the official news. Another ethical brand, Plantlife, are interested in placing an order. Unlike Garb, they visit you at the factory before committing to the order. They are impressed by what they see, but they want you to reveal your labour costs.

Be scrupulously honest and say what you pay.

▶ 29

Give Plantlife the impression you pay more than you do so that you do not lose the order; you pay at reasonable level for the industry, although still a little under a living wage.

▶ 200 IF accepted heating grant
▶ 201 IF declined heating grant

You complete the school-uniform dresses. Sydney Workwear call you: they have not received the waterproof trousers. Your shipping company tell you the order has got stuck at the port and that customs report that it is in a queue for checking, and it could take months. You ring Ku Fang in the municipal authorities business department to see if he can help but he is somewhat cool with you on the phone.

Ku Fang is clear that if he is to help, you must use a local cotton mill he recommends, and make a significant contribution to his Factory Development Fund.

Spend 25,000.

▶ **98a**

EFFICIENCY IS LIFE

Are you a member of the
All-China Union?

YES	NO
Did you move to piecework?	Did you pay a regular wage?

YES	NO	YES	NO
243		**247**	
	321		**227**

You complete the Christmas jumpers. You get an order for men's checked shirts from Zina at the cheaper end of the market. The new workers settle in quickly; like all your workers, they do not have hukou (city residency) and therefore do not have any rights in the city. As the wages are so low, like most other factories, you rent dormitories for them. Your workers' dormitories are on site, but no additional rooms are currently available for the new workers.

Provide additional beds for the current dormitories; there is space and 5 to a room is not unusual.

 32

Take out an annual lease on new dormitories; it cannot be covered by your running costs so will have to come from your capital.

Spend 12,000.

 109

You complete the baby clothes on time; you make a small profit, and Plantlife place a new order. An environmental NGO is on to you: they keep sending you reports. One reveals that the fabric factory you bought from actually source their cotton from Uzbekistan, where child labour is state-sanctioned.

Keep exploring the options for organic cotton. You are determined to find a clean source, even though it will cost you time and money.

Receive 8,000.

 151

Decline the order. The issues with sourcing organic cotton are too time-consuming: you cannot be held responsible for the whole supply chain.

Receive 15,000.

 139

Paying wages, guaranteeing workers a stable income, rather than paying per piece, is just about manageable at this wage level. Li Pengjian tells you the workers want to make whole garments, rather than just a single part of a garment. This will vary the work and mean that the fastest ones will be able to work more quickly. You do need to increase productivity. You consult with fellow factory managers including Madame Wang and find that she has already made this change. You agree to trial it.

Ku Fang calls you: factories in the vicinity are letting workers make key operative decisions outside the Union; he reminds you that independent collectivisation is illegal.

▶ **51** IF taught workers English
▶ **38** IF did not teach English

It is very difficult to find a replacement for your pattern-cutter and you lose the suit-jacket order. Your workers are frustrated by you only having enough work for them for half-days. Liu Huiquan from the factory on the other side of the complex calls to see if you have capacity for handling some jeans? They need to be sandblasted to make them look preworn. She has the equipment, but needs additional labour. If you take the order, you will make a huge profit.

Ask to see the sandblasting equipment before agreeing to provide workers: you have heard it can be dangerous.

▶ **296**

Provide the workers; it is better not to know more. You need the income, and your workers will not be exposed to the sandblasting particles for long; it is only a temporary arrangement.

▶ **301**

You complete the Marvellous shirts and are preparing to ship them. Yuan Bao comes to see you; she tells you that after you sacked her, Lu Qingmin ended up in unpaid bonded labour in an electronics factory in Shenzhen. For 3 days now she has not turned up to work or answered her phone; all Yuan Bao's efforts to locate her have come to nothing. Marvellous cancel their order and tell you to destroy the shirts.

Have the clothes incinerated on the insistence of Marvellous. This is the standard way of protecting the identity of a global brand.

Spend 40,000.

⟩ **95**   IF accepted heating grant

⟩ **91**   IF declined heating grant

Sell the garments on to a textile reseller who has outlets in inland China.

Spend 20,000.

⟩ **237**

"A retailer might have certain factory criteria, which means a factory has to be ethically compliant. It costs the factories a lot of money to have these tests done – so, they'll spend all this money to be audited, and then that retailer might just use them for one order. Even though they might have done ten different prototypes, which is a massive cost to them. That's the shame – there's no regular continuity with the [factories] – it's just standard exploitation. But it's very competitive, it's just the industry and how it works…"

Knitwear designer for the fast-fashion market, Manchester, 2015

Plantlife are happy with your response and place an order for women's organic vest tops. Geosync call to say they have not received the kaftans: they have got stuck in customs at the port. You ring Ku Fang in the municipal authorities business department to see if he can help. He says he will see what he can do; and gives you a strong recommendation for a local fabric factory he hopes you will use.

You place an order with the fabric factory immediately; by the end of the day you get a call from customs to say the clothes have been cleared for shipping.

▶ **104a**

IT'S A WIN-WIN SITUATION

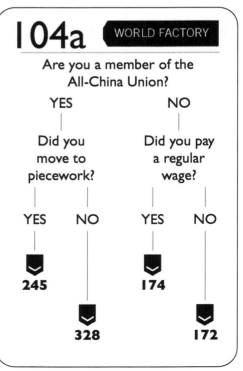

Are you a member of the
All-China Union?

YES   NO

Did you move to piecework?   Did you pay a regular wage?

YES   NO   YES   NO

245   **174**

328   **172**

Plantlife are happy with your response and place an order for women's vest tops made from organic cotton. Geosync call to say they have not received the kaftans: they have got stuck in customs at port. You ring Ku Fang in the municipal authorities business department to see if he can help and he is somewhat cool with you on the phone.

Ku Fang is clear that if he is to help, you must use a local cotton mill he recommends, and make a significant contribution to his Factory Development Fund.

Spend 30,000.

▶ 105a

PRECARITY IS LIFE

105a WORLD FACTORY

Are you a member of the All-China Union?

YES   NO

Did you move to piecework?   Did you pay a regular wage?

YES   NO   YES   NO

245   **174**

328   **172**

You complete the school-uniform dresses and make a profit. Sydney Workwear call you: they have not received the waterproof trousers. Your shipping company tell you they are stuck in customs at the port; it could take months to clear. You ring Ku Fang in the municipal authorities business department to see if he can help. Ku Fang says he will see what he can do, and gives you a strong recommendation for a local fabric factory: if you mention his name, they will give you an excellent price.

You place an order with the fabric factory immediately; by the end of the day you get a call from customs to say the clothes have been cleared for shipping.

Receive 8,000.

▶ **106a**

WORK HARD SO YOUR CHILDREN WON'T HAVE TO

Are you a member of the
All-China Union?

YES   NO

Did you   Did you pay
move to   a regular
piecework?   wage?

YES   NO   YES   NO

243   **174**

          321   **172**

107

Hong Kong sportswear company Run Rabbit place an order for organic-cotton sports T-shirts. A storm cloud is gathering. Regardless of Rainbow Plan rules for measured implementation of wage increases, managed by the Union, Liang Qiang is gathering support for an independent strike in protest at the low pay. Li Pengjian, your factory-floor supervisor, thinks you should take the threat seriously. Although there are ways of dealing with strikes (you help subsidise the local police), it will cost you in productivity.

Sack Liang Qiang. Tell the other workers you will increase pay if they finish the order on time.

Lose 1 worker.

▶ 195 IF hired child workers
▶ 60 IF refused to hire children

Put the pay up.

▶ 123 IF hired child workers
▶ 221 IF refused to hire children

108

Footage from the social evening of the workers' band playing a cover of Bob Dylan's 'The Times They Are A-Changin'" goes viral on Tudou.com and then YouTube. Mick Fletcher from Run Rabbit congratulates you and retweets the link. An ethical lingerie company, Meow, give you a small order for lace bodysuits with a generous deposit. You make a profit again.

Worker Watch, an international NGO, adds you to its list of recommended factories.

Receive 30,000.

 114

The workers seem happy with their accommodation, and productivity is good. However, Carol Zhang is finding it hard to get orders for you in the fast-fashion world, as your labour costs are too high for you to be competitive in this market. She strongly recommends lowering the workers' pay in line with industry standards.

Implement lower wages.

 273

Source cheaper, low-quality cloth to enable you to keep workers' wages up.

 275

Your wiring is declared unsafe by the electrician you hired to check it. He recommends a complete overhaul; this will be very expensive. Your workers are in the middle of a small order of dresses and tops for retailer Garb. They need an especially quick turnaround as it is a near copy of a dress worn by Angelina Jolie at the BAFTAs 24 hours ago.

Go ahead with having the factory completely rewired. Luckily so many of your orders are outsourced it shouldn't slow production by more than a day.

Spend 15,000.

 116

You do not want to upset this important order just when your business is starting to grow. You will review the situation once the dresses are complete.

 239

WORLD FACTORY

Zina do not notice and pay the balance; you just about break even. They place another order for American flag vest tops. After many cold calls to ethically branded retailers, eventually Plantlife call you back. Unusually for fashion, they will give a deposit of a third upfront, which you will then be able to use for fabric and your wage bill. They visit the factory; you send everyone home early that day. They place a large order for men's long-sleeved T-shirts.

To handle the order, hire 3 new workers on the recommendation of your best machinist, Tian Jianying. The deposit makes it affordable.

Gain 3 workers.

 290

WORLD FACTORY

The strikes spread across factories, and then onto the streets. Your workers get caught up in it. Several of them, for example Yan Rong, Yao Lin and Zhu Qing, who are all highly skilled, are unable to get into work. This slows production by 2 days. Your outgoings are crippling.

Pay everyone the full amount for the month. This means dipping into your capital.

Spend 34,000.

 73

Dock pay for the week that workers could not get into work.

Spend 17,000.

 389

You get more orders thanks to Carole Zhang's efforts in Milan. But the phone will not stop ringing for another reason. Your clients have heard a BBC World Service programme about Chinese factories. You listen to it online: Lu Qingmin has given an interview about being a child worker. You go onto the factory floor to find her, but she did not turn up today. A new client, Marvellous, cancels its order, insisting you destroy the garments.

Have the clothes incinerated on the insistence of Marvellous. This is the standard way of protecting the identity of a global brand.

Lose 1 worker.

92 IF accepted heating grant
115 IF declined heating grant

Sell the garments on to a textile reseller who has outlets in inland China.

Receive 8,000. Lose 1 worker.

166

A workers' rights group approach you to ask if they can convert one of the factory storerooms into a small 'museum' for garment workers to counteract the negative image portrayed in the media.

Allow the workers' rights group to set up a museum to value the contribution that garment workers make to society.

381

Say no to the museum; it will distract the workers and the emphasis on workers' rights may draw unwelcome attention from the authorities.

223

The municipal authorities are clamping down on the increasingly unbearable smog; you are fined for using the city incinerators. Zina call you: they have not received the dresses. Your shipping company tell you they are stuck at the port and that customs report that it is in a queue for checking; it could take months. You steel yourself to ring Ku Fang in the municipal authorities business department to ask for help. He is rather cool with you on the phone.

Ku Fang is clear that if he is to help, you must use a local fabric factory as your main supplier for organic cotton and contribute to his Factory Development Fund.

Spend 30,000.

▶ 41

Due to the delay you have to air-freight the evening dresses to get them into the shops in time, which takes any profit you would have made. However, you discover while your factory is shut that you can run the business quite well by paying the factory downstairs to do small orders, and outsourcing everything else to Vietnam. The overheads for only maintaining an office, rather than a whole factory, are much less.

Reduce your workforce to the 5 best workers, who will be able to do all your samples for you.

Retain 5 workers.

▶ 133

Reopen: the balance between outsourcing and employing Chinese workers works well; now you have overhauled the electrics you can be more efficient.

 136

WORLD FACTORY

You complete the workshirt order for Workers Comfort. Your accountant Wang Lin has done the accounts and you find you have made a reasonable profit. However, she is worried about the factory's productivity, as your workers have varying levels of skills.

Spend part of your profit on training workers.

Receive 15,000.

 159

Keep the profit. Your income is too precarious to risk additional outlay at the moment; you have not had any complaints about the quality of the garments.

Receive 30,000.

 169

WORLD FACTORY

Your profits are small this month, due to a series of late payments that have disrupted cashflow. The workers' rights group introduces you to an ethical lingerie company, Meow, who give you a small order for lace bodysuits with a deposit to cover fabric costs. You have been trying to get hold of Qiu Lian, who you outsourced to, to find out when she will complete your recent order. It is now well overdue.

Decide to go round to Qiu Lian's factory in person tomorrow.

Receive 10,000.

 119

119

A fire has engulfed Qiu Lian's factory: Qiu Lian has disappeared, and so have your orders. It turns out the illegal makeshift construction on the roof of the building meant that it was impossible for the workers to escape and 15 lives were lost. A press investigation quickly links Qiu Lian's factory to your own and the famous David Beckham-modelled Run Rabbit T-shirt campaign. Athlete and Meow both cancel their orders.

Keep your full workforce on whilst lowering their pay level; with your expected income cancelled, this will have to come from your capital.

Spend 25,000.

 122

Lose 10 of your workers. It is hard to decide who should go. Everyone is in shock from the news of Qiu Lian's factory.

Lose 10 workers.

 223

120

The workers are pleasantly surprised; they had not expected you to agree. You get an order for men's checked shirts from Zina at the cheaper end of the market. Liang Qiang catches you as you leave the factory office: the workers understood the low pay level while you were starting up. But they would now like the wages to be returned to 3,000 a month. Currently, Liang Qiang points out, they have barely enough to cover food bills, and certainly can't save anything to send home.

Tell the workers they will have to be patient; workwear pays a deposit upfront, but fashion brands do not, and therefore your income is not yet stable enough to raise pay.

273

Put the wages back up. Source cheap fabric so that you can afford it.

275

The workers are pleasantly surprised; they had not expected you to agree. Liang Qiang catches you as you leave the factory office: the workers understood the low pay level while you were starting up. But they would now like the wages to be returned to 3,000 a month. Currently, Liang Qiang points out, they have barely enough to cover food bills, and certainly can't save anything to send home.

Put the wages back up. Source cheaper fabric to balance the books.

》 274

Do not put up the wages as you cannot afford it.

》 276

Your reputation is destroyed. None of your regular clients are currently willing to place an order with you, although you are aware it may well blow over in a few weeks. You can't sleep at night as you deliberate over how you can continue to operate in an industry that regularly overlooks the rights and welfare of workers. You have to keep going somehow, to survive.

Commit part of any future income to a local NGO to fight for workers' rights.

》 378

Put all your efforts into seeking orders to ensure you can pay your workers.

》 223

123 WORLD FACTORY

The pay rise appears to have calmed relations for the time being, and you finish the waterproof trousers, bringing in a profit. Garb unexpectedly send a compliance officer to inspect you: the agreed signal sends the young workers out the back, but she sees them as she leaves, and Garb do not place another order. You also discover organic cotton is very costly but Run Rabbit say they cannot raise the price: their research shows that people will not pay more. Zina place an order for dresses with a frill skirt.

Outsource to Vietnam: the labour costs are lower there. Your pattern-cutter cuts and bundles the fabric, which is then sent to Vietnam for sewing.

Receive 30,000.

▶ 123a

Take the hit yourself on the organic cotton: you want to use it for environmental reasons, but decide outsourcing is not for you.

Receive 18,000.

▶ 49

MAXIMUM DESIGN WOW AT MINIMUM COST

123a WORLD FACTORY

Are you a member of the All-China Union?

YES — Did you move to piecework?
  YES → 248
  NO → 322

NO — Did you pay a regular wage?
  YES → 177
  NO → 176

You immediately start to get more orders thanks to Carol Zhang's efforts. But today the phone will not stop ringing for another reason. Your clients have heard a BBC World Service programme about Chinese factories. You listen to the interview online, and realise that Lu Qingmin has given an interview about being a child worker. You go onto the factory floor to talk to her, and find she did not turn up to work today. Your new client, Marvellous, cancel their order, insisting you destroy the garments.

Have the skirts incinerated: this is standard for unwanted branded goods.

▶ 124a

Sell the garments on to a textile reseller who has outlets in inland China.

Receive 15,000.

▶ 161

BITTER FIRST SWEET LATER

124a WORLD FACTORY

Are you a member of the
All-China Union?

YES	NO
Did you move to piecework?	Did you pay a regular wage?

YES	NO	YES	NO
⌄ 249		⌄ 164	
	⌄ 326		⌄ 34

125

You complete the baby clothes for Plantlife and make a profit. Run Rabbit would like to place another order, also for garments made with organic cotton. An environmental NGO you contacted keep sending you reports. One reveals that the fabric factory you bought the non-organic cotton from source it from Uzbekistan, where child labour is state-sanctioned.

Keep exploring the options for organic cotton. You are determined to find a clean source, even though it will cost you time and money.

Receive 5,000.

 151

Decline the order. The issues with sourcing organic cotton are too time-consuming: you cannot be held responsible for the whole supply chain.

Receive 10,000.

 139

126

Paying per piece means your workers are reluctant to take time to train the new workers. Ku Fang calls. He wants your factory to set up a Union, belonging to the All-China Federation of Trade Unions. He reassures you that you will have some say in appointing the Union committee. Liang Qiang immediately makes a formal request that you implement the Rainbow Plan for improving workers' pay.

Tell Liang Qiang you hear him, but the Rainbow Plan is for the long term: pay will go up when your revenue goes up.

▶ **203**

Put the pay up in accordance with the Union long-term plan, although you will have to pay part of this month's pay from your capital.

Spend 12,000.

 150

WORLD FACTORY

You complete the Run Rabbit T-shirts. Setting up an office in Beijing was an excellent idea; the internal market is on the up due to the rapid expansion of the Chinese consumer base. You are already making a profit. You are inundated with orders, including one from a Chinese high-street brand, Peace&Love, for skinny jeans.

Expand your workforce to cope with demand.

Receive 30,000. Gain 8 workers.

▶ **127a**

KEEP GOING FORWARD

127a WORLD FACTORY

Are you a member of the All-China Union?

YES — Did you move to piecework? — YES → **242** / NO → **267**

NO — Did you pay a regular wage? — YES → **182** / NO → **181**

WORLD FACTORY

Liang Qiang comes to see you to say that the workers have voted unanimously for the pay to be returned at least to its previous level. The other workers selected Liang Qiang to be their spokesperson, and he wishes to represent their needs. You have other concerns on your mind. Of 15 free samples you have sewn for fast-fashion clients in recent weeks, only 2 placed an order.

Put the pay up as requested by the workers, although to start with it will have to come from your capital.

Spend 10,000.

 131

Tell Liang Qiang you hear him, but your hand cannot be forced. Pay levels will go up when your revenue goes up.

▶ **23**

WORLD FACTORY

Qiu Lian, a former worker of yours, has set up her own small factory; she offers to take part of the order. You have also heard of high-quality garment factories in Vietnam. The running costs of factories there are much lower than in China. According to your projections for cost for each, you are likely to make double the profit if you outsource to Vietnam.

Source the organic fabric and have your pattern-cutter cut and bundle it, to be sent to Vietnam for sewing.

▶ **278**

Outsource to Qiu Lian: then you can keep an eye on production.

▶ **36**

Morale is high: most of your younger workers have taken up the offer of English and computing lessons. You get a rush order for dresses with a frill skirt from Zina. You make a reasonable profit this month. You receive an email from Run Rabbit saying they cannot raise the price for the organic-cotton sports T-shirt as their research shows that people will not pay more. You find a company in Vietnam who have half the labour costs you do, and produce very high-quality work.

Outsource to Vietnam in order to cover the cost of the organic cotton. Your pattern-cutter cuts and bundles the fabric, which is then sent to Vietnam for sewing.

Receive 30,000.

 130a

Take the hit yourself on the organic cotton: you want to use it for environmental reasons, but decide outsourcing is not for you.

Receive 8,000.

▶ 49

BELIEVE IN THE FUTURE

130a   WORLD FACTORY

Are you a member of the All-China Union?

YES

Did you move to piecework?

YES — 248

NO — 322

NO

Did you pay a regular wage?

YES — 177

NO — 176

131 WORLD FACTORY

You get an order for ladies' New York couture tops from Zina. You have dinner with merchandiser Gloria Yeung and neighbouring factory owner, Madame Wang. The conversation turns to rumours of strikes in other provinces: there is no information in the official news. Madame Wang is providing her workers with free tuition in computing and English. Gloria talks about the night school where she learnt English, which helped her fulfil her dream of a desk job.

Decide to invest in training workers in skills that are useful to the factory. It is not your role to direct the education of the workers.

Spend 3,000.

 224

Offer free extra tuition to your workers at the end of their working day, as well as improving their sewing skills.

Spend 6,000.

 188

---

132 WORLD FACTORY

You have to find a way out of the impasse.

Sack the entire workforce so that you can hire new more cooperative workers.

Lose your workforce.

 143

Agree to some demands for raising pay and improved working conditions; you hire 5 workers to reduce the workload.

Spend 20,000. Gain 5 workers.

 223

WORLD FACTORY

You complete the Chinese print tops for Garb. Your profits immediately increase and Garb arrange to visit you to discuss new orders. You decide to come clean to all your clients about your practice of outsourcing the cheaper end of your business. Run Rabbit are not happy about this but Garb do not mind: although they take the opportunity to negotiate a lower price for the tops.

Make the possibility of outsourcing a standard part of your contracts from now on. You can afford to lose Run Rabbit's custom.

Receive 45,000.

》 191

Agree with Run Rabbit that you will continue to make their orders in house. Rehire 10 workers.

Receive 45,000. Gain 10 workers.

》 223

WORLD FACTORY

You complete the T-shirts for Plantlife and the skirts for Geosync. You get your first order from a British ethical retailer site, as Greenlee, for patterned tops: you now have to design and make them. Qiu Lian, a former worker, has set up her own small factory; she needs orders and has fewer overheads than you. You've also heard of high-quality garment factories in Vietnam: the running costs of factories there are much lower than in China. According to your projections, you are likely to make double the profit if you outsource to Vietnam.

Source the fabric and have your pattern-cutter cut and bundle it, to be sent to Vietnam for sewing.

Receive 60,000.

》 198

Outsource the whole of production locally, to Qiu Lian: then you can keep an eye on it.

Receive 30,000.

》 145

You get a phone call: it is Marvellous, cancelling the order for skirts that they placed with you. What is awkward is that they only officially ordered 500, which they will pay for: but they had indicated they would be likely to want 5,000, and therefore, since the fabric was so much cheaper in bulk, you bought enough for 5,000 and had started making them.

Have the skirts incinerated: this is standard practice for unwanted branded goods.

 135a

Sell the garments on to a textile reseller who has outlets in inland China.

Receive 15,000.

▶ **161**

WORK HARD DREAM HARDER

Are you a member of the All-China Union?

YES	NO
Did you move to piecework?	Did you pay a regular wage?

YES	NO	YES	NO
249		**164**	
	326		**34**

You now need to find new orders if you are to survive. Liu Huiquan from the factory on the other side of the complex gives you a call. Her factory escaped the fire, and she wonders whether you could handle some jeans? They need to be sandblasted to make them look preworn. She has the equipment, but not enough workers to get the order completed in time. If you provide 7 workers, you will make a huge profit: much more than your usual profit from a single order.

Ask to see the sandblasting equipment before agreeing to provide workers: you have heard it can be dangerous.

 296

Provide the workers. It is better not to know; you need the income, and they will not be exposed to the sandblasting particles for long, as it is only a temporary arrangement.

 301

"In plain words, starting a business is a path of no return. There's no retreat. I not only have to make enough for myself to survive, I also need to make enough for those I'm leading – the employees, and their families – and their development, so that they can buy a flat and buy a car in Shanghai. All these dreams, I can't not... keep going forward."

Madame Wang, owner of the Zhengxing Clothing Co. factory, Shanghai (manufacturer of the World Factory shirt), 2014

You complete the Marvellous skirts and are preparing to ship them. Yuan Bao comes to see you; she tells you that after you sacked her, Lu Qingmin ended up in unpaid bonded labour in an electronics factory in Shenzhen. For 3 days now she has not turned up to work or answered her phone; all Yuan Bao's efforts to locate her have come to nothing. And then you get a phone call: It is Marvellous, who cancel the order.

Have the skirts incinerated: this is standard for unwanted branded goods.

▶ 137a

Sell the garments on to a textile reseller who has outlets in inland China.

Receive 15,000.

▶ 161

CHINA FIRST

Are you a member of the All-China Union?

YES   NO

Did you move to piecework?   Did you pay a regular wage?

YES   NO   YES   NO

⌄ 249   **⌄ 164**

      ⌄ 326   **⌄ 34**

138

Your Vietnamese workers are quickly back to work, once the official has gone, and promise you they will stay late to finish. You have dinner with Madame Wang from ZhengXing Clothing Co., and your friend, the merchandiser Gloria Yeung. The major topic of conversation is a new police crackdown on illegal immigrants. The conversation later turns to rumours of strikes in other provinces, although there is no information in the official news.

Arriving at your factory mid-morning the next day, there is no sign of your Vietnamese workers. They have simply vanished: you never find out what happened to them.

Lose 5 workers.

▶ 183

139

Your pattern-cutter Liu Chengtian slices a finger off, ruining a stack of fabric worth 5,000. As a migrant worker, he does not have any access to health care.

Pay Liu Chengtian's medical bills and compensation; you have to dig into your capital to cover the costs.

Spend 15,000.

▶ 88

Sack Liu Chengtian for negligence; you have to dig into your capital to cover the cost of the ruined fabric.

Spend 5,000. Lose 1 worker.

 244

140

◀ WORLD FACTORY

You have dinner with Madame Wang from ZhengXing Clothing Co. and your friend, the merchandiser Gloria Yeung. The major topic of conversation is a new police crackdown on illegal immigrants. The conversation later turns to rumours of strikes in other provinces, although there is no information in the official news. Sportswear company Run Rabbit place an order for 100% organic-cotton T-shirts.

Arriving at your factory mid-morning the next day, there is no sign of your Vietnamese workers. They have simply vanished: you never find out what happened to them.

▶ 107

141

◀ WORLD FACTORY

You complete the vest tops, and receive more orders for organic items, including baby clothes. International brand Zina, who make clothes for the Chinese market, have heard about the copycat Marbleous shop. They are keen to know if you will make other copies of fashion garments for them. You will just have to change 5 details to avoid copyright; they have lawyers to handle that sort of thing.

Take the order. You are happy to oblige; producing copies of fashion garments should be a lucrative line of business.

Receive 30,000.

▶ 125

Refuse to copy other brands; you believe in the integrity of the designer.

 100

Thanks to Carole Zhang, in Milan, you get an order from Marvellous, a British brand with global outlets. Yuan Bao comes to see you; she tells you that after you sacked her, Lu Qingmin ended up in unpaid bonded labour in an electronics factory in Shenzhen. For 3 days now she has not turned up to work or answered her phone; all Yuan Bao's efforts to locate her have come to nothing. Marvellous cancel their order, although you have already started it.

Have the clothes incinerated on the insistence of Marvellous. This is the standard way of protecting the identity of a global brand.

92 IF accepted heating grant
115 IF declined heating grant

Sell the garments on to a textile reseller who has outlets in inland China.

Receive 8,000.

166

Having sacked your workers, you realise it will not be as easy as you thought to get new ones in the city: the labour market is changing, and there is a shortage of workers who have the skills you require.

Move the factory out to the provinces where pay levels are lower; you can hire workers locally, and rent larger premises at the same price.

Gain 40 workers.

155

Decide to stay in the city and rehire a smaller number of workers at a better pay level, to manage outsourcing the easier work overseas.

Gain 10 workers.

396

144

You complete the order for skirts from Marvellous. Setting up an office in Beijing was an excellent idea; you immediately start to make more profit. The internal market is on the up due to the rapid expansion of the Chinese consumer base. You are inundated with orders including one from a Chinese high-street brand, Peace&Love, for skinny jeans.

Expand your workforce to cope with demand.

Receive 30,000. Gain 8 workers.

 144a

TIME IS MONEY

144a

WORLD FACTORY

Are you a member of the
All-China Union?

YES   NO

Did you   Did you pay
move to   a regular
piecework?   wage?

YES   NO   YES   NO

242   **182**

            267   **181**

Profits are pouring in; however, the quality of the completed order from Qiu Lian is variable; there are quite a lot of differences between the tops made in-house and those made in Qiu Lian's factory. You are on your way to see her about it, when you hear that there has been a serious fire that has engulfed her factory. It appears that several of her workers were trapped inside as she did not have proper safety exits.

Shut down the Greenlee website; you cannot in all conscience market these garments as 'ethical' any longer. You go back to making workwear.

Receive 60,000.

 213

Donate a substantial amount to the local labour rights organisation, who are trying to improve the situation for workers.

Spend 20,000.

 223

You complete the Run Rabbit T-shirt order. Zina call you: they have not received the dresses. Your shipping company tell you they are stuck at the port and that customs report that they are in a queue for checking; it could take months. You steel yourself to ring Ku Fang in the municipal authorities business department to see if he can help but he is somewhat cool with you on the phone.

Ku Fang is clear that if he is to help, you must use a local fabric factory as your main supplier for organic cotton and contribute to his Factory Development Fund.

Spend 30,000.

 41

147

WORLD FACTORY

You have dinner with Madame Wang from ZhengXing Clothing Co., Ltd and your friend, the merchandiser Gloria Yeung. The major topic of conversation is a new police crackdown on illegal immigrants. The conversation later turns to rumours of strikes in other provinces, although there is no information in the official news.

Arriving at your factory mid-morning the next day, there is no sign of your Vietnamese workers. They have simply vanished: you never find out what happened to them.

Lose 5 workers.

▶ 183

148

WORLD FACTORY

You discover while your factory is shut that you can run the business quite well by paying the factory downstairs to do small orders, and outsourcing everything else to Vietnam. The overheads for only maintaining an office, rather than a whole factory, are much less.

Reopen. You have paid a lot to repair the factory, and you do not want to lose direct contact with the workforce making your orders.

▶ 136

Reduce your workforce to the 5 best workers, who will be able to do all your samples for you

Retain 5 workers.

 133

The radio report is unsettling. Whilst you are pleased that your own factory passes stringent international compliance regulations for ethical practices, you do not know the exact conditions in your Vietnamese factory. You have made a good profit this month. However, to bring production at current levels back to your own factory, you would have to hire a lot more people and your own workers would have to take a significant drop in pay.

Continue to outsource to Vietnam for the time being.

Receive 45,000.

》110

Decide to investigate the working conditions in Vietnam yourself, and use some capital for a flight to Hanoi.

Receive 42,000.

》61

You have dinner with Madame Wang from ZhengXing Clothing Co. and your friend, the merchandiser Gloria Yeung. The major topic of conversation is a new police crackdown on illegal immigrants. The conversation later turns to rumours of strikes in other provinces, although there is no information in the official news. Sportswear company Run Rabbit place an order for 100% organic-cotton T-shirts.

Go home after the dinner relieved that you have put the pay up; hopefully it will prevent trouble spreading your way.

》123 IF hired child workers
》221 IF refused to hire children

151

Your research leads you to Benin in West Africa, where crops are watered by rain rather than depleting rivers. For organic certification it must be free of chemicals for 3 years before it can be sold at the higher price organic cotton attracts. You decide to support farmers attempting this transition. Meanwhile, on the factory floor, your pattern-cutter Liu Chengtian slices a finger off, ruining a stack of fabric worth 5,000.

Pay Liu Chengtian's medical bills and compensation; you have to dig into your capital to cover the costs.

Spend 15,000.

 88

Sack Liu Chengtian for negligence; you have to dig into your capital to cover the cost of the ruined fabric.

Spend 5,000. Lose 1 worker.

 102

152

You complete the Run Rabbit T-shirt order. Zina call you: they have not received the dresses. Your shipping company tell you they are stuck at the port and that customs report that it is in a queue for checking; it could take months. You ring Ku Fang in the municipal authorities business department to see if he can help. Ku Fang says he will see what he can do, and gives you a strong recommendation for a local fabric factory: if you mention his name, they will give you an excellent price.

You place an order with the fabric factory immediately; by the end of the day you get a call from customs to say the clothes have been cleared for shipping.

 41

Sewing whole garments is hard for some workers, but your skilled machinists help out: this slows productivity but in the longer term will improve everyone's skills. For now, the garments are less neatly sewn than previously, but you have had no complaints. It turns out to be very expensive to source organic cotton for the Plantlife order, but they claim they cannot raise the price, as their research shows that people will not pay more. You also receive an order from Marvellous, a British brand, for suit jackets.

Decline the Plantlife order: you cannot afford to take the financial risk on it given your commitment to paying your workers at this level.

 43

Take the Plantlife order and try to make it work; organic cotton does not use pesticides which damage the health of cotton pickers.

▶ 379

Yuan Bao comes to see you; she tells you that after you sacked her, Lu Qingmin ended up in unpaid bonded labour in an electronics factory in Shenzhen. For 3 days now she has not turned up to work or answered her phone; all Yuan Bao's efforts to locate her have come to nothing. And then Run Rabbit cancel their order halfway through.

Have the garments incinerated: this is standard practice for unwanted branded goods.

▶ 67

Sell the garments on to a textile reseller who has outlets in inland China.

Receive 15,000.

▶ 70

155

WORLD FACTORY

Moving to the province of Chongqing almost immediately proves profitable: the relocation costs are soon covered by your increased income, due to the lower pay levels. Your workers will now have average journeys of only 5–6 hours to get home, rather than 18–24. A few are local. With the new lower target prices you can offer, you are excited to receive an order from Anna Morgan, a high-end fashion brand. You are now in a position to increase the workforce further.

Recruitment is time-consuming at this scale so you hire a temporary recruitment manager to take care of it.

Receive 50,000. Gain 40 workers.

▶ **178**

156

WORLD FACTORY

The phone will not stop ringing. Your clients have heard a BBC World Service programme about Chinese factories. You listen to the interview online, and realise that Lu Qingmin has given an interview about being a child worker. You go onto the factory floor to talk to her, and find she did not turn up to work today. Run Rabbit cancels its order, insisting you destroy the garments.

Have the garments incinerated: this is standard practice for unwanted branded goods.

▶ **67**

Sell the garments on to a textile reseller who has outlets in inland China.

Receive 15,000.

▶ **70**

Marvellous call you: reporters from the BBC World Service have called them to ask if they realise that they are working with factories employing underage workers. You go to find Lu Qingmin to talk to her and find she did not come in to work today. Marvellous pull their shirt order; they want to expand internationally and this could badly affect their reputation. As well as a trade deficit, you now have stockpiles of cancelled clothing.

Have the shirts incinerated on the insistence of Marvellous. This is the standard way of protecting the identity of a global brand.

▶ **95**   IF accepted heating grant
▶ **91**   IF declined heating grant

Sell the garments on to a textile reseller who has outlets in inland China.

Receive 10,000.

▶ **237**

Your new workers settle in quickly and are very diligent. Tian Jianying provides the ID and you arrange a signal by which they would all exit the back door of the factory in the unlikely event of an inspection. Wang Lin advises you to move to piecework, a different financial model for paying your workers. Workers are paid per item they complete, which incentivises them to work faster. Apparently skilled workers tend to like it, as it means they can earn more to send home.

Change to piecework. From now on you will pay workers according to how many garments they make, rather than paying a set monthly wage.

▶ **37**

Enquire as to the attitudes of your workers by asking your factory-floor supervisor, Li Pengjian, before you change your pay structure.

▶ **293**

WORLD FACTORY

Your factory-floor supervisor, Li Pengjian, tells you that other local factories have started to provide free tuition in subjects such as computing and English for their workers, and that the workers would like this opportunity as well. Carol Zhang has been telling them about the night school she went to, to learn English, which helped her fulfil her dream of a desk job.

Offer free extra tuition to your workers at the end of their working day, as well as improving their sewing skills.

Spend 7,000.

 21

Tell Li Pengjian that you will only invest in training workers in skills that are useful to the factory.
It is not your role to direct the education of the workers.

> **334**

WORLD FACTORY

You complete the Garb distressed T-shirt order; it took longer than anticipated to make them look old and worn. You get an order from Sydney Workwear for waterproof trousers. Under your guidance, your newly unionised workers form a committee to move towards implementing the government-sponsored Rainbow Plan, for increasing wages over the longer term. However, Liang Qiang demands pay is put up immediately.

Tell Liang Qiang you hear him, but the Rainbow Plan is for the long-term: pay will go up when your revenue goes up.

> **203**

Put the pay up in accordance with the Union long-term plan, although you will have to pay part of this month's pay from your capital.

Spend 12,000.

 150

It is not a good day: Marvellous send you photos of a fake 'Marbleous' shop in Chongqing selling their garments you made. They set legal proceedings in motion for breach of contract. In this globalised economy, brand recognition reaches everywhere, and Marvellous are increasingly protective of their identity.

You are unable to avoid being sued; and have to dig into your capital to afford it.

Spend 7,000.

▶ **161a**

CHEAP AND QUICK

Are you a member of the All-China Union?

YES — NO

YES:
Did you move to piecework?

YES — NO

NO:
Did you pay a regular wage?

YES — NO

YES (piecework): **50**

NO (piecework): **84**

YES (wage): **101**

NO (wage): **90**

162

International brand Zina, who make clothes for the Chinese market, have heard about the copycat Run Rabbie shop. They want you to make a T-shirt inspired by the Run Rabbit design. You will just have to change 5 details to avoid copyright.

Take the order. You are happy to oblige; producing copies of fashion garments could be lucrative.

 89

Refuse to copy other brands: you believe in artistic integrity.

223

163

You finally complete the Garb distressed T-shirt order, it took longer than anticipated to make them look old and worn. You get an order from Sydney Workwear for waterproof trousers. Ku Fang calls: they would like you to appoint a workers' rep for consultation between the union and management. He recommends Zhu Qing. You think she will be a good source of information regarding the workers. Advised by their local headquarters, a workers' delegation comes to see you to ask for a small increase in pay.

Tell Liang Qiang you hear him, but your hand cannot be forced. Pay levels will go up when your revenue goes up.

203

Put the pay up in accordance with the Union long-term plan, although you will have to pay part of this month's pay from your capital.

Spend 12,000.

 150

WORLD FACTORY

The municipal authorities are clamping down on the unbearable smog; you are fined 5,000 for using the city incinerators. Paying wages, guaranteeing workers a stable income, rather than paying per piece, is manageable. Li Pengjian tells you the workers want to make whole garments, rather than just a single part, to vary the work and enable the fastest to work more quickly. You need to increase productivity. You consult with Madame Wang and find she has already made this change. You agree to trial it.

Ku Fang calls you: factories in the vicinity are letting workers make key operative decisions outside the Union; he reminds you that independent collectivisation is illegal.

Spend 5,000.

▶ **51** IF taught workers English

▶ **38** IF did not teach English

WORLD FACTORY

You complete the Mud workshirts, and make a profit. You invite Yan Rong, Yao Lin, Zhu Qing and Li Pengjian into your office. They tell you the move to piecework has divided the workforce, as it discriminates against those who are highly skilled but older and therefore slower. They tell you that life is precarious enough without the uncertainty each month of not knowing how much they will earn. They would like to be able to monitor the situation and meet with you again to discuss it.

Help your workers set up a legal Union under government auspices.

Receive 15,000.

▶ **160**

Agree to the request for regular consultation, although it will be unofficial as independent unionisation is illegal.

Receive 15,000.

▶ **218**

166

WORLD FACTORY

It is not a good day: Marvellous send you photos of a fake 'Marbleous' shop in Chongqing selling their garments you made. They cancel the cropped trousers and set legal proceedings in motion for breach of contract. In this globalised economy, brand recognition reaches everywhere, and Marvellous are increasingly protective of their identity.

You are unable to avoid being sued; and have to dig into your capital to afford it.

Spend 7,000.

▶ 175

167

WORLD FACTORY

You complete the Garb distressed T-shirt order; it took longer than anticipated to make them look old and worn. You get an order from Sydney Workwear for waterproof trousers. Liang Qiang comes to see you to say that the workers have voted unanimously for the pay to be returned at least to its previous level. The other workers selected Liang Qiang to be their spokesperson, and he wishes to represent their needs.

Tell Liang Qiang you hear him, but your hand cannot be forced. Pay levels will go up when your revenue goes up.

▶ 204

Put the pay up in accordance with the Union long-term plan, although you will have to pay part of this month's pay from your capital.

Spend 12,000.

 150

It was a good decision: Zina place a steady stream of orders. You hire 2 workers to handle the workload. Sydney Workwear call you: they have not received the waterproof trousers. Your shipping company tells you they are stuck in customs at the port; it could take months to clear. You ring Ku Fang in the municipal authorities business department to see if he can help. Ku Fang says he will see what he can do, and gives you a strong recommendation for a local fabric factory.

You place an order with the fabric factory immediately; by the end of the day you get a call from customs to say the clothes have been cleared for shipping.

Gain 2 workers.

▶ 41

You get an order for waterproof trousers. However, production is slowed by a day, because Xie Qingfang, Liu Luiquan and Cao Tao suddenly leave, having got jobs in larger factories that offer on-site educational facilities. This causes ripples of discontent: many of your workers are frustrated with the lack of potential in their work for developing their education or skills.

Hire replacements for Xie Qingfang, Liu Luiquan and Cao Tao.

Lose 3 workers. Gain 3 workers.

 376

WORLD FACTORY

The new workers from Teke Village arrive, and set to work quickly. However, they are complaining that the food served in the canteen is far too bland for their taste. You receive some late payments on orders that you delivered over a month ago.

Increase the choice on the canteen menu to include 3 main dishes per day with varying degrees of spiciness.

Receive 30,000.

▶ **74**

Keep the menu the same. Not everyone wants to eat such spicy food.

Receive 30,000.

▶ **223**

WORLD FACTORY

The Marvellous suit jackets and the second order of Workers Comfort workshirts are completed and shipped. Your agent has organised a visit from the ethical sports brand Run Rabbit, who send their compliance officer. He reports that you don't have enough fire extinguishers and that the exposed and worn electrical wiring in the factory is dangerous. He says that if you don't get Worldwide Responsible Apparel Production (WRAP) certification they cannot work with you.

Pay for fire extinguishers and new electrical cabling and proceed with the process of getting full certification.

Spend 15,000.

▶ **395** IF accepted heating grant
▶ **394** IF declined heating grant

Tell Run Rabbit you will move towards compliance, but decide not to interfere with the electrics for now; it has been that way for years with no issues arising.

 85

Paying the workers per piece of garment rather than a wage has significantly increased productivity, and your profits. Li Pengjian reports that Yan Rong and Yao Lin, who are older, are earning less due to their slower working speeds, despite the quality of their work. Would you be willing to meet with them informally to discuss an idea for changing how the pay is structured?

Meet Li Pengjian and other workers to negotiate the pay structure; you offer them tea.

 347

Decline to meet Li Pengjian and other worekrs; you are aware that the authorities are currently nervous about independent collective bargaining.

▶ **31**

You complete the Mud workshirts and Garb distressed T-shirts and make a profit, once the balance is paid. You notice that as a result of your treatment of the troublemakers, your workforce is more deferential; and productivity is increasing. You go to the labour exchange to find new workers, and discover it will not be as easy as you thought. Most who are there looking for work want to join a large factory with more onsite benefits than you are in a position to offer.

Hire untrained Chinese migrant workers willing to take low pay. You will have to train them.

Receive 15,000. Gain 5 workers.

▶ **391**

Hire illegal Vietnamese economic migrants who are desperate for work and highly skilled.

Receive 15,000. Gain 5 workers.

 297

174

WORLD FACTORY

Paying wages, guaranteeing workers a stable income, is tough at this wage level; you have to use part of your capital again for this month's pay. Li Pengjian tells you the workers want to make whole garments, rather than just a single part of a garment. This will vary the work and mean that the fastest ones will be able to work faster. You consult with fellow factory managers including Madame Wang and find that she has already made this change. You agree to trial it.

Ku Fang calls you: factories in the vicinity are letting workers make key operative decisions outside the Union; he reminds you that independent collectivisation is illegal.

Spend 10,000.

▶ **153**

175

WORLD FACTORY

International brand Zina, who make clothes for the Chinese market, have heard about the copycat Marbleous shop. They are keen to know if you will make other copies of fashion garments for them. You will just have to change 5 details to avoid copyright; they have lawyers to handle that sort of thing.

Take the order. You are happy to oblige; producing copies of fashion garments could be a lucrative line of business.

Receive 30,000.

▶ **168** IF accepted heating grant
▶ **197** IF declined heating grant

Refuse to copy other garments; you believe in the integrity of the designer.

▶ **152** IF accepted heating grant
▶ **146** IF declined heating grant

You complete the dresses with a frill skirt and ship them to Zina. Outsourcing, as well as paying the workers per piece of garment rather than a wage has significantly increased productivity, and your profits. Li Pengjian reports that Yan Rong and Yao Lin, who are older, are earning less due to their slower working speeds, despite the quality of their work. He would like to see a pay increase: would you be willing to meet with them informally to discuss an idea for changing how the pay is structured?

Meet Li Pengjian and other workers to negotiate the payment structure; you offer them tea.

Receive 30,000.

 356

Keep a distance, you are aware that such independent negotiations are not welcomed by the authorities.

Receive 30,000.

▶ **57**

You complete the dresses and ship them to Zina. Paying wages, guaranteeing workers a stable income, rather than paying per piece, is just about manageable thanks to outsourcing some of the work. Li Pengjian tells you the workers want to make whole garments, rather than individual parts, which would vary the work and mean that the fastest could work more quickly. You do need to increase productivity. You consult with fellow factory manager Madame Wang and find that she has already made this change. You agree to trial it.

Ku Fang calls you: factories in the vicinity are letting workers make key operative decisions outside the Union; he reminds you that independent collectivisation is illegal.

▶ **55**   IF accepted heating grant
▶ **57**   IF declined heating grant

178

All is going well, and you are making steady profits. There does seem to be a high turnover of staff; you need to do something to keep them, as it is affecting the quality of the work, and morale in the factory. The brands generally do not seem to notice quality as long as the price is right, but you would like to stabilise the workforce.

Plan to build more spacious dormitories, with broadband access for wifi, using most of your profit this month.

Receive 20,000.

 186

Organise a social club where workers can gather for activities. You are on the edge of an industrial city and their homes are still too far for them to travel regularly.

Receive 60,000.

 338

179

Paying the workers per piece of garment rather than a wage has significantly increased productivity, and your profits. Li Pengjian reports that Yan Rong and Yao Lin, who are older, are earning less due to their slower working speeds, despite the quality of their work. He would like to see a pay increase: would you be willing to meet with them informally to discuss an idea for changing how the pay is structured?

Meet Li Pengjian and other workers to negotiate the payment structure; you offer them tea.

▶ **359**

Put pay up a little: you know that is what your workers want.

▶ **171**

Paying wages, guaranteeing workers a stable income, rather than paying per piece, is just about manageable at this wage level. Li Pengjian tells you the workers want to make whole garments, rather than just a single part of a garment. This will vary the work and mean that the fastest ones will be able to work more quickly. You do need to increase productivity. You consult with fellow factory managers including Madame Wang and find that she has already made this change. You agree to trial it.

Ku Fang calls you: factories in the vicinity are letting workers make key operative decisions outside the Union; he reminds you that independent collectivisation is illegal.

 171

You complete the Run Rabbit T-shirts. Paying the workers per piece of garment rather than a wage has significantly increased productivity, and your profits. Li Pengjian reports that Yan Rong and Yao Lin, who are older, are earning less due to their slower working speeds, despite the quality of their work. He would like to see a pay increase: would you be willing to meet with them informally to discuss an idea for changing how the pay is structured?

Meet Li Pengjian and other workers to negotiate the payment structure; you offer them tea.

 365

182

Paying wages, guaranteeing workers a stable income, rather than paying per piece, is just about manageable at this wage level. Li Pengjian tells you the workers want to make whole garments, rather than just a single part of a garment. This will vary the work and mean that the fastest ones will be able to work more quickly. You do need to increase productivity. You consult with fellow factory managers including Madame Wang and find that she has already made this change. You agree to trial it.

Ku Fang calls you: factories in the vicinity are letting workers make key operative decisions outside the Union; he reminds you that independent collectivisation is illegal.

▶ 265

183

You get an order for skirts with zip details from British brand Marvellous. Your factory-floor supervisor, Li Pengjian, tells you that other local factories have started to provide free tuition in subjects such as computing and English for their workers, and that the workers would like this opportunity as well. Carol Zhang has been telling them about the night school she went to, to learn English, which helped her fulfil her dream of a desk job.

Offer free extra tuition to your workers at the end of their working day, as well as improving their sewing skills.

Spend 15,000.

▶ 47 IF accepted heating grant
▶ 40 IF declined heating grant

Tell Li Pengjian that you will only invest in training workers in skills that are useful to the factory.
It is not your role to direct the education of the workers.

▶ 58 IF accepted heating grant
▶ 59 IF declined heating grant

Thanks to Carole Zhang, in Milan, you get an order from Marvellous, a famous British brand with global outlets, who market themselves on sustainability. They place an order for slim-fit cropped trousers but ring up 2 days later to say they now want slim-fit long trousers. To protect their brand they insist that you destroy the trousers you have made already.

Have the trousers incinerated on the insistence of Marvellous. This is the standard way of protecting the identity of a global brand.

> **92** IF accepted heating grant
> **115** IF declined heating grant

Sell the garments on to a textile reseller who has outlets in inland China.

Receive 8,000.

> **166**

You complete the waterproof trousers. Whilst training your workers is a long-term investment, in the short term you are in danger of missing your deadlines. A man turns up at your office looking for his 15-year-old daughter, Yang Lin, who he says works in your factory. He lost contact with her when she left their village to find work in the city 8 months ago. He has travelled for 26 hours.

Usher Yang Lin's father quickly out of the door, telling him to return at the end of the shift and you will see what you can do.

Receive 30,000.

> **404**

Tell Yang Lin's father that you have a fast turnover of staff and that you do not recognise his daughter: you worry he might be a compliance inspector.

Receive 30,000.

> **220**

186

You discover you will have to engage with local officials to be able to buy more land to build the new dormitories for your workers.

Invite a couple of the officials to your factory, and then take them out for dinner. The dinner will cost 5,000, including an unstinting flow of rice wine.

Spend 5,000.

▶ **199**

Apply in writing to build more dormitories.

▶ **338**

187

Paying the workers per piece of garment rather than a wage has significantly increased productivity, and your profits. Li Pengjian reports that Yan Rong and Yao Lin, who are older, are earning less due to their slower working speeds, despite the quality of their work. He would like to see a pay increase: would you be willing to meet with them informally to discuss an idea for changing how the pay is structured?

Meet Li Pengjian and other workers to negotiate the payment structure; you offer them tea.

▶ **368**

Put pay up a little: you know that is what your workers want.

▶ **196**

You complete the faux-fur jackets and the couture tops and make a profit. Your younger workers sign up for English lessons with alacrity. Yang Lin tells you it makes her feel valued: she is glad to be working for you. You get a rush order of dresses with a frill skirt from Zina and an order of organic-cotton T-shirts from sportswear company Run Rabbit. You soon discover how expensive organic cotton is, but Run Rabbit won't raise the price as their research shows that people won't pay more. You cannot afford to lose the order.

Outsource to Vietnam: the labour costs are lower there. Your pattern-cutter cuts and bundles the fabric, which is then sent to Vietnam for sewing.

Receive 30,000.

▶ **188a**

Take the hit yourself on the organic cotton: you want to use it for environmental reasons, but decide outsourcing is not for you.

Receive 8,000.

▶ **49**

THERE'S ONLY AN UP OR A DOWN

Are you a member of the All-China Union?

YES — Did you move to piecework?
- YES → **248**
- NO → **322**

NO — Did you pay a regular wage?
- YES → **177**
- NO → **176**

The Workers Comfort order is finished, resulting in a good profit. Kwok Han, the WRAP compliance officer, has looked over your factory and says you need emergency-exit signs, smoke detectors, ear protectors and dust masks for workers, automatic shut-off switches for machines and secure handrails on stairways. If you get WRAP compliance, fast-fashion brands Garb and Mud say they will place new orders with you.

Spend most of your profit from the Workers Comfort order on upgrades required to get WRAP certification.

Receive 5,000.

 223

Decide that achieving compliance is too risky, financially. There are plenty of retailers who do not require it.

Receive 30,000.

 86

"No idea who wears [the clothes we make]; it's the boss who gets the business. Sometimes we get foreign business, so they'd be worn by foreigners. Sometimes we make workwear, so those are probably sent to factories to be worn by workers. Sometimes I do think about it."

Yang Huafeng (machinist who made the World Factory shirt), Shanghai, 2014

Plantlife want to showcase your factory in a documentary. They promise you a new order of vest tops if you agree.

Take the order and allow the documentary.

 190a

Decline the order, saying that filming the documentary would slow productivity.

▶ 25

KEEP GOING FORWARD

Are you a member of the All-China Union?

YES   NO

YES → Did you move to piecework?

NO → Did you pay a regular wage?

Did you move to piecework?
YES → 262
NO → 329

Did you pay a regular wage?
YES → 192
NO → 187

191 ◀ WORLD FACTORY

You can now handle large orders without huge overheads, increasing profits. The future is less certain — some samples for a UK supermarket only led to 1 order. Liu Huiquan from the factory opposite gives you a call. Do you have capacity to handle some jeans? They need to be sandblasted to make them look preworn. She has the equipment, but too few workers to complete the order in time. If you help, you will make a huge profit. You know some of your former workers are still looking for work.

Ask to see the sandblasting equipment before agreeing to provide workers: you have heard it can be dangerous.

Receive 35,000.

 296

Provide the workers. They need the work and you need the income — they will not be exposed to sandblasting particles for long, as it is only a temporary arrangement.

Receive 35,000.

 301

192 ◀ WORLD FACTORY

Paying wages, guaranteeing workers a stable income, rather than paying per piece, is just about manageable at this wage level. Li Pengjian tells you the workers want to make whole garments, rather than just a single part of a garment. This will vary the work and mean that the fastest ones will be able to work more quickly. You do need to increase productivity. You consult with fellow factory managers including Madame Wang and find that she has already made this change. You agree to trial it.

Ku Fang calls you: factories in the vicinity are letting workers make key operative decisions outside the Union; he reminds you that independent collectivisation is illegal.

 196

WORLD FACTORY

Paying the workers per piece of garment rather than a wage has significantly increased productivity, and your profits. Li Pengjian reports that Yan Rong and Yao Lin, who are older, are earning less due to their slower working speeds, despite the quality of their work. He would like to see a pay increase: would you be willing to meet with them informally to discuss an idea for changing how the pay is structured?

Meet Li Pengjian and other workers to negotiate the pay structure; you offer them tea.

 371

Put pay up a little: you know that is what they want.

193a

PRECARITY IS LIFE

WORLD FACTORY

Did a compliance inspector ask to see ID for all your workers?

YES   NO

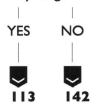

184

Did you allow Lu Qingmin to keep working despite her looking very young?

YES   NO

113   **142**

Paying wages, guaranteeing workers a stable income, rather than paying per piece, is just about manageable at this wage level. Li Pengjian tells you the workers want to make whole garments, rather than just a single part of a garment. This will vary the work and mean that the fastest ones will be able to work more quickly. You do need to increase productivity. You consult with fellow factory managers including Madame Wang and find that she has already made this change. You agree to trial it.

Ku Fang calls you: factories in the vicinity are letting workers make key operative decisions outside the Union; he reminds you that independent collectivisation is illegal.

 194a

WORK IS ENTERTAINMENT

Did a compliance inspector ask to see ID for all your workers?

YES   NO

184

Did you allow Lu Qingmin to keep working despite her looking very young?

YES   NO

113   142

You complete the waterproof trousers. Fashion brand Mud unexpectedly send a compliance officer to inspect you: the agreed signal works to get your underage workers out the back, but the officer spots them on her way out. Mud pull their next order. The unrest in the factory is palpable; the workers are angry that you sacked Liang Qiang, and do not believe your promise of increasing pay. You come in the next day to find them sitting silently at their machines, not working.

Give in to your workers and put the pay up, despite the hit to your profits both this month and in the longer term.

Receive 10,000.

 236

Negotiate a one-off bonus if they return to work immediately, which will still leave you with a reasonable profit this month.

Receive 25,000.

216 IF accepted heating grant

80 IF declined heating grant

You complete the order for women's vest tops for Plantlife and they give you a small order for fairtrade dresses. The documentary-makers would like to visit the factory that supplies your fabric. You have never visited the factory yourself.

Give the documentary crew the address of your fabric supplier and book them a taxi.

202

Agree to drive the documentary crew to your fabric supplier yourself, although it is a couple of hours outside the city.

 222

It was a good decision: Zina place a steady stream of orders. You hire 2 workers to handle the workload. Sydney Workwear call you: they have not received their waterproof trousers. Your shipping company tell you the order has got stuck at the port and that customs report that it is in a queue for checking, and it could take months. You steel yourself to ring Ku Fang in the municipal authorities business department to see if he can help but he is somewhat cool with you on the phone.

Ku Fang is clear that if he is to help, you must use a local fabric factory as your main supplier for organic cotton and contribute to his Factory Development Fund.

Spend 30,000. Gain 2 workers.

▶ 41

Greenpeace do a major investigation into poisons in dyes in clothing that can have carcinogenic effects on those who wear them, as well as causing long-term pollution where the waste is released into local rivers. You discover by doing a bit of research that the factory that Ku Fang 'invited' you to buy your fabric from is on the list of factories using these dyes.

Inform Ku Fang of the problem with the dyes and put a warning notice on your website about the fabric; dump the remaining fabric and find a new source.

Spend 20,000.

▶ 261

The order is underway now; it is too late to do anything about it.

 223

At the dinner, one of the officials recommended obtaining your fabric from a good source, his brother, and you agreed to this. Soon after, the papers for you to convert the use of land come through with no problem. You have paid off all the peasants who had rights to the land, apart from one guy, who has built a small house on it, right in the middle of the plot you want to develop.

Send round heavies to encourage the gentleman to vacate his land.

Receive 10,000.

 288

Up the level of compensation offered to the remaining resident.

Spend 30,000.

 338

Plantlife are happy with your response and place an order for women's vest tops. Geosync call to say they have not received the kaftans: they got stuck in customs at the port. You ring Ku Fang in the municipal authorities business department to see if he can help. Ku Fang says he will see what he can do, and gives you a strong recommendation for a local fabric factory: if you mention him you will get a good price. You make some profit after receiving the balance on a couple of orders.

You place an order with the fabric factory immediately; by the end of the day you get a call from customs to say the clothes have been cleared for shipping.

Receive 15,000.

 190

201

Plantlife are happy with your response and place an order for women's vest tops. Geosync call to say they have not received the kaftans: they have got stuck in customs at the port. You ring Ku Fang in the municipal authorities business department to see if he can help, and he is somewhat cool with you on the phone.

Ku Fang is clear that if he is to help, you must use a local cotton mill he recommends, and make a significant contribution to his Factory Development Fund.

Spend 20,000.

 190

202

The documentary-makers return from the fabric factory: they have footage of river pollution pouring out of the factory. You complete the fairtrade dresses for Plantlife and once all your costs are covered, discover you have made a small profit.

Email Plantlife and promise to source a better factory for dyeing the cloth. You have to dip into your capital, and production is slowed by 2 days.

Receive 8,000.

 217

Explain to Plantlife that dumping is common practice and that rivers in China are large and fast-flowing so it isn't a problem.

Receive 8,000.

▶ 205

You have dinner with Madame Wang from ZhengXing Clothing Co. and your friend, the merchandiser Gloria Yeung. The major topic of conversation is a new police crackdown on illegal immigrants. The conversation later turns to rumours of strikes in other provinces, although there is no information in the official news. Sportswear company Run Rabbit place an order for 100% organic-cotton T-shirts.

Go home after dinner unsettled; your own relations with your workers are not as strong as they could be; hopefully the party-backed Union will keep them in check.

▶ 107

You have dinner with Madame Wang from ZhengXing Clothing Co. and your friend, the merchandiser Gloria Yeung. The major topic of conversation is a new police crackdown on illegal immigrants. The conversation later turns to rumours of strikes in other provinces, although there is no information in the official news. Hong Kong sportswear company Run Rabbit place an order for organic-cotton sports T-shirts.

Go home after the dinner unsettled; your own relations with your workers are not as strong as they could be, despite your willingness to negotiate with them directly.

▶ 298

You are fully expecting – and dreading – the exposure that must come from the documentary, despite your excuses; you fully expect Plantlife to end their relationship with you. But before the documentary is edited, the fairtrade dress is launched at Paris Fashion Week. Kate Middleton buys one, and suddenly Plantlife want you to sew another 25,000 on an extremely short timescale.

Point out you cannot handle the Plantlife order without outsourcing (in which case you cannot guarantee ethical quality), or making the workers do an inhumane level of work.

 225

It is great that a celebrity is promoting ethical clothing, and you should make a profit: take the Plantlife order.

 295

Greenpeace do a major investigation into poisons in dyes in clothing that can have carcinogenic effects on those who wear them, as well as causing long-term pollution where the waste is released into local rivers. You discover by doing a bit of research that the factory that Ku Fang 'invited' you to buy your fabric from is on the list of factories using these dyes. You are in the middle of making your Run Rabbit order from the fabric.

Inform Ku Fang of the problem with the dyes and cancel the order, costing you the trust of your client. Due to the lost profits you have to dip into your capital to cover payday. **Spend 20,000.**

268

Do nothing. The order is underway now; it is too late to do anything about it.

223

The municipal authorities are clamping down on the increasingly unbearable smog; you are fined for using the city incinerators. Peace&Love call you: the skinny jeans you shipped for their export market never reached their destination. Your shipping company say they are stuck in customs and could take months to clear. You steel yourself to ring Ku Fang to ask for help. He is rather cool with you on the phone.

Ku Fang is clear that if he is to help, you must use a local fabric factory as your main supplier for organic cotton and contribute to his Factory Development Fund.

Spend 30,000.

▶ 139

Low on orders having turned away Run Rabbit, you quickly get started on an order of ladies shorts from Fasttrac. Then you hear that Greenpeace are doing a major investigation into poisons in dyes in clothing that can have carcinogenic effects, as well as causing long-term pollution when released into local rivers. You discover that the factory that Ku Fang 'invited' you to buy your fabric from is on the list of factories using these dyes. You are in the middle of making the shorts from the fabric.

Inform Ku Fang of the problem with the dyes and cancel the shorts, costing you the trust of your client. Due to the lost profits you have to dip into your capital to cover payday.

Spend 20,000.

▶ 114

Do nothing. The order is underway now; it is too late to do anything about it.

 223

209 ◀ WORLD FACTORY

Greenpeace do a major investigation into poisons in dyes in clothing that can have carcinogenic effects on those who wear them, as well as causing long-term pollution where the waste is released into local rivers. You discover by doing a bit of research that the factory that Ku Fang 'invited' you to buy your fabric from is on the list of factories using these dyes. You are in the middle of making Run Rabbit hoodies from the fabric.

Inform Ku Fang of the problem with the dyes and cancel the hoodies, costing you the trust of your client. Due to the lost profits you have to dip into your capital to cover payday.

Spend 20,000.

▶ **101**

Do nothing. The order is underway now; it is too late to do anything about it.

▶ **223**

210 ◀ WORLD FACTORY

Greenpeace do a major investigation into poisons in dyes in clothing that can have carcinogenic effects on those who wear them, as well as causing long-term pollution where the waste is released into local rivers. You discover by doing a bit of research that the factory that Ku Fang 'invited' you to buy your fabric from is on the list of factories using these dyes. You are in the middle of making the bibs from the fabric.

Inform Ku Fang of the problem with the dyes and cancel the bibs, costing you the trust of your client Savaday. Due to the lost profits you have to use your capital to cover payday.

Spend 20,000.

▶ **223**

Do nothing. The order is underway now; it is too late to do anything about it.

▶ **139**

WORLD FACTORY

Greenpeace do a major investigation into poisons in dyes in clothing that can have carcinogenic effects on those who wear them, as well as causing long-term pollution where the waste is released into local rivers. You discover by doing a bit of research that the factory that Ku Fang 'invited' you to buy your fabric from is on the list of factories using these dyes. You are in the middle of making the bibs from the fabric.

Inform Ku Fang of the problem with the dyes and cancel the bibs, costing you the trust of your client Savaday. Due to the lost profits you have to use your capital to cover payday.

Spend 20,000.

 139

Do nothing. The order is underway now; it is too late to do anything about it.

 223

WORLD FACTORY

The municipal authorities are clamping down on the increasingly unbearable smog; you are fined for using the city incinerators. Peace&Love call you: the skinny jeans you shipped for their export market have disappeared. Your shipping company tells you the order has got stuck in customs at the port; it could take months to clear. You ring Ku Fang in the municipal authorities business department to see if he can help. He says he will see what he can do, and recommends a local fabric factory you should use.

Place an order with the fabric factory immediately; by the end of the day you get a call from customs to say the clothes have been cleared for shipping.

▶ **139**

213

WORLD FACTORY

You complete the T-shirts for Plantlife. You feel a strong responsibility to all your workers; you do not now have enough work for them. Liu Huiquan from the factory on the other side of the complex gives you a call. Would you have capacity for handling some jeans? They need to be sandblasted to make them look preworn. She has the equipment, but not enough workers to get the order completed in time. If you provide 7 workers, you will make a hefty profit.

Ask to see the sandblasting equipment before agreeing to provide workers: you have heard it can be dangerous.

> **296**

Provide the workers; it is better not to know more; you need the income, and your workers will not be exposed to sandblasting particles for long; it is only a temporary arrangement.

> **301**

214

WORLD FACTORY

Tony gets an order from Run Rabbit and comes to thank you. Meanwhile, you are yourself in desperate need of new orders: Plantlife do not want to place another order yet; Geosync have come back with an order of skirts but it only covers paying the workers at your previous rate, just below the living wage – like Plantlife, they claim they can't raise the end price. How do you fulfil your obligation to the new pay levels for the workers?

Dig into your capital to enable you to market yourself as an ethical brand online called Greenlee.

Spend 20,000.

> **87**

Reduce the number of workers you have, and partially outsource any large orders somewhere cheaper.

Lose 6 workers.

 134

You now have more orders than you can possibly handle. You realise it is impossible to achieve the fast turnaround required 'ethically'; even if you pay the workers at your very reasonable rate, they are going to have to work very long hours.

Decide the ethical message is as important as the reality: making a large profit means you can pay the workers well; keep making the dresses.

Receive 30,000.

 226

Place a 'sold out' notice on the website, and then auction the remaining 20 dresses for increasingly astronomical prices on eBay.

Receive 8,000.

 213

2 skilled machinists jump to another factory, but the other workers accept the bonus and return to work, completing the Run Rabbit T-shirts. Classic brand Marvellous place an order for zip-detail skirts. Sydney Workwear call you: they haven't received the waterproof trousers. Your shipping company tell you the order is stuck in customs and could take months to clear. You ring Ku Fang in the municipal authorities business department; he says he'll see what he can do, and recommends a local fabric factory he is supporting.

Place an order with the fabric factory immediately; by the end of the day you get a call from customs to say the clothes have been cleared for shipping.

Lose 2 workers.

▶ **409**

217

The fairtrade dress is launched at Paris Fashion Week. Kate Middleton buys one, and suddenly Plantlife want you to sew another 25,000 on an extremely short timescale.

Point out you cannot make so many dresses so quickly without outsourcing (with no guarantee of ethical quality), or making the workers do an inhumane level of work.

 225

It is great that a celebrity is promoting ethical clothing; and you should make a profit: agree to make the dresses.

▶ 295

218

You complete the Garb distressed T-shirt order; it took longer than anticipated to make them look old and worn. You get an order from Sydney Workwear for waterproof trousers. Liang Qiang comes to see you to say that the workers have voted unanimously for the pay to be returned at least to its previous level. The other workers selected Liang Qiang to be their spokesperson, and he wishes to represent their needs.

Tell Liang Qiang you hear him, but your hand cannot be forced. Pay levels will go up when your revenue goes up.

▶ 204

Put the pay up, although you will have to pay part of this month's pay from your capital.

Spend 12,000.

 150

Mick Fletcher from Run Rabbit also offers you a very large order for 100% organic-cotton hoodies if you adhere to their ethical guidelines and allow your factory to be inspected. Tony Nie, whose factory is a couple of blocks away, was telling you the other day about how achieving compliance with international standards can get extremely complicated; they tend to pry into all your affairs, whether relevant or not.

Decline the order from Run Rabbit, to avoid being inspected.

 208

Take the order from Run Rabbit and allow your factory to be inspected. It is just as well you let Yang Lin go.

393

After her shift, Yang Lin rushes up to you; she heard from another worker that her father was asking for her; she is desperate to be reunited: she lost her phone and her parents' numbers. When she finds out you sent him away she is very upset. You now know that Yang Lin is underage: the legal working age is 16. Yang Lin tells you she will be 16 in 6 months, and claims she can get fake ID.

Give Yang Lin a week's notice: you do not believe in employing underage workers.

Lose 1 worker.

 219

Arrange with Yang Lin that she will get ID and if you play a particular piece of music in the factory she will slip out the back.

 325

221 WORLD FACTORY

The pay rise appears to have calmed relations for the time being, and you complete the waterproof trousers, bringing in a profit. Tian Jianying comes to see you, upset: the underage workers you did not employ have ended up in unpaid bonded labour in a Shenzhen electronics factory. Zina place an order for dresses, and you discover the organic cotton for Run Rabbit is very costly. However, they say they cannot raise the price: their research shows that people will not pay more. You cannot afford to lose the order.

Outsource to Vietnam: the labour costs are lower there. Your pattern-cutter cuts and bundles the fabric, which is then sent to Vietnam for sewing.

Receive 30,000.

▶ **221a**

Take the hit yourself on the organic cotton: you want to use it for environmental reasons, but decide outsourcing is not for you.

Receive 18,000.

▶ **49**

TIME IS MONEY

221a WORLD FACTORY

Are you a member of the All-China Union?

YES	NO
Did you move to piecework?	Did you pay a regular wage?

YES	NO	YES	NO
248		**177**	
	322		**176**

Just as your workers are completing the fairtrade dresses for Plantlife, you pile the documentary-makers into your car. But as you are driving up towards the factory, with the documentary-makers avidly filming everything, you see that the fabric factory you have been using is pouring textile waste into the local river, with the dye turning it an unnatural shade of green.

Drive past the fabric factory and pretend you are lost.

Receive 8,000.

 217

Explain that dumping is common practice and that rivers in China are large and fast-flowing, so it isn't a problem.

Receive 8,000.

 205

You complete a number of orders and after several emails chasing late payments, you receive the balance. Liu Huiquan from the factory on the other side of the complex gives you a call. Would you have capacity for handling some jeans? They need to be sandblasted to make them look preworn. She has the equipment, but not enough workers to get the order completed in time. If you provide 7 workers, you will make a hefty profit: much more than your usual profit from a single order.

Ask to see the sandblasting equipment before agreeing to provide workers: you have heard it can be dangerous.

Receive 25,000.

▶ **296**

Provide the workers. It is better not to know details; you need the income, and they will not be exposed to sandblasting particles for long, as it is only a temporary arrangement.

Receive 25,000.

▶ **301**

WORLD FACTORY

You complete the faux-fur jacket order for SexiBabi and the couture tops for Zina. Productivity is increasing, and you make a reasonable profit. You get new orders: a rush order of dresses with a frill skirt from Zina and organic-cotton T-shirts from sportswear company Run Rabbit. You soon discover that organic cotton is very expensive. Run Rabbit tell you they cannot raise the price, as their research shows that people will not pay more. You cannot afford to lose the order.

Outsource to Vietnam: the labour costs are lower there. Your pattern-cutter cuts and bundles the fabric, which is then sent to Vietnam for sewing.

Receive 30,000.

▶ **224a**

Take the hit yourself on the organic cotton: you want to use it for environmental reasons, but decide outsourcing is not for you.

Receive 8,000.

▶ **49**

EQUALITY IS A MIRAGE

Plantlife are very keen for you to do the order; it is clear that they do not mind how you achieve it. The problem remains: how do you actually make that many dresses so quickly?

Recruit 8 new workers and get everyone to do overtime to complete the Plnatlife order.

Gain 8 workers.

▶ **246**

Outsource to other factories to complete the Plantlife order.

▶ **129**

You complete the T-shirts for Plantlife. Now you have to work out how to keep up with this sudden short-term demand, although the high sales of this dress are also impacting positively on sales of other items on your Greenlee website. You could expand the factory whilst demand lasts, letting workers go after; or you could outsource elsewhere.

Get an agency to hire you new workers quickly: at the rate you are paying this is not difficult.

Gain 10 workers.

▶ **228**

Outsource production.

▶ **145**

227

Sydney Workwear thank you for getting the clothes out of customs and pay the balance. Paying the workers per piece of garment they make has significantly increased productivity, and profit. Li Pengjian reports that Yan Rong and Yao Lin, who are older, are earning less due to their slower working speeds, despite the quality of their work. He would like to see a pay increase: would you be willing to meet informally to discuss how the pay is structured?

Meet Li Pengjian and other workers to negotiate the pay structure; you offer them tea.

Receive 30,000.

 344

Put pay up a little: you know that is what your workers want.

Receive 25,000.

 39

228

The facilities are extremely cramped; you have not had time to sort out dormitory arrangements for everyone, so there are extra people in each room, and the factory floor is extremely crowded.

You arrive the following day to find the workers have gone on strike; you are forced to abandon all ongoing orders. Production is halted for 3 days.

132

It is not a good day: Marvellous send you photos of a fake 'Marbleous' shop in Chongqing selling their garments you made. They cancel the ladies' suits and set legal proceedings in motion for breach of contract. In this globalised economy, brand recognition reaches everywhere, and Marvellous are increasingly protective of their identity.

You are unable to avoid being sued; and have to dig into your capital to afford it.

Spend 7,000.

》 **235**

Hong Kong-based sportswear company Run Rabbit place an order for organic-cotton sports T-shirts. You invite Yan Rong, Yao Lin, Zhu Qing, and Li Pengjian, the supervisor, into your office. They tell you that the move to piecework has divided the workforce: it discriminates against the older, and therefore slower, workers. They tell you life is precarious enough without the uncertainty each month of not knowing how much they will earn. They would like to monitor the situation and meet with you again to discuss it.

Help your workers set up a legal Union under government auspices.

》 **411**

Agree to your workers' request for regular consultation, although it will be unofficial as independent unionisation is illegal.

》 **408**

231 WORLD FACTORY

You have dinner with Madame Wang from ZhengXing Clothing Co., Ltd and your friend, the merchandiser Gloria Yeung. The major topic of conversation is a new police crackdown on illegal immigrants. The conversation later turns to rumours of strikes in other provinces, although there is no information in the official news. The following day, machinist Liang Qiang accosts you as you leave the office to ask how you plan to move forward with enabling workers' rights.

Suggest your workers set up a legal Union under government auspices, linked to the All-China Federation of Trade Unions.

 375

Agree to the workers' request for regular consultation, although it will be unofficial as independent unionisation is illegal.

▶ 390

232 WORLD FACTORY

Liang Qiang accosts you as you leave the office to ask how you plan to move forward with enabling workers' rights.

Suggest your workers set up a legal Union under government auspices, linked to the All-China Federation of Trade Unions.

 309

Agree to your workers' request for regular consultation, although it will be unofficial as independent unionisation is illegal.

▶ 415

This cooperative sharing of profit calms relations for the time being. But now you need new orders. Liu Huiquan from the factory on the other side of the complex gives you a call. Would you have capacity for handling some jeans? They need to be sandblasted to make them look preworn. She has the equipment, but not enough workers to get the order completed in time. If you provide 7 workers, you will make a hefty profit.

Ask to see the sandblasting equipment before agreeing to provide workers: you have heard it can be dangerous.

▶ 296

Provide the workers; it is better not to know more; you need the income, and your workers will not be exposed to sandblasting particles for long; it is only a temporary arrangement.

▶ 301

Payment finally arrives for the garments you recently completed, and you make a profit. Run Rabbit, a Hong Kong-based sportswear company, place an order for organic-cotton sports T-shirts. Liang Qiang accosts you as you leave the office to ask how you plan to move forward with enabling workers' rights.

Suggest your workers set up a legal Union under government auspices, linked to the All-China Federation of Trade Unions.

Receive 15,000.

▶ 386

Agree to the workers' request for regular consultation, although it will be unofficial as independent unionisation is illegal.

Receive 15,000.

▶ 263

International brand Zina, who make clothes for the Chinese market, have heard about the copycat Marbleous shop. They are keen to know if you will make other copies of fashion garments for them. You will just have to change 5 details to avoid copyright; they have lawyers to handle that sort of thing.

Take the order. You are happy to oblige; producing copies of fashion garments could be a lucrative line of business.

Receive 20,000.

》93 IF accepted heating grant
》83 IF declined heating grant

Refuse to copy other brands; you believe in the integrity of the designer.

》77 IF accepted heating grant
》78 IF declined heating grant

The pay rise seems to have calmed the workforce but you now need to broaden your market and increase profits to enable you to cover their pay next month. Setting up a sales office in another city will make you stand out and lead to orders in new markets. Carol Zhang, your most successful salesperson, will run the new office.

Set up a sales office in Milan; rental costs are on a par with Beijing. You'll benefit from the city's association with high-quality clothing in attracting European clients.

Spend 10,000.

》48

Set up a sales office in Beijing; this could put you in a better position to pick up orders from Chinese brands, as well as lucrative government orders.

Spend 5,000.

 127

It is not a good day: Marvellous send you photos of a fake 'Marbleous' shop in Chongqing selling their garments you made. They set legal proceedings in motion for breach of contract. In this globalised economy, brand recognition reaches everywhere, and Marvellous are increasingly protective of their identity.

You are unable to avoid being sued; and have to dig into your capital to afford it.

Spend 7,000.

 139

You complete the Mud workshirt order and make a profit. Productivity is increasing. Able and willing, your younger workers work fast and neatly. Productivity is increasing. Liang Qiang accosts you as you leave the office to ask how you plan to move forward with enabling workers' rights.

Suggest your workers set up a legal Union under government auspices, linked to the All-China Federation of Trade Unions.

Receive 15,000.

163

Agree to your workers' request for regular consultation, although it will be unofficial as independent unionisation is illegal.

Receive 15,000.

167

239

WORLD FACTORY

That very evening, perhaps as a result of the electrics being handled by the inspector, a fire starts that damages your factory and spreads to several buildings in the complex. 3 workers, who worked in the next-door factory, and were sleeping overnight there, are killed. The dresses you were working on are destroyed, and Garb take the order elsewhere.

Move fast to repair your factory to a higher safety standard before starting work again. Give your workers a week's paid holiday to ensure they do not jump to another factory.

Spend 30,000.

 148

Set up the machines that are still working, and bring in builders to do repairs around the workers while they work: you cannot afford to stop production.

Spend 15,000.

 7

240

WORLD FACTORY

Bringing production back to your Chinese factory is not, however, simple. You have a number of orders on the go: the short-term challenge is to complete them on schedule whilst increasing the capacity of your factory. The long-term challenge is how to afford the labour costs in China.

Get your current workers to work 16-hour days until you have stabilised the situation and can afford to hire more workers.

 258

Hire 6 new workers and delay paying everyone this month until you have completed all current orders and got new ones underway.

Gain 6 workers.

 251

Your workers are managing valiantly, but the fire loses you the trust of some clients, who stop using your factory. Liu Huiquan from the factory on the other side of the complex gives you a call. Would you have capacity for handling some jeans? They need to be sandblasted to make them look preworn. She has the equipment, but not enough workers to get the order completed in time. If you provide 7 workers, you will make a huge profit: much more than your usual profit from a single order.

Ask to see the sandblasting equipment before agreeing to provide workers: you have heard it can be dangerous.

》 296

Provide the workers. It is better not to know; you need the income, and they will not be exposed to sandblasting particles for long, as it is only a temporary arrangement.

》 301

Paying the workers per piece of garment rather than a wage has significantly increased productivity, and your profits. Zhu Qing has taken on the leadership of the Union: you are surprised Li Pengjian is not involved, as he has always taken an interest in workers' rights. Zhu Qing reports that Yan Rong and Yao Lin, who are older, are earning less due to their slower working speeds, despite the quality of their work.

Do nothing about the pay. The Union is controlled centrally and therefore workers' demands are managed by protocol.

Receive 30,000.

》 265

Agree to a request from Li Pengjian for a meeting external to the Union, to explore an idea the workers would like to put to you regarding how the pay is calculated. You offer them tea.

Receive 30,000.

》 364

243

Sydney Workwear thank you for getting the clothes out of customs and pay the balance. Paying the workers per piece of garment they make has increased productivity, and profit. Zhu Qing has taken on the leadership of the Union. You are surprised Li Pengjian is not involved: he has always taken an interest in workers' rights. Zhu Qing reports that Yan Rong and Yao Lin, who are older, are earning less due to their slower working speeds, despite the quality of their work.

Do nothing about the pay. The Union is controlled centrally and therefore workers' demands are managed by protocol.

Receive 30,000.

 39

Agree to a request from Li Pengjian for a meeting external to the Union, to explore an idea the workers would like to put to you regarding how the pay is calculated. You offer them tea.

Receive 30,000.

 351

244

WORLD FACTORY

When you come in the next day, the workers are sitting silently at their machines. Upset by the accident, and in protest at the increasingly cramped conditions since the increase in workers, as well as the low pay, they are refusing to work. Production stops for 3 days.

Incurring building/rental costs without generating income to match means you have to pay your bills from your capital.

Spend 20,000.

 132

WORLD FACTORY

Paying the workers per piece of garment rather than a wage has significantly increased productivity, and your profits. Zhu Qing has taken on the leadership of the Union: you are surprised Li Pengjian is not involved, as he has always taken an interest in workers' rights. Zhu Qing reports that Yan Rong and Yao Lin, who are older, are earning less due to their slower working speeds, despite the quality of their work.

Do nothing about the pay. The Union is controlled centrally and therefore workers' demands are managed by protocol.

Receive 30,000.

 31

Agree to a request from Li Pengjian for a meeting external to the Union, to explore an idea the workers would like to put to you regarding how the pay is calculated. You offer them tea.

Receive 30,000.

 353

WORLD FACTORY

The facilities are extremely cramped; you have not had time to sort out dormitory arrangements for everyone, so there are extra people in each room. The factory is very overcrowded, and there is not enough ventilation.

You arrive the following day to find the workers have gone on strike; production is halted for 3 days.

 253

Sydney Workwear thank you for getting the clothes out of customs and pay the balance. Paying wages, ensuring stability for workers, rather than paying per piece, is just manageable at this wage level. Li Pengjian says the workers want to make whole garments, rather than individual parts. This would vary the work and mean the fastest could work more quickly. You do need to increase productivity. You consult with fellow factory manager Madame Wang and find that she has already made this change. You agree to trial it.

Ku Fang calls you: factories in the vicinity are letting workers make key operative decisions outside the Union; he reminds you that independent collectivisation is illegal.

 39

You complete the dresses with a frill skirt and ship them. Outsourcing to Vietnam and paying the workers per piece of garment rather than a wage has significantly increased productivity, and your profits. Zhu Qing has taken on the leadership of the Union: you are surprised Li Pengjian is not involved, as he has always taken an interest in workers' rights. Zhu Qing reports that Yan Rong and Yao Lin, who are older, are earning less due to their slower working speeds, despite the quality of their work.

Do nothing. The Union is controlled centrally and therefore workers' demands are managed by protocol.

Receive 60,000.

55 IF accepted heating grant
57 IF declined heating grant

Agree to a request from Li Pengjian for a meeting external to the Union; the workers would like to put an idea to you regarding how the pay is calculated. You offer them tea.

Receive 60,000.

 348

249 ◀ WORLD FACTORY

The municipal authorities are clamping down on the unbearable smog; you are fined for using the city incinerators, reducing this month's profit by 5,000. Paying the workers per piece of garment has, however, increased productivity. Zhu Qing has taken on the leadership of the Union: you are surprised Li Pengjian is not involved, as he usually takes an interest in workers' rights. Zhu Qing reports that Yan Rong and Yao Lin, who are older, are earning less despite being highly skilled, as they work more slowly.

Do nothing about the pay. The Union is controlled centrally and therefore workers' demands are managed by protocol.

Receive 25,000.

▶ **51** IF taught workers English
▶ **38** IF did not teach English

Agree to a request from Li Pengjian for a meeting external to the Union, to explore an idea the workers would like to put to you regarding how the pay is calculated. You offer them tea.

Receive 25,000.

▶ **346**

250 ◀ WORLD FACTORY

Paying the workers per piece of garment rather than a wage has significantly increased productivity, and your profits. Zhu Qing has taken on the leadership of the Union: you are surprised Li Pengjian is not involved, as he has always taken an interest in workers' rights. Zhu Qing reports that Yan Rong and Yao Lin, who are older, are earning less due to their slower working speeds, despite the quality of their work.

Do nothing about the pay. The Union is controlled centrally and therefore workers' demands are managed by protocol.

Receive 30,000.

▶ **171**

Agree to a request from Li Pengjian for a meeting external to the Union, to explore an idea the workers would like to put to you regarding how the pay is calculated. You offer them tea.

Receive 30,000.

▶ **358**

251

Liu Huiquan from the factory on the other side of the complex gives you a call. Would you have capacity for handling some jeans? They need to be sandblasted to make them look preworn. She has the equipment, but not enough workers to get the order completed in time. If you provide 7 workers, you will make a hefty profit: much more than your usual profit from a single order, enabling you to pay everyone.

Ask to see the sandblasting equipment before agreeing to provide workers: you have heard it can be dangerous.

 296

Provide the workers. It is better not to know; you need the income, and they will not be exposed to sandblasting particles for long, as it is only a temporary arrangement.

 301

252

Huang Jiao and Yan Rong point out that the fan system that they currently have in the factory works fine; an additional fan might be useful when it gets particularly warm, but what is more important to them than air conditioning is that their dormitories are rather cramped, and there is nowhere for couples to stay. You must decide whether to comply with Garb, in order to get the order for blue-striped skirts.

Take the order, and follow the compliance directives. You need it; your running costs are not yet covered by your income. Promise to address the workers' concerns later.

Spend 10,000.

 337

Turn down Garb, as compliance is costly and does not always benefit workers. Rent new more spacious dorms for your workers.

Spend 15,000.

 397

You are in despair: one of the workers has complained to Plantlife about your treatment of them, and it has come to light that you lied about what you were paying them. The documentary is now going to be an uncovering of malpractice, but all along you have been trying to do your best in difficult circumstances. You complete the order for 20,000 dresses.

Share your profit with all the workers: this is the best way to improve the situation with them.

Receive 15,000.

 233

Decide that there is very little point attempting to be ethical, as it creates more problems than it solves. Keep the profit.

Receive 90,000.

 132

Carol Zhang, your salesperson who speaks English, gets you an order for blue vest tops from British chain, Zina. They refuse to negotiate on price so the profit margin is small. You are invited to dinner by Ku Fang, an official from the local municipal authorities business department, who wines and dines you royally. A couple of days later you find out you have been awarded a grant from the Factory Development Fund for improving the factory's facilities, which will enable you to replace your highly unreliable heating system.

Accept gratefully the offer of a new heating system.

 311

Decline gently the offer of a new heating system, citing your respect for socialist principles: that all factories should be treated equally.

 11

255

Your English-speaking salesperson, Carol Zhang, immediately gets you a small trial order for blue vest tops from British chain, Zina. You are invited to dinner by Ku Fang, an official from the local municipal authorities business department, and you are wined and dined royally. A couple of days later, you receive a call to say you have been awarded an exclusive grant from the Factory Development Fund for improving the general facilities in the factory, which will enable you to replace your highly unreliable heating system.

Accept the grant gratefully: Ku Fang tells you the system can be installed immediately.

 312

Decline gently the offer of a new heating system, citing your respect for socialist principles: that all factories should be treated equally.

 8

256

You complete the mining jackets and make a profit. You get a small trial order for blue vest tops from fashion brand Zina, who have a target price and won't pay more. You are invited to dinner by Ku Fang, an official from the local municipal authorities, and you are wined and dined royally. A couple of days later, you receive a call to say you have been awarded an exclusive grant from the Factory Development Fund for improving the general facilities in the factory, which will enable you to replace your highly unreliable heating system.

Accept the grant gratefully: Ku Fang tells you the system can be installed immediately.

Receive 15,000.

 314

Decline gently the offer of a new heating system, citing your respect for socialist principles: that all factories should be treated equally.

Receive 15,000.

 12

You get a new order for workshirts from Workers Comfort. You are invited to dinner by Ku Fang, an official from the local municipal authorities, and you are wined and dined royally. A couple of days later, you receive a call to say you have been awarded an exclusive grant from the Factory Development Fund for improving the general facilities in the factory, which will enable you to replace your highly unreliable heating system.

Accept the grant gratefully: Ku Fang tells you the system can be installed immediately.

 313

Decline gently the offer of a new heating system, citing your respect for socialist principles: that all factories should be treated equally.

▶ 10

Although there is some grumbling at the compulsory long days, you have the impression that your workers are glad that you are no longer outsourcing work. You have just completed your current orders, when Liu Huiquan from the factory on the other side of the complex gives you a call: do you have capacity for handling some jeans that need sandblasting so they look preworn? She has the equipment, but not enough workers to get the order done. If you provide 7 workers, you will make a hefty profit.

Ask to see the sandblasting equipment before agreeing to provide workers: you have heard it can be dangerous.

▶ 296

Provide the workers. It is better not to know; you need the income, and they will not be exposed to sandblasting particles for long, as it is only a temporary arrangement.

 301

Paying the workers per piece of garment rather than a wage has significantly increased productivity, and your profits. Zhu Qing has taken on the leadership of the Union: you are surprised Li Pengjian is not involved, as he has always taken an interest in workers' rights. Zhu Qing reports that Yan Rong and Yao Lin, who are older, are earning less due to their slower working speeds, despite the quality of their work.

Do nothing about the pay. The Union is controlled centrally and therefore workers' demands are managed by protocol.

Receive 30,000.

 259a

Agree to a request from Li Pengjian for a meeting external to the Union, to explore an idea the workers would like to put to you regarding how the pay is calculated. You offer them tea.

Receive 30,000.

 370

CHINA FIRST

Did a compliance inspector ask to see ID for all your workers?

YES   NO

184

Did you allow Lu Qingmin to keep working despite her looking very young?

YES   NO

113   142

You complete the mining jackets, and get a new order for workshirts from Workers Comfort. You are invited to dinner by Ku Fang, an official from the local municipal business authorities department, and you are wined and dined royally. The next day, you receive a call to say you have been awarded an exclusive grant from the Factory Development Fund for improving the general facilities in the factory, which will enable you to replace your highly unreliable heating system. Your monthly accounts show you've made a profit.

Accept the grant gratefully: Ku Fang tells you the system can be installed immediately.

Receive 20,000.

 315

Decline gently the offer of a new heating system, citing your respect for socialist principles: that all factories should be treated equally.

Receive 20,000.

▶ **16**

The slump in sales as a result of coming clean to your customers about the fabric means you are desperate for new orders. Liu Huiquan from the factory on the other side of the complex gives you a call. Would you have capacity for handling some jeans? They need to be sandblasted to make them look preworn. She has the equipment, but not enough workers to get the order completed in time. If you provide 7 workers, you will make a hefty profit.

Ask to see the sandblasting equipment before agreeing to provide workers: you have heard it can be dangerous.

▶ **296**

Provide the workers; it is better not to know more. You need the income, and your workers will not be exposed to sandblasting particles for long; it is only a temporary arrangement.

▶ **301**

262

Paying the workers per piece of garment rather than a wage has significantly increased productivity, and your profits. Zhu Qing has taken on the leadership of the Union: you are surprised Li Pengjian is not involved, as he has always taken an interest in workers' rights. Zhu Qing reports that Yan Rong and Yao Lin, who are older, are earning less due to their slower working speeds, despite the quality of their work.

Do nothing about the pay. The Union is controlled centrally and therefore workers' demands are managed by protocol.

 196

Agree to a request from Li Pengjian for a meeting external to the Union, to explore an idea the workers would like to put to you regarding how the pay is calculated. You offer them tea.

367

263

Li Pengjian, your factory-floor supervisor, tells you morale is high among the workers, thanks to your willingness to hear their perspective. You have made a profit this month, but discover that sourcing organic cotton is more expensive than you thought. You email Run Rabbit with a higher price. You have dinner with Madame Wang from ZhengXing Clothing Co., Ltd and your friend, the merchandiser Gloria Yeung. The major topic of conversation is a new police crackdown on illegal immigrants.

The conversation later turns to rumours of strikes in other provinces, although there is no information in the official news.

Receive 20,000.

 17

You receive an order for school-uniform dresses. You are making a profit, but it is low, so your accountant Wang Lin advises you to move to piecework, a different financial model for paying your workers. Instead of being paid a fixed monthly wage, workers are paid per item they complete, which incentivises them to work faster. Apparently skilled workers tend to like it, as it means they can earn more to send home.

Change to piecework. From now on you will pay workers according to how many garments they make, rather than paying a fixed monthly wage.

Receive 8,000.

 343

Enquire as to the attitudes of your workers by asking your factory-floor supervisor, Li Pengjian, before you change your pay structure.

Receive 8,000.

 277

"The Far East was becoming a major player. But we did notice that a lot of the things that they were producing were the easier… not a lot of natural yarns. Plus people found with your man-made fibres: 'Oh, it's cheap so we'll buy it'. Whereas the worsted yarns [made in the UK] were expensive. Down in Savile Row you still get your niche that will buy it but the masses won't pay the price for the worsted. Years ago, you didn't have your central heating, you didn't have your car. So everybody wore an overcoat, everybody wore woollen trousers or worsted trousers. But nowadays, with modern things, you don't need that."

Andy Smith, former weaver in a textile mill, Bradford, 2014

WORLD FACTORY

You complete the skinny jeans for Peace&Love, who have also recommended you to Marvellous, a British classic brand who want to expand into the Chinese market, and place a small order for denim-detail shirts. Through your Beijing office's efforts, you receive a large order for military uniforms for an unspecified African country. The fabric factory has already been contracted; now garment factories are required to fulfil the order.

Refuse the order, it is against company policy to produce military gear.

Receive 15,000.

 265a

Take the order of military uniforms, which comes with such a large deposit that you can already bank some as profit, and hire new workers.

Receive 75,000. Gain 10 workers.

▶ 62

MAXIMUM DESIGN WOW AT MINIMUM COST

265a 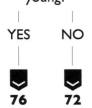 WORLD FACTORY

Did a compliance inspector ask to see ID for all your workers?

YES   NO

▼ 71

Did you allow Lu Qingmin to keep working despite her looking very young?

YES   NO

▼ 76   **▼ 72**

Having sacked the workers, you realise it will not be as easy as you thought to get new ones: the labour market is changing, and there is a shortage of workers who have the skills you need. You have to give up the Athlete order.

Rather than rehiring in the city, move the factory out to the provinces where pay levels are lower. You will be able to get larger premises at the same price.

 155

Decide to stay in the city and rehire a smaller number of workers at a better pay level, to oversee outsourcing the easier work overseas.

Gain 10 workers.

▶ **396**

You complete the Run Rabbit T-shirts. Paying wages, guaranteeing workers a stable income, rather than paying per piece, is just about manageable at this wage level. However, the workers want to return the wages to their previous levels. Zhu Qing has taken on the leadership of the Union: you are surprised Li Pengjian is not involved, as he has always taken an interest in workers' rights. Zhu Qing tells you the faster workers would rather be paid by piece so they can earn more to send home.

Continue paying wages. You do not like how Zhu Qing is trying to ingratiate herself with you.

▶ **265**

Reconsider your decision and move to piecework, which will increase your productivity, which you desperately need, and satisfy your more ambitious workers.

 366

268

WORLD FACTORY

Athlete, a major UK sports retailer, place an order for bikinis in 5 colours. You are worried you cannot understand the local dialect that the workers from Teke in Sichuan Province speak; you fear they may be planning to strike. You ask the advice of neighbouring factory owners: Liu Huiquan from the factory on the other side of the complex says she asks workers to hand in their mobiles at the start of shifts, to make it harder for them to engage in collective action as well as preventing distraction.

Form a workers' rock band and hold a social evening to encourage integration amongst the workforce.

 108

Take Liu Huiquan's advice and confiscate phones when people come on shift, handing them back at the end of the day.

287

269

WORLD FACTORY

Recruiting workers with sewing skills is not easy but Li Pengjian has a chat with an associate in rural Sichuan and arranges the recruitment of new workers. You complete the order for military uniforms on time and make a large profit. As your workforce grows it is harder to keep track of who should be doing what, so you introduce a colour-coded uniform to help keep control. You are offered a long-term (1-year) contract for the supply of UN peacekeeping uniforms.

Continue to supply military uniforms. This will bring a stable income, with an upfront deposit paid on signing the contract.

Receive 80,000.

75

Refuse the contract; you would rather focus on other orders. You bank this profit and move on.

Receive 60,000.

103 IF sacked young worker

157 IF kept young worker

Sydney Workwear don't notice the bad-quality sewing and place an order for waterproof trousers. After paying your bills, you make a small profit. You now need to rebuild your workforce.

Seek out the workers you sacked previously with the aim of giving them their job back: they were highly skilled and loyal.

Receive 3,000.

> **271**

Hire contacts of Tian Jianying's from Sichuan. They are all trained in tailoring, and looking for work in the city.

Receive 3,000. Gain 10 workers.

> **272**

Looking for your workers reminds you about Spring Festival, celebrating Chinese New Year, when all factories close for 2 weeks and migrant workers make the long journey back to their home provinces. Your skilled workers are an important asset. You were told that last year a number of them did not return after the holiday due to finding work that was better paid or nearer their families. You need to take action to ensure that productivity is not affected.

Book a minibus to take the workers home, then bring them back. The journey can take more than 2 days and getting train tickets is difficult.

> **18**

Pay the workers to stay in the city during the holiday rather than returning to their home villages. This will cost you half as much.

> **330**

272

WORLD FACTORY

It takes a whole day for your new workers to get to the city, which reminds you that you were planning to put measures in place for the Chinese New Year, when all factories close and the migrant workers all go back home for Spring Festival. Last year apparently some workers did not return afterwards, having found better-paid work closer to their families. Even with your new workers you only have 22 in total; they are an important asset.

Book a minibus to take the workers home, then bring them back. The journey can take more than 2 days and getting train tickets is difficult.

 264

Pay the workers to stay in the city rather than returning to their villages. This will cost you half as much.

332

273

WORLD FACTORY

Dealing with the workers' demands reminds you about Spring Festival, celebrating Chinese New Year, when all factories close for 2 weeks and migrant workers make the long journey back to their home provinces. Your skilled workers are an important asset; and they are unhappy about the pay level. Last year a number of them did not return after the holiday due to finding work that was better paid or nearer their families. You need to take action to ensure that productivity is not affected.

Book a minibus to take the workers home, then bring them back. The journey can take more than 2 days and getting train tickets is difficult.

20

Pay the workers to stay in the city during the holiday rather than returning to their home villages. This will cost you half as much.

 333

Responding to your workers' demands reminds you about Spring Festival, celebrating Chinese New Year, when all factories close for 2 weeks and migrant workers make the long journey back to their home provinces. Your skilled workers are an important asset. You were told that last year a number of them did not return after the holiday due to finding work that was better paid or nearer their families. You need to take action to ensure that productivity is not affected.

Book a minibus to take the workers home, then bring them back. The journey can take more than 2 days and getting train tickets is difficult.

 117

Pay the workers to stay in the city during the holiday rather than returning to their home villages. This will cost half as much.

▶ 388

Responding to your workers' demands reminds you about Spring Festival, celebrating Chinese New Year, when all factories close for 2 weeks and the workers make the long journey back to their home provinces. Your skilled workers are an important asset. You were told that last year a number of them did not return after the holiday due to finding work that was better paid or nearer their families. You need to take action to ensure that productivity is not affected.

Book a minibus to take the workers home, then bring them back. The journey can take more than 2 days and getting train tickets is difficult.

▶ 53

Promise the workers you will pay them if they stay in the city during the holiday rather than returning to their home villages.

 335

You complete the workshirts. Dealing with your workers' demands reminds you about Spring Festival, celebrating Chinese New Year, when all factories close for 2 weeks and the workers make the long journey back to their home provinces. Your skilled workers are an important asset. You were told that last year a number of them did not return after the holiday due to finding work that was better paid or nearer their families. You need to take action to ensure that productivity is not affected.

Book a minibus to take the workers home, then bring them back. The journey can take more than 2 days and getting train tickets is difficult.

 81

Pay the workers to stay in the city rather than returning to their home villages. This will cost you half as much.

▶ 336

The workers tell you that more than half of them would prefer to keep to a monthly wage, as then they are able to rely on a stable income; and it will not discriminate against those who are highly skilled but older and therefore a little slower. Your workshop supervisor Li Pengjian also tells you that 2 of your most adept machinists, Huang Jiao and Tian Jianying, want to move to piecework.

Decide to stick with paying wages and to investigate how to move forward with consultation in future. Your accountant is not impressed.

▶ 231

Move to piecework and, now you know the attitude of your workers, plan to replace some of those who wanted wages with more ambitious ones.

Lose 5 workers.

 357

In the end you have to outsource to Liu Huiquan next door, as well as to Vietnam, as the latter cannot manage the turnaround time. The dresses are sent out as completed and are flying off the shelves. No one seems to notice that each factory has different ways of making them and that the fabric differs significantly in quality. You make a massive profit. However, you had to let down other clients to get the order done, and will soon be in need of new orders.

Bank your profit first, and drink a toast to Kate Middleton for wearing your dress and bringing you good fortune.

Receive 90,000.

▶ **223**

You complete the waterproof trousers and receive new orders: organic-cotton T-shirts from Run Rabbit and orange gilets from Sportex. You are again in danger of missing your deadlines. You have dinner with Madame Wang from the neighbouring factory. The conversation turns to rumours of major strikes in other provinces. Madame Wang tells you that Qiu Lian, a former worker, has set up her own small factory in a makeshift extension on the roof of a nearby building and needs orders.

Outsource to Qiu Lian; you admire her entrepreneurial spirit. Furthermore you can pay for the work she does from your running costs, without touching your capital.

▶ **106** IF accepted heating grant
▶ **221** IF declined heating grant

Hire 2 new workers, which means having to dig into your capital this month. Outsourcing is out of the question.

Spend 6,000. Gain 2 workers.

 405

280

Losing Lu Qingmin so abruptly slows productivity by a day as there is no one to iron and prepare the cut fabric for the machinists. Your accountant Wang Lin advises you to move to piecework, a different financial model for paying your workers. Workers are paid per item they complete, which incentivises them to work faster. Apparently skilled workers tend to like it, as it means they can earn more to send home.

Change to piecework. From now on you will pay workers according to how many garments they make, rather than paying a fixed monthly wage.

 354

Enquire as to the attitudes of your workers by asking your factory-floor supervisor, Li Pengjian, before you change your pay structure.

281

281

You complete the vest tops for Zina, the mens' long-sleeved T-shirts for Plantlife and the knickers for Poppy. The workers tell you that more than half of your workers would prefer to keep to a monthly wage, as then they are able to rely on a stable income; and it will not discriminate against those who are highly skilled but older and therefore a little slower. Your factory-floor supervisor Li Pengjian also tells you that 2 of your most adept machinists, Huang Jiao and Tian Jianying, want to move to piecework.

Decide to stick with paying wages and to investigate how to move forward with consultation in future. Your accountant is not impressed.

234

Move to piecework and, now you know the attitude of your workers, plan to replace some of those who wanted wages with more ambitious ones hungry to work hard and earn more. **Lose 5 workers.**

 352

Zina's compliance officer is satisfied with the documentation you provide for Lu Qingmin, and having agreed a signal (a whistle) for her to hide in case there is ever another inspection, the matter is closed. Wang Lin advises you to move to piecework, a different financial model for paying your workers. Workers are paid per item they complete, incentivising them to work faster. Apparently skilled workers like it, as they can earn more to send home.

Change to piecework. From now on you will pay workers according to how many garments they make, rather than paying a fixed monthly wage.

 354

Enquire as to the attitudes of your workers by asking your factory-floor supervisor, Li Pengjian, before you change your pay structure.

▶ **281**

Productivity is slowed by losing a day's work from your 5 Vietnamese workers. You also discover that organic cotton is more expensive than you thought; you email Run Rabbit with a higher price. You have dinner with Madame Wang from ZhengXing Clothing Co. and your friend, the merchandiser Gloria Yeung. The major topic of conversation is a new police crackdown on illegal immigrants. The conversation later turns to rumours of strikes in other provinces, although there is no information in the official news.

Arriving at your factory mid-morning the next day, there is no sign of your Vietnamese workers. They have simply vanished: you never do find out what happened to them.

Lose 5 workers.

▶ **26**

284

You complete the men's checked shirts for Zina; and are paid for other orders, putting you in profit. Losing Lu Qingmin so abruptly has slowed productivity by a day as there is no one to iron and prepare the cut fabric for the machinists. Your accountant Wang Lin advises you to move to piecework: workers are paid per item they complete, which incentivises them to work faster. Skilled workers tend to like it, as they can earn more to send home.

Change to piecework. From now on you will not have to pay a monthly wage, but a proportion of your income will be deducted to pay your workers.

Receive 30,000.

 307

Enquire as to the attitudes of your workers by asking your factory-floor supervisor, Li Pengjian, before you change your pay structure.

Receive 30,000.

 285

285

You get a new order from Chinese fashion brand SexiBabi for faux-fur jackets. The workers tell you that more than half of them would prefer to keep to a monthly wage, as then they are able to rely on a stable income; and it will not discriminate against those who are highly skilled but older and therefore a little slower. Your workshop supervisor Li Pengjian also tells you that 2 of your most adept machinists, Huang Jiao and Tian Jianying, want to move to piecework.

Decide to stick with paying wages and to investigate how to move forward with consultation in future. Your accountant is not impressed.

232

Move to piecework and, now you know the attitude of your workers, plan to replace some of those who wanted wages with more ambitious ones hungry to work hard and earn more.

Lose 5 workers.

339

Zina's compliance officer is satisfied with the documentation you provide for Lu Qingmin and you complete the checked shirts. After receiving late payments on a couple of orders you make a profit this month, but productivity could be improved. Your accountant advises you to move to piecework: workers are paid per item they complete, which incentivises them to work faster. Skilled workers tend to like it, as they can earn more to send home.

Change to piecework. From now on you will not have to pay a monthly wage, but a proportion of your income will be deducted to pay your workers.

Receive 30,000.

 307

Enquire as to the attitudes of your workers by asking your factory-floor supervisor, Li Pengjian, before you change your pay structure.

Receive 30,000.

 285

When you come in the next day, the workers are sitting silently at their machines. They are refusing to work until they receive their phones back. Merchandiser Gloria Yeung turns up unexpectedly, and is horrified by the strike. You beg her not to tell her clients. Incurring building rental costs without generating income to match means you have to pay your bills from your capital.

Tell Li Pengjian, your factory-floor supervisor, that if they start work again you will say no more about confiscating phones.

Spend 10,000.

 316

Sack your workforce and seek new more compliant workers.

Spend 10,000. Lose your workforce.

 266

288

Your shift in the World Factory is now over. That was a year in the life of a Chinese clothing factory, but the World Factory goes on. In China, the cost of labour is rising, as are living standards, and workers are increasingly organised – in spite of government restrictions. The World Factory is therefore seeking new locations and new markets. Where will it end up?

Please now turn to the end of the cards to explore different options for how to continue.

▶ Turn to page 247

289

After the official has gone, your Vietnamese workers go straight back to work. It turns out that organic cotton is more expensive than you thought; you email Run Rabbit with a higher price. You have dinner with Madame Wang from ZhengXing Clothing Co. and your friend, the merchandiser Gloria Yeung. The main topic of conversation is a new police crackdown on illegal immigrants. You also discuss rumours of strikes in other provinces, although there is no information in the official news.

Arriving at your factory mid-morning the next day, there is no sign of your Vietnamese workers. They have simply vanished: you never do find out what happened to them.

Lose 5 workers.

▶ 26

You get an order for ladies' knickers from European brand Poppy. Rob Baxter, Zina's international compliance inspector, suddenly appears one morning, asking questions. You realise that he has been staying in the hotel opposite the factory and spying on you. He is keen to see ID showing age for all your workers. It occurs to you that you do not have a record for Lu Qingmin, who looks very young.

Ask Lu Qingmin to take 'unpaid holiday' for the foreseeable future, and tell Rob Baxter she has left the company.

Lose 1 worker.

 280

Ask Lu Qingmin to bring ID; you do not care if it is fake. She is a good worker and you would like to keep her.

▶ **282**

All your workers are pleased with the improved facilities. Liu Huiquan from the factory on the other side of the complex gives you a call. Would you have capacity for handling some jeans? They need to be sandblasted to make them look preworn. She has the equipment, but not enough workers to get the order completed in time. If you provide 7 workers, you will make a hefty profit: much more than your usual profit from a single order.

Ask to see the sandblasting equipment before agreeing to provide workers: you have heard it can be dangerous.

▶ **296**

Provide the workers. It is better not to know; you need the income, and they will not be exposed to sandblasting particles for long, as it is only a temporary arrangement.

▶ **301**

292

Production has been slowed by a day; it was hard to hire different workers after refusing to employ Tian Jianying's contacts; skilled workers are not attracted by the low level of pay. Wang Lin advises you to move to piecework, a different financial model for paying your workers. Workers are paid per item they complete, which incentivises them to work faster. Apparently skilled workers tend to like it, as it means they can earn more to send home.

Change to piecework. From now on you will pay workers according to how many garments they make, rather than paying a fixed monthly wage.

Gain 10 workers.

 37

Enquire as to the attitudes of your workers by asking your workshop supervisor, Li Pengjian, before changing your pay structure.

Gain 10 workers.

 293

293

The workers tell you that more than half of them would prefer to keep to a monthly wage, as then they are able to rely on a stable income; and it will not discriminate against those who are highly skilled but older and therefore a little slower. Your workshop supervisor Li Pengjian also tells you that 2 of your most adept machinists, Huang Jiao and Tian Jianying, want to move to piecework. Mud recommend you to fashion brand Garb, who place a large order for distressed T-shirts.

Decide to stick with paying wages and to investigate how to move forward with consultation in future. Your accountant is not impressed.

▶ **238**

Move to piecework and, now you know the attitude of your workers, plan to replace some of those who wanted wages with more ambitious ones.

Lose 5 workers.

▶ **173**

You get a substantial order for bibs from Savaday and complete the leggings order. New orders are coming thick and fast, your turnover is higher, and you are making regular profits. You can afford to expand, so you get an agency to recruit 15 new workers for you. You are in negotiations with Savaday, the supermarket, who need to lower their prices as it is discount season. You start to notice that everyone is more deferential. You notice they are scared they might be sacked, too.

You have barely any contact with your new workers, but they seem to settle in fine, although the factory is now much more cramped.

Receive 60,000. Gain 15 workers.

▶ 211

The work is relentless: you have to put everyone on overnight shifts, and you still will not get the order done in time.

Recruit 8 new workers, and get everyone to do overtime.

Gain 8 workers.

▶ 246

Outsource to other factories.

▶ 129

As you feared, the factory is using illegal equipment for sandblasting: this involves firing abrasive sand at denim under high pressure. The factory is badly ventilated, and the workers are wearing no safety equipment, although Liu Huiquan says she will supply some. You know that sandblasting in the long-term exposes workers to silicosis, a deadly lung disease.

Tell Liu Huiquan you won't consent to your workers sandblasting, but that you will happily sew part of the order of jeans. Liu Huiquan is happy with this.

 317

Tell Liu Huiquan that under no circumstances will you have anything to do with practices that are so damaging to the health of your workers.

▶ **340**

You get an order from Sydney Workwear for waterproof trousers. Your new workers are very fast: they are desperate to earn enough to repay the Snakehead gang that brought them across the border into China. Ku Fang calls. Your factory must set up a Union, belonging to the All-China Federation of Trade Unions. He reassures you that you will have some say in appointing the Union committee. Liang Qiang immediately makes a formal request that you implement the Rainbow Plan for improving workers' pay.

Tell Liang Qiang you hear him, but the Rainbow Plan is for the long term: pay will go up when your revenue goes up.

▶ **140**

Put the pay up in accordance with the Union long-term plan, although you will have to pay part of this month's pay from your capital.

Spend 12,000.

 302

WORLD FACTORY

Despite your engagement with the workers, Liang Qiang appears to be gathering support for an independent strike in protest at the continuance of low pay. Li Pengjian, your factory-floor supervisor, thinks you should take the threat seriously. Although there are ways of dealing with strikes (you, like everyone else, help subsidise the local police), it is likely to cost you in productivity.

Sack Liang Qiang. Tell the other workers you will increase pay if they finish the order on time.

Lose 1 worker.

195 IF hired child workers

60 IF refused to hire children

Put the pay up.

123 IF hired child workers

221 IF refused to hire children

WORLD FACTORY

The kaftan order is completed and shipped. You are a little unsettled; a clique of workers seem unhappy that you changed the method of pay without discussion. Your factory-floor supervisor, Li Pengjian, is working long hours to keep track of the different work rates. You ask him about the workers' attitudes but he tells you it is difficult to get an overview as several talk in dialect or use their mobiles to share information. He suggests that you hear their demands directly if you are worried.

Adopt a policy of lowering the pay of the troublemakers until they find work elsewhere.

Lose 5 workers.

304

Agree to meet Yan Rong, Yao Lin and Zhu Qing, informally.

416

300

You are invited to dinner by Ku Fang, an official from the local municipal authorities business department, and you are wined and dined royally. A couple of days later, you receive a call to say you have been awarded an exclusive grant from the Factory Development Fund for improving the general facilities in the factory, which will enable you to have a new heating system installed.

Accept the grant gratefully: Ku Fang tells you the heating system can be installed immediately.

 310

Decline gently the offer of a new heating system, citing your respect for socialist principles: that all factories should be treated equally.

▶ 13

301

The work on the jeans goes well, and your workers seem pleased to be paid the higher rate it attracts due to the health issues. You notice that Yuan Bao has been working much more slowly than usual, for a little while, and seems to be taking a lot of breaks, and be on her phone a lot. You ask your workshop supervisor, Li Pengjian, what the trouble is. He does not know.

Let Yuan Bao go. You cannot afford to have any laziness in a factory like yours.

Receive 50,000. Lose 1 worker.

▶ 319

Tell Li Pengjian to ask Yuan Bao what the problem is.

Receive 50,000.

 327

WORLD FACTORY

You have dinner with Madame Wang from ZhengXing Clothing Co. and your friend, the merchandiser Gloria Yeung. The major topic of conversation is a new police crackdown on illegal immigrants. The conversation later turns to rumours of strikes in other provinces, although there is no information in the official news. Sportswear company Run Rabbit place an order for 100% organic-cotton T-shirts.

Arriving at your factory the next day, there is no sign of your Vietnamese workers. They have simply vanished: you never find out what happened to them.

> **123** IF hired child workers
> **221** IF refused to hire children

WORLD FACTORY

Profits are pouring in: sharing the workload in this way means you do not have to take responsibility for the relationship with the client. You notice that Yuan Bao has been working much more slowly than usual for a little while, and seems to be taking a lot of breaks, and be on her phone a lot. You ask your workshop supervisor, Li Pengjian, what the trouble is. He does not know.

Let Yuan Bao go. You cannot afford to have any laziness in a factory like yours.

Receive 25,000. Lose 1 worker.

> **382**

Tell Li Pengjian to ask Yuan Bao what the problem is.

Receive 25,000.

> **384**

304

You get an order for waterproof trousers. You notice that as a result of your treatment of the troublemakers, your workforce is more deferential; and productivity is increasing. You go to the labour exchange to find new workers, and discover it will not be as easy as you thought. Most who are there looking for work want to join a large factory with more onsite benefits than you are in a position to offer.

Hire untrained Chinese migrant workers willing to take low pay. You will have to train them.

Gain 5 workers.

▶ **361**

Hire illegal Vietnamese economic migrants who are desperate for work and highly skilled.

Gain 5 workers.

▶ **350**

305

WORLD FACTORY

Yuan Bao accepts gratefully. Your workers have not been wearing the safety equipment provided for the sandblasting, as it makes it almost impossible to do the work quickly, and they are being paid by the piece. When they come off the order, all of them have a bad cough. However, they were well paid, and you have made yet more profit. Li Pengjian comes to see you – since you were willing to pay Yuan Bao's health costs, would you be willing to pay for your other workers to receive medical attention?

Agree to pay for your workers who are involved in sandblasting to see a doctor to receive advice about how protect themselves.

Spend 8,000.

▶ **400**

Let your workers off overtime for a few days, which slows production a little.

▶ **331**

WORLD FACTORY

Ku Fang calls: they would like you to appoint a workers' rep for consultation between the Union and management on pay levels. He recommends Zhu Qing. You think she will be a good source of information regarding the situation of the workers. Another ethical brand, Plantlife, are interested in placing an order. Unlike Garb, they visit you at the factory before committing to the order. They are impressed by what they see, but they want you to reveal your labour costs.

Be honest and tell Plantlife what you pay.

》 29

Tell Plantlife you pay more than you actually do: you do not want to lose the order.

》 200 IF accepted heating grant
》 201 IF declined heating grant

WORLD FACTORY

You get an order for faux-fur jackets from Chinese high-street brand, SexiBabi. You are a little unsettled; a clique of workers seem unhappy that you changed the method of calculating pay without discussion. Your factory-floor supervisor, Li Pengjian, is working long hours to keep track of the different work rates. You ask him about the workers' attitudes but he tells you it is difficult to get an overview because several talk in dialect or use their mobiles to share information. He suggests that you hear their demands directly.

Adopt a policy of lowering the pay of the troublemakers until they find work elsewhere.

Lose 5 workers.

》 339

Agree to meet Yan Rong, Yao Lin and Zhu Qing, informally.

》 308

308

 WORLD FACTORY

You invite Yan Rong, Yao Lin and Zhu Qing, along with Li Pengjian, the supervisor, into your office. They tell you that the move to piecework has divided the workforce, as it discriminates against those who are highly skilled but older and therefore a little slower. They tell you that the life is precarious enough without the uncertainty each month of not knowing how much they will earn. They would like to be able to monitor the situation and meet with you again to discuss it.

Help them set up a legal Union under government auspices.

▶ 373

Agree to their request for regular consultation, although it will be unofficial as independent unionisation is illegal.

▶ 128

309

WORLD FACTORY

Of 15 free samples you have sewn for fast-fashion clients in the recent weeks, only 2 placed an order. Ku Fang calls: they would like you to appoint a workers' rep for consultation between the Union and management on pay levels. He recommends Zhu Qing. You think she will be a good source of information regarding the situation of the workers. Advised by their local headquarters, a workers' delegation comes to see you to ask for a small increase in their pay.

Put the pay up as requested by the workers, although to start with it will have to come from your capital.

Spend 10,000.

 131

Tell the workers you hear them, but your hand cannot be forced. Pay levels will go up when your revenue goes up.

▶ 23

Installing the heating system has slowed production by a day and there is a technical problem: it will not switch off. Your already-warm factory is now unbearably hot. Ku Heating Co. demand 5,000 to fix it, which will have to come out of your capital. Your 12 workers are working very long hours, resulting in the red lab coats being shoddily sewn. You do not have enough fabric or time to redo them.

Offer Sydney Workwear a discounted price.

Spend 5,000.

 9

Iron and pack the lab coats really neatly, and cross your fingers and hope that Sydney Workwear do not notice.

Spend 5,000.

 270

Installing the heating system has slowed production by a day and there is a technical problem: it will not switch off. Your already-warm factory is now unbearably hot. You get a new order to assemble Christmas jumpers subcontracted from a neighbouring factory.

Ku Heating Co. demand 5,000 to fix it, which will have to come out of your capital.

Spend 5,000.

▶ 11

312 ◀ WORLD FACTORY

You complete the order for the hi-vis jackets for Sydney Workwear, and also the vest tops for Zina. You let your new workers (Hou Yu, He Na, Yang Weina, Qian Yufen and Liu Fang) go again as you have no more work for them. Installing the heating system has slowed production by a day and there is a technical problem: it will not switch off. Your already-warm factory is now unbearably hot. Ku Heating Co. demand 5,000 to fix it; after your other running costs of bills, rent and fabric costs, it absorbs all your profit.

Next morning you receive a letter from Hou Yu, who, in despair at the hiring and firing, asks you to appreciate his skills and consider him if you are ever re-recruiting.

Spend 5,000. Lose 5 workers.

▶ 14

313 ◀ WORLD FACTORY

You complete the order for the hi-vis vests for Sydney Workwear. You let your new workers (Hou Yu, He Na, Yang Weina, Qian Yufen, Liu Fang) go again as you have no more work for them. Installing the heating system has slowed production by a day and there is a technical problem: it will not switch off. Your already-warm factory is now unbearably hot. Ku Heating Co. demand 5,000 to fix it; after your other running costs of bills, rent and fabric costs, it absorbs all your profit.

Next morning you receive a letter from Hou Yu, who, in despair at the hiring and firing, asks you to appreciate his skills and consider him if you are ever re-recruiting.

Spend 5,000. Lose 5 workers.

▶ 19

314

Installing the heating system slows production by a day. There is a problem: it won't switch off. Your already-warm factory is now unbearable; Ku Heating Co. demand 5,000 to fix it. You just meet the deadline for the vest tops and the hi-vis vests but your workers are exhausted from the 16-hour days required. Liang Qiang comes to see you, demanding an extra week's wages; equivalent to paying double for the extra hours worked. You don't have enough cash to pay from your running costs, so you will have to use your capital.

Pay the workers the rate that they ask for, as well as paying for the heating to be fixed. After all, their wages are already low.

Spend 10,000.

 120

Pay the workers for all the additional hours worked at their normal rate – you cannot afford more, given the heating bill.

Spend 5,000.

14

315

You complete the hi-vis vests. Installing the heating system slows production by a day. There is a problem: it won't switch off. Your already-warm factory is now unbearable; Ku Heating Co. demand 5,000 to fix it. You meet the deadline for the vests but the workers are exhausted from the 16-hour days required. Your factory-floor supervisor Li Pengjian requests you pay the overtime at double rate. You don't have enough cash to pay from your running costs so you will have to use your capital.

Pay for the heating and pay the workers the rate that they ask for; after all, their wages are already low.

Spend 15,000.

121

Pay for the heating and pay the workers for all the additional hours worked at their normal rate. You cannot afford more at the moment and they know this.

Spend 10,000.

 407

316

When you arrive the next morning, your workers are back at their machines, sewing. However, you have lost the Athelete bikini order due to the strike. Neighbouring factory manager, Liu Huiquan, gives you a call. Would you have capacity for handling some jeans? They need to be sandblasted to make them look preworn. She has the equipment, but not enough workers to get the order completed in time. You will make a huge profit.

Ask to see the sandblasting equipment before agreeing to provide workers: you have heard it can be dangerous.

 296

Provide the workers; it is better not to know more. You need the income, and your workers will not be exposed to sandblasting particles for long; it is only a temporary arrangement.

301

317

You receive the jeans already cut into the pattern. They also supply the buttons, which are genuine Levi rivets. You get the order done quickly, and hand them over to Liu Huiquan who pays you in cash for the work, and tells you that they are, in fact, counterfeit. The reason the profit margin is so high is that because she managed to source genuine Levi rivets, they cannot be distinguished from the real thing, and fetch a high price in both Chinese and foreign markets.

Make an agreement with Liu Huiquan to continue the collaboration, guaranteeing a steady profit.

Receive 40,000.

303

Tell Liu Huiquan you do not want to be involved.

Receive 40,000.

340

Your new workers are very fast: they are desperate to earn enough to repay the Snakehead gang that brought them across the border into China. Ku Fang calls. He asks you if you have come across the Rainbow Plan for improving workers' pay; your factory does not have a Union, belonging to the All-China Federation of Trade Unions. It is imperative you set one up. He reassures you that you will have a say in appointing the Union committee. The next day another official, Chen Jianlin, arrives to monitor the first meeting.

Send your illegal Vietnamese workers out the back while the party official is presiding over your first Union meeting.

》289

Give your illegal Vietnamese workers the day off to ensure they are not discovered by the party official.

》283

Yuan Bao writes you a letter claiming that the working conditions in the factory are responsible for the 3 miscarriages that she has had. She has only been working for your factory for a couple of years, but she started in the industry as a child, and when you read up on it, you discover that there are adverse reproductive effects associated with inhalation of synthetic fibres. As Yaun Bao is a migrant worker, gaining access to health care in the city is extremely expensive for her.

Extend your sympathies to Yuan Bao, offer her 5,000 towards getting medical help and tell her she can have her job back if she would like it.

Spend 5,000.

》305

Extend your sympathies to Yuan Bao but point out that it is her previous employment history and not your factory that is the cause of her present troubles.

》320

320

Your workers have not been wearing the safety equipment provided for the sandblasting, as it makes it almost impossible to do the work quickly, and they are being paid by the piece. When they come off the order, all of them have a bad cough. However, they were well paid, and you have made yet more profit. Liu Huiquan wants to continue the collaboration: she still needs some additional workers to handle the sandblasting, but also wonders if she can outsource some of the sewing to you.

Provide workers and take on the jeans for sewing on Liu Huiquan's behalf.

Receive 40,000.

 288

Take on the jeans for sewing on Liu Huiquan's behalf, but tell Liu Huiquan she will have to find workers herself, as you will no longer provide them, given the health issues.

Receive 20,000.

 338

321

Sydney Workwear thank you for getting the clothes out of customs and pay the balance. Paying wages, guaranteeing workers a stable income, rather than paying per piece, is manageable at this wage level. However, the workers want a payrise. Zhu Qing has taken on the leadership of the Union: you are surprised Li Pengjian is not involved; he has always been interested in workers' rights. Zhu Qing tells you the faster workers would rather be paid by piece so they can earn more to send home.

Continue paying wages. You do not like how Zhu Qing is trying to ingratiate herself with you.

 39

Reconsider your decision and move to piecework, which will increase your productivity, which you desperately need, and satisfy your more ambitious workers.

 345

WORLD FACTORY

You complete the dresses with a frill skirt and ship them to Zina. Paying wages, guaranteeing workers a stable income, rather than paying per piece, is manageable due to your decision to outsource. However, the workers want a payrise. Zhu Qing has taken on the leadership of the Union: you are surprised Li Pengjian is not involved; he has always been interested in workers' rights. Zhu Qing tells you the faster workers would rather be paid by piece so they can earn more to send home.

Continue paying wages. You do not like how Zhu Qing is trying to ingratiate herself with you.

Spend 15,000.

55 IF accepted heating grant
57 IF declined heating grant

Reconsider your decision and move to piecework, which will increase your productivity, which you desperately need, and satisfy your more ambitious workers.

349

WORLD FACTORY

Paying wages, guaranteeing workers a stable income, rather than paying per piece, is manageable at this wage level: you have been able to cover the wage bill this month through your income. However, the workers want a payrise. Zhu Qing has taken on the leadership of the Union: you are surprised Li Pengjian is not involved, as he has always taken an interest in workers' rights. Zhu Qing tells you the faster workers would rather be paid by piece so they can earn more to send home to their families.

Continue paying wages. You do not like how Zhu Qing is trying to ingratiate herself with you.

171

Reconsider your decision and move to piecework, which will increase your productivity, which you desperately need, and satisfy your more ambitious workers.

363

WORLD FACTORY

Paying wages, guaranteeing workers a stable income, rather than paying per piece, is manageable at this wage level: you have been able to cover the wage bill this month through your income. However, the workers want a payrise. Zhu Qing has taken on the leadership of the Union: you are surprised Li Pengjian is not involved, as he has always taken an interest in workers' rights. Zhu Qing tells you the faster workers would rather be paid by piece so they can earn more to send home to their families.

Continue paying wages. You do not like how Zhu Qing is trying to ingratiate herself with you.

 324a

Reconsider your decision and move to piecework, which will increase your productivity, which you desperately need, and satisfy your more ambitious workers.

▶ 372

UNCERTAINTY MEANS PROGRESS

WORLD FACTORY

Did a compliance inspector ask to see ID for all your workers?

YES   NO
|
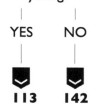
184

Did you allow Lu Qingmin to keep working despite her looking very young?

| |
YES   NO
| |
113   **142**

325 WORLD FACTORY

Mick Fletcher from Run Rabbit offers you a new order for 100% organic-cotton hoodies if you adhere to their ethical guidelines and allow your factory to be inspected. Tony Nie, whose factory is a couple of blocks away, was telling you the other day about how achieving compliance with international standards can get extremely expensive.

Decline the order from Run Rabbit, to avoid being inspected.

 208

Take the order from Run Rabbit and allow your factory to be inspected.

 209

---

326 WORLD FACTORY

The municipal authorities are clamping down on the unbearable smog; you are fined 5,000 for using the city incinerators. Paying wages rather than paying per piece is manageable at this wage level and ensures stability for your workers. However, they want a pay rise. Zhu Qing has taken on the leadership of the Union: you are surprised Li Pengjian is not involved, as he has always taken an interest in workers' rights. Zhu Qing tells you the faster workers would rather be paid per piece so they could earn more to send home.

Continue paying wages. You do not trust how Zhu Qing is trying to ingratiate herself with you as management.

Spend 5,000.

51 IF taught workers English
38 IF did not teach English

Reconsider your decision and move to piecework, which will increase your productivity, which you desperately need, and satisfy your more ambitious workers.

Spend 5,000.

383

327

Li Pengjian tells you Yuan Bao has just suffered a third miscarriage and has been told she will probably never have a child. She has only been working for your factory for a couple of years, but started in the industry as a child, and when you read up on it, you discover that there are adverse reproductive effects associated with inhalation of synthetic fibres. As Yaun Bao is a migrant worker, gaining access to health care in the city is extremely expensive for her.

Extend your sympathies to Yuan Bao, and offer her 5,000 towards getting medical help.

Spend 5,000.

 305

Extend your sympathies to Yuan Bao but point out that it is her previous employment history and not your factory that is the cause of her present troubles.

320

328

Paying wages, guaranteeing workers a stable income, rather than paying per piece, is tough at this wage level, and you have to use part of your capital again this month to pay workers. Zhu Qing has taken on the leadership of the Union: you are surprised Li Pengjian is not involved, as he has always taken an interest in workers' rights. Zhu Qing tells you the faster workers would rather be paid by piece so they can earn more to send home to their families.

Continue paying wages. You do not like how Zhu Qing is trying to ingratiate herself with you.

Spend 10,000.

31

Move to piecework; paying wages at this level is unsustainable; piecework will increase productivity and satisfy your more ambitious workers.

Spend 10,000.

 399

WORLD FACTORY

Paying wages, guaranteeing workers a stable income, rather than paying per piece, is manageable at this wage level. However, the workers want a payrise. Zhu Qing has taken on the leadership of the Union: you are surprised Li Pengjian is not involved, as he has always been interested in workers' rights. Zhu Qing tells you the faster workers would rather be paid by piece so they can earn more to send home to their families.

Continue paying wages. You do not like how Zhu Qing is trying to ingratiate herself with you.

 196

Reconsider your decision and move to piecework, which will increase your productivity, which you desperately need, and satisfy your more ambitious workers.

 369

WORLD FACTORY

Your workers aren't happy at the idea of not going home and may not accept your offer: it is their only chance to see their families. The search for your old workers takes a long time: 6 have new jobs; Wang Haiyan has moved city; Sang Hong's mobile number doesn't work; and Xu Daiqun had a heart attack and is unfit to work. In the end you can only reinstate Xie Qingfang, Liu Lequn and Cao Tao. Due to the delay in rebuilding your workforce, you must turn down an order from a regular client.

Hire another 7 new people, in addition to giving jobs to your 3 former workers.

Gain 10 workers.

369 377

WORLD FACTORY

You receive the balance of payment on the order from Liu Huiquan. She would like to continue the collaboration: she still needs some additional workers to handle the sandblasting, but also wonders if she can outsource some of the sewing to you.

Provide workers and take on the jeans for sewing on Liu Huiquan's behalf.

Receive 40,000.

 288

Take on the jeans for sewing on Liu Huiquan's behalf, but tell Liu Huiquan she will have to find workers herself, as you will no longer provide them, given the health issues.
Receive 20,000.

 338

WORLD FACTORY

Your workers are not happy about not going home for Spring Festival to see family, and may not accept your offer. You receive an order for school-uniform dresses. Your accountant Wang Lin advises you to move to piecework, a different financial model for paying your workers. Instead of being paid a fixed monthly wage, workers are paid per item they complete, which incentivises them to work faster. Apparently skilled workers tend to like it, as it means they can earn more to send home.

Change to piecework. From now on you will pay workers according to how many garments they make, rather than paying a fixed monthly wage.

343

Enquire as to the attitudes of your workers by asking your factory-floor supervisor, Li Pengjian, before you change your pay structure.

 277

Your workers are not happy at the idea of not going home at New Year: this is the only time of year when they see their families. You need to get more orders so you can cover your outgoings. Rob Baxter, Zina's compliance inspector, suddenly turns up. It appears he has been staying in the hotel opposite and spying on you. He asks to see ID for all your workers. You do not have a record for Lu Qingmin, who looks really young.

Ask Lu Qingmin to take 'unpaid holiday' for the foreseeable future, and tell Rob Baxter she has left the company.

Lose I worker.

▶ **284**

Ask her to bring ID: you do not care if it is fake. She is a good worker and you would like to keep her.

▶ **286**

You receive a new order of grey polo shirts from Sydney Workwear. Training is increasing productivity. After advertising on MadeInChina.com about your pay levels and workers' training, you are surprised to hear from fashion line Garb, who are bringing out an 'ethical' range. They will place a large order of blue-striped skirts if you comply with a number of international directives, including providing air conditioning.

Install air conditioning and make a thorough check to ensure you comply with international standards for working conditions.

Spend 15,000.

▶ **337**

Ask Li Pengjian to find out, subtly, whether the workers are likely to appreciate the installation of air conditioning.

▶ **252**

335

The workers are not happy about not going home at New Year and some refuse your offer: this is the only time of year when they see their families. Despite lots of orders, you struggle to pay the newly increased wages, and have to let 4 workers go. You research ethical retailers to see if they pay a fairer price. The cheaper fabric you bought frays easily and proves difficult to sew; around 7,000 shirts turn out shoddy, with misaligned buttons.

Get Lu Qingmin to iron and pack the shirts really neatly and cross your fingers that Zina do not notice.

Lose 4 workers.

 111

Confess the error to Zina and offer a discounted price.

Lose 4 workers.

▶ **52**

336

The workers reject your offer: New Year is the only time of year they see their families. International brand Mud call you. A celebrity has been seen wearing one of the workshirts you made for Workers Comfort. They want to place a huge order (for 10,000) with their brand label, immediately, which means prioritising them ahead of other orders. You need more workers to manage. Your best machinist, Tian Jianying, suggests hiring contacts of hers from home, all trained in tailoring.

Refuse to hire Tian Jianying's contacts when they arrive from Sichuan late the next day, after travelling all night; they look very young and do not have ID.

▶ **292**

Tell Tian Jianying she must provide ID for her contacts; you don't mind how. You have tested their skills, and are impressed; they must have been working for several years.

Gain 10 workers.

 158

WORLD FACTORY

You quickly finish Garb's order for blue-striped skirts, and make a profit. You have the air conditioning installed, but no one uses it, and Garb do not ask you about it again. Wang Lin advises you to move to piecework, a different financial model for paying your workers. Workers are paid per item they complete, incentivising them to work faster. Apparently skilled workers like it, as it means they can earn more to send home. Your financial situation is currently highly precarious.

Change to piecework. From now on you will pay workers according to how many garments they make, rather than paying a fixed monthly wage.

Receive 30,000.

 299

Enquire as to the attitudes of your workers by asking your factory-floor supervisor, Li Pengjian, before you change your pay structure.

Receive 30,000.

▶ **94**

WORLD FACTORY

Your shift in the World Factory is now over. That was a year in the life of a Chinese clothing factory, but the World Factory goes on. In China, the cost of labour is rising, as are living standards, and workers are increasingly organised – in spite of government restrictions. The World Factory is therefore seeking new locations and new markets. Where will it end up?

Please now turn to the end of the cards to explore different options for how to continue.

▶ Turn to page 247

339

You notice that as a result of your treatment of the troublemakers, your workforce is more deferential. Productivity is increasing – and so are profits. However, when you go to the labour exchange to find new workers, you discover that at the level that you are currently paying, it is hard to find anyone willing to work for you. Of 15 free samples you have sewn for fast-fashion clients in the recent weeks, only 2 placed an order.

Hire untrained Chinese migrant workers willing to take low pay. You will have to train them.

Receive 40,000. Gain 5 workers.

▶ 414

Hire illegal Vietnamese economic migrants who are desperate for work and highly skilled.

Receive 40,000. Gain 5 workers.

▶ 362

340

You notice that Yuan Bao has been working much more slowly than usual for a little while, and seems to be taking a lot of breaks, and be on her phone a lot. You ask your workshop supervisor, Li Pengjian, what the trouble is. He does not know.

Let Yuan Bao go. You cannot afford to have any laziness in a factory like yours.

Lose 1 worker.

▶ 382

Tell Li Pengjian to ask Yuan Bao what the problem is.

 384

You discover that sourcing organic cotton is more expensive than you thought and email Run Rabbit with a higher price. You have dinner with Madame Wang from ZhengXing Clothing Co. and your friend, the merchandiser Gloria Yeung. The conversation turns to rumours of strikes in other provinces, although there is no information in the official news. Madame Wang is trying a new scheme: offering her workers free tuition in computing and English. Gloria talks about the night school she went to, to learn English.

Invest in training workers in skills that are useful to the factory.
It is not your role to direct the education of the workers.

 17

Offer free extra tuition to your workers at the end of their working day, as well as improving their sewing skills.

Spend 3,000.

▶ 130

Training your workers causes friction as, now that the workers are paid by piece, no one wants to spend time training others. Ku Fang calls and asks you if you have come across the Rainbow Plan for improving workers' pay. It has come to his attention that your factory does not have a Union, belonging to the All-China Federation of Trade Unions. He insists you set one up, but reassures you that you will have some say in appointing its committee.

Another official, Chen Jianlin, turns up the next day to monitor the first meeting. He has useful suggestions for increasing productivity.

▶ 279

343 ◀ WORLD FACTORY

You are a little unsettled; a clique of workers seem unhappy that you changed the method of calculating pay without discussion. Your factory-floor supervisor, Li Pengjian, is working long hours to keep track of the different work rates. You ask him about the workers' attitudes, but he tells you it is difficult to get an overview because several talk in dialect or use their mobiles to share information. He suggests that you hear their demands directly, if you are worried.

Adopt a policy of lowering the pay of the troublemakers until they find work elsewhere.

Lose 5 workers.

 357

Agree to meet Yan Rong, Yao Lin and Zhu Qing, informally.

 355

344 ◀ WORLD FACTORY

Huang Jiao tells you that, as well as a small pay increase, they would like to alter the working method so that they each make whole garments rather than just a single part of a garment. This will vary the work and mean that the fastest ones will not be slowed down by the slowest not finishing their part of the garment as quickly. You consult with fellow factory managers including Madame Wang and find that she has already made this change, at the request of her workers. You agree to trial it.

Ku Fang calls you: factories in the vicinity are letting workers make key operative decisions outside the Union; he reminds you that independent collectivisation is illegal.

 39

A few later Li Pengjian asks you whether you will trial a method that your neighbouring factory manager, Madame Wang, has adopted. Rather than each making a single part of a garment, they would like to make whole garments. That way the fastest will not be held up by those who are slower, and it will vary the work. You consult with Madame Wang who recommends it, although she does admit the quality of the garments is sometimes lower. You agree to a short-term trial.

Ku Fang calls you: factories in the vicinity are letting workers make key operative decisions outside the Union; he reminds you that independent collectivisation is illegal.

》39

Huang Jiao tells you that, as well as a small pay increase, they would like to alter the working method so that they each make whole garments rather than just a single part of a garment. This will vary the work and mean that the fastest ones will not be held up by the slowest not finishing their part of the garment as quickly. You consult with fellow factory managers including Madame Wang and find that she has already made this change, at the request of her workers. You agree to trial it.

Ku Fang calls you: factories in the vicinity are letting workers make key operative decisions outside the Union; he reminds you that independent collectivisation is illegal.

》51 IF taught workers English
》38 IF did not teach English

347 ◀ WORLD FACTORY

Huang Jiao tells you that they would like to alter the working method so that they each make whole garments rather than just a single part of a garment. This will vary the work and mean that the fastest ones will not be slowed down by the slowest not finishing their part of the garment as quickly. You consult with fellow factory managers including Madame Wang and find that she has already made this change, at the request of her workers. You agree to trial it.

Ku Fang calls you: factories in the vicinity are letting workers make key operative decisions outside the Union; he reminds you that independent collectivisation is illegal.

▶ 153

---

348 ◀ WORLD FACTORY

Huang Jiao tells you that, as well as a small pay increase, they would like to alter the working method so that they each make whole garments rather than just a single part of a garment. This will vary the work and mean that the fastest ones will not be held up by the slowest not finishing their part of the garment as quickly. You consult with fellow factory managers including Madame Wang and find that she has already made this change, at the request of her workers. You agree to trial it.

Ku Fang calls you: factories in the vicinity are letting workers make key operative decisions outside the Union; he reminds you that independent collectivisation is illegal.

▶ 55   IF accepted heating grant
▶ 57   IF declined heating grant

A few later, Li Pengjian asks you whether you will trial a method that your neighbouring factory manager, Madame Wang, has adopted. Rather than each making a single part of a garment, they would like to make whole garments. That way the fastest will not be held up by those who are slower, and it will vary the work. You consult with Madame Wang who recommends it, although she does admit the quality of the garments is sometimes lower. You agree to a short-term trial.

Ku Fang calls you: factories in the vicinity are letting workers make key operative decisions outside the Union; he reminds you that independent collectivisation is illegal.

▶ **55**   IF accepted heating grant
▶ **57**   IF declined heating grant

You get an order for school-uniform dresses. Your new workers are fast: they are desperate to repay the Snakehead gang that smuggled them into China. Ku Fang calls. He asks you if you have come across the Rainbow Plan for improving workers' pay; your factory does not have a Union belonging to the All-China Federation of Trade Unions. It is imperative you set one up; another party official, Chen Jianlin, is on his way to you to help out.

Send your illegal Vietnamese workers out the back while the party official is presiding over your first Union meeting.

▶ **27**

Give your illegal Vietnamese workers the day off to ensure they are not discovered by the party official.

▶ **46**

351

Huang Jiao tells you that as well as a small pay increase, they would like to alter the working method so that they each make whole garments rather than just a single part of a garment. This will vary the work and mean that the fastest ones will not be held up by the slowest not finishing their part of the garment as quickly. You consult with fellow factory managers including Madame Wang and find that she has already made this change, at the request of her workers. You agree to trial it.

Ku Fang calls you: factories in the vicinity are letting workers make key operative decisions outside the Union; he reminds you that independent collectivisation is illegal.

▶ 39

352

You notice that as a result of your treatment of the troublemakers, your workforce is more deferential; and productivity is increasing. You make a reasonable profit this month, but need to rebuild the workforce. You go to the labour exchange, and discover it will not be as easy as you thought. Most workers want to join a large factory with more onsite benefits than you are in a position to offer. Run Rabbit, a Hong Kong based sportswear company place an order for organic-cotton T-shirts.

Hire untrained Chinese migrant workers willing to take low pay. You will have to train them.

Receive 25,000. Gain 5 workers.

▶ 341

Hire illegal Vietnamese economic migrants who are desperate for work and highly skilled.

Receive 25,000. Gain 5 workers.

 318

353 ◀ WORLD FACTORY

Huang Jiao tells you they would like to alter the working method so that they each make whole garments rather than just a single part of a garment. This will vary the work and mean that the fastest ones will not be held up by the slowest not finishing their part of the garment as quickly. You consult with fellow factory managers including Madame Wang and find that she has already made this change, at the request of her workers. You agree to trial it.

Ku Fang calls you: factories in the vicinity are letting workers make key operative decisions outside the Union; he reminds you that independent collectivisation is illegal.

▶ 153

354 ◀ WORLD FACTORY

You complete the vest tops for Zina, the mens' long sleeve T-shirts for Plantlife, and the knickers for Poppy. You are a little unsettled; a clique of workers seem unhappy that you changed the method of pay without discussion. Li Pengjian is working long hours to keep track of the different work rates. You ask him about the workers' attitudes; he tells you it is difficult to get an overview as several talk in dialect or use their mobiles to share information. He suggests that you hear their demands directly if you are worried.

Adopt a policy of lowering the pay of the troublemakers until they find work elsewhere.

Lose 5 workers.

▶ 352

Agree to meet Yan Rong, Yao Lin and Zhu Qing, informally.

▶ 230

You invite Yan Rong, Yao Lin and Zhu Qing, along with Li Pengjian, the supervisor, into your office. They tell you that the move to piecework has divided the workforce, as it discriminates against those who are highly skilled but older and therefore a little slower. They tell you that life is precarious enough without the uncertainty each month of not knowing how much they will earn. They would like to be able to monitor the situation and meet with you again to discuss it.

Help your workers set up a legal Union under government auspices.

 360

Agree to your workers' request for regular consultation, although it will be unofficial as independent unionisation is illegal.

▶ **28**

Huang Jiao tells you that as well as a small pay increase, they would like to alter the working method so that they each make whole garments rather than just a single part of a garment. This will vary the work and mean that the fastest ones will not be slowed down by the slowest not finishing their part of the garment as quickly. You consult with fellow factory managers including Madame Wang and find that she has already made this change, at the request of her workers. You agree to trial it.

Ku Fang calls you: factories in the vicinity are letting workers make key operative decisions outside the Union; he reminds you that independent collectivisation is illegal.

▶ **55** IF accepted heating grant
▶ **57** IF declined heating grant

You notice that as a result of your treatment of the troublemakers, your workforce is more deferential; productivity is increasing, and after being paid for several orders you find you have made a profit. You go to the labour exchange to find new workers, and discover it will not be as easy as you thought. Most who are there looking for work want to join a large factory with more onsite benefits than you are in a position to offer.

Hire untrained Chinese migrant workers willing to take low pay. You will have to train them.

Receive 10,000. Gain 5 workers.

 342

Hire illegal Vietnamese economic migrants who are desperate for work and highly skilled.

Receive 10,000. Gain 5 workers.

 380

Huang Jiao tells you that as well as a small pay increase, they would like to alter the working method so that they each make whole garments rather than just a single part of a garment. This will vary the work and mean that the fastest ones will not be held up by the slowest not finishing their part of the garment as quickly. You consult with fellow factory managers including Madame Wang and find that she has already made this change, at the request of her workers. You agree to trial it.

Ku Fang calls you: factories in the vicinity are letting workers make key operative decisions outside the Union; he reminds you that independent collectivisation is illegal.

▶ **171**

Huang Jiao tells you that as well as a small pay increase, they would like to alter the working method so that they each make whole garments rather than just a single part of a garment. This will vary the work and mean that the fastest ones will not be slowed down by the slowest not finishing their part of the garment as quickly. You consult with fellow factory managers including Madame Wang and find that she has already made this change, at the request of her workers. You agree to trial it.

Ku Fang calls you: factories in the vicinity are letting workers make key operative decisions outside the Union; he reminds you that independent collectivisation is illegal.

▶ 171

You allow your newly unionised workers to form a committee to move towards implementing the Rainbow Plan to increase wages over the longer term. This is a plan devised by the All-China Federation of Trade Unions, for implementation nationally, supported by the government.

An official, Chen Jianlin, turns up the next day to monitor the first meeting. He has useful suggestions for increasing productivity.

▶ 279

Training is slow as, now that your workers are paid by piece, they are reluctant to take the time to train others. Ku Fang calls. He asks you if you have come across the Rainbow Plan for improving workers' pay. It has been brought to his attention that your factory does not have a Union, belonging to the All-China Federation of Trade Unions. It is imperative you set one up. He reassures you that you will have some say in appointing the Union committee.

Another official, Chen Jianlin, turns up the next day to monitor the first meeting. He has useful suggestions for increasing productivity.

▶ 66

Your new workers are very fast: they are desperate to earn enough to repay the Snakehead gang that brought them across the border into China. Ku Fang calls. He asks you if you have come across the Rainbow Plan for improving workers' pay. It has been brought to his attention that your factory does not have a Union, belonging to the All-China Federation of Trade Unions. It is imperative you set one up. The next day another official, Chen Jianlin, arrives to appoint the Union committee.

Send your illegal Vietnamese workers out the back while the party official is presiding over your first Union meeting.

▶ 138

Give your illegal Vietnamese workers the day off to ensure they are not discovered by the party official.

▶ 147

363 ◀ WORLD FACTORY

A few days later Li Pengjian asks you whether you will trial a method that your neighbouring factory manager, Madame Wang, has adopted. Rather than each making a single part of a garment, they would like to make whole garments. That way the fastest will not be held up by those who are slower, and it will vary the work. You consult with Madame Wang who recommends it, although she does admit the quality of the garments is sometimes lower. You agree to a short-term trial.

Ku Fang calls you: factories in the vicinity are letting workers make key operative decisions outside the Union; he reminds you that independent collectivisation is illegal.

▶ 171

364 ◀ WORLD FACTORY

Huang Jiao tells you that as well as a small pay increase, they would like to alter the working method so that they each make whole garments rather than just a single part of a garment. This will vary the work and mean that the fastest ones will not be held up by the slowest not finishing their part of the garment as quickly. You consult with fellow factory managers including Madame Wang and find that she has already made this change, at the request of her workers. You agree to trial it.

Ku Fang calls you: factories in the vicinity are letting workers make key operative decisions outside the Union; he reminds you that independent collectivisation is illegal.

 ▶ 265

WORLD FACTORY

Huang Jiao tells you that as well as a small pay increase, they would like to alter the working method so that they each make whole garments rather than just a single part of a garment. This will vary the work and mean that the fastest ones will not be slowed down by the slowest not finishing their part of the garment as quickly. You consult with fellow factory managers including Madame Wang and find that she has already made this change, at the request of her workers. You agree to trial it.

Ku Fang calls you: factories in the vicinity are letting workers make key operative decisions outside the Union; he reminds you that independent collectivisation is illegal.

》 265

WORLD FACTORY

A few days later Li Pengjian asks you whether you will trial a method that your neighbouring factory manager, Madame Wang, has adopted. Rather than each making a single part of a garment, they would like to make whole garments. That way the fastest will not be held up by those who are slower, and it will vary the work. You consult with Madame Wang who recommends it, although she does admit the quality of the garments is sometimes lower. You agree to a short-term trial.

Ku Fang calls you: factories in the vicinity are letting workers make key operative decisions outside the Union; he reminds you that independent collectivisation is illegal.

 265

367 WORLD FACTORY

Huang Jiao tells you that as well as a small pay increase, they would like to alter the working method so that they each make whole garments rather than just a single part of a garment. This will vary the work and mean that the fastest ones will not be held up by the slowest not finishing their part of the garment as quickly. You consult with fellow factory managers including Madame Wang and find that she has already made this change, at the request of her workers. You agree to trial it.

Ku Fang calls you: factories in the vicinity are letting workers make key operative decisions outside the Union; he reminds you that independent collectivisation is illegal.

 196

368 WORLD FACTORY

Huang Jiao tells you that as well as a small pay increase, they would like to alter the working method so that they each make whole garments rather than just a single part of a garment. This will vary the work and mean that the fastest ones will not be slowed down by the slowest not finishing their part of the garment as quickly. You consult with fellow factory managers including Madame Wang and find that she has already made this change, at the request of her workers. You agree to trial it.

Ku Fang calls you: factories in the vicinity are letting workers make key operative decisions outside the Union; he reminds you that independent collectivisation is illegal.

196

A few days later Li Pengjian asks you whether you will trial a method that your neighbouring factory manager, Madame Wang, has adopted. Rather than each making a single part of a garment, they would like to make whole garments. That way the fastest will not be held up by those who are slower, and it will vary the work. You consult with Madame Wang who recommends it, although she does admit the quality of the garments is sometimes lower. You agree to a short-term trial.

Ku Fang calls you: factories in the vicinity are letting workers make key operative decisions outside the Union; he reminds you that independent collectivisation is illegal.

▶ 196

"We really want to be like you British, have a carefree life – gentlemanlike – but we can't yet. We – our generation, and the generation before us, and the generation after – they've strived and struggled hard. But maybe the generation after, when it's our grandchildren's time, maybe then they might be able to live like you, and have an easy life. When we started our business, that we'd ever live like you British was unimaginable. It really was. We worked all day and at night we slept on the floor. That's what it was like. Really, it's hard to imagine. For our children and grandchildren, nothing will make them do that."

Tony Nie, Shanghai Xiaosa Garment Co. Ltd, Shanghai, 2014

WORLD FACTORY

Huang Jiao tells you that as well as a small pay increase, they would like to alter the working method so that they each make whole garments rather than just a single part of a garment. This will vary the work and mean that the fastest ones will not be held up by the slowest not finishing their part of the garment as quickly. You consult with fellow factory managers including Madame Wang and find that she has already made this change, at the request of her workers. You agree to trial it.

Ku Fang calls you: factories in the vicinity are letting workers make key operative decisions outside the Union; he reminds you that independent collectivisation is illegal.

 370a

TIME IS MONEY

370a

WORLD FACTORY

Did a compliance inspector ask to see ID for all your workers?

YES   NO

184

Did you allow Lu Qingmin to keep working despite her looking very young?

YES   NO

113   142

Huang Jiao tells you that as well as a small pay increase, they would like to alter the working method so that they each make whole garments rather than just a single part of a garment. This will vary the work and mean that the fastest ones will not be slowed down by the slowest not finishing their part of the garment as quickly. You consult with fellow factory managers including Madame Wang and find that she has already made this change, at the request of her workers. You agree to trial it.

Ku Fang calls you: factories in the vicinity are letting workers make key operative decisions outside the Union; he reminds you that independent collectivisation is illegal.

▶ 371a

KEEP GOING FORWARD

371a

Did a compliance inspector ask to see ID for all your workers?

YES | NO

184

Did you allow Lu Qingmin to keep working despite her looking very young?

YES | NO

113 | **142**

A few days later Li Pengjian asks you whether you will trial a method that your neighbouring factory manager, Madame Wang, has adopted. Rather than each making a single part of a garment, they would like to make whole garments. That way the fastest will not be held up by those who are slower, and it will vary the work. You consult with Madame Wang who recommends it, although she does admit the quality of the garments is sometimes lower. You agree to a short-term trial.

Ku Fang calls you: factories in the vicinity are letting workers make key operative decisions outside the Union; he reminds you that independent collectivisation is illegal.

 172a

SURVIVAL IS WINNING

Did a compliance inspector ask to see ID for all your workers?

YES   NO

184

Did you allow Lu Qingmin to keep working despite her looking very young?

YES   NO

113   142

373

WORLD FACTORY

You allow your newly unionised workers to form a committee to move towards implementing the Rainbow Plan to increase wages over the longer term. This is a plan devised by the All-China Federation of Trade Unions, for implementation nationally, supported by the government. When you do your accounts you find you have made excellent profits this month.

Another official, Chen Jianlin, turns up the next day to monitor the first meeting. He has useful suggestions for increasing productivity.

Receive 40,000.

▶ **23**

374

WORLD FACTORY

Your new workers finish the order of shorts in record time, but despite the compliance costs absorbing all your profit, Run Rabbit say they do not currently have another order for you. Liu Huiquan from a nearby factory gives you a call; do you have capacity for handling some jeans? They need to be sandblasted to make them look preworn. She has the equipment, but not enough workers to get the order completed in time. If you provide 7 workers, you will make a significant profit.

Ask to see the equipment before agreeing to provide workers: you have heard it can be dangerous.

▶ **296**

Provide the workers. It is better not to know; you need the income, and they will not be exposed for long, as it is only a temporary arrangement.

▶ **301**

You complete the waterproof trousers and receive new orders: organic-cotton T-shirts from Run Rabbit and orange gilets from Sportex. Despite having doubled your workforce, you are again in danger of missing your deadlines. A former worker, Qiu Lian, has set up her own small factory in a makeshift extension on the roof of a nearby building. You admire her entrepreneurial spirit, and you know her work is of a high quality.

Outsource to Qiu Lian; you can pay for the work she does from your running costs, without touching your capital.

▶▶ 106 IF accepted heating grant
▶▶ 98 IF declined heating grant

Hire 4 new workers, which will mean having to dig into your capital this month to pay the additional cost. Outsourcing is out of the question.

Spend 12,000. Gain 4 workers.

▶▶ 216 IF accepted heating grant
▶▶ 405 IF declined heating grant

You receive an order for school-uniform dresses. Your accountant Wang Lin advises you to move to piecework, a different financial model for paying your workers. Instead of being paid a fixed monthly wage, workers are paid per item they complete, which incentivises them to work faster. Apparently skilled workers tend to like it, as it means they can earn more to send home.

Change to piecework. From now on you will pay workers according to how many garments they make, rather than paying a fixed monthly wage.

▶▶ 343

Enquire as to the attitudes of your workers by asking your factory-floor supervisor, Li Pengjian, before you change your pay structure.

▶▶ 277

You receive an order for school uniform dresses. You are making a profit, but it is low, so your accountant Wang Lin advises you to move to piecework, a different financial model for paying your workers. Instead of being paid a fixed monthly wage, workers are paid per item they complete, which incentivises them to work faster. Apparently skilled workers tend to like it, as it means they can earn more to send home.

Change to piecework. From now on you will pay workers according to how many garments they make, rather than paying a fixed monthly wage.

Receive 8,000.

 343

Enquire as to the attitudes of your workers by asking your factory-floor supervisor, Li Pengjian, before you change your pay structure.

Receive 8,000.

▶ **277**

Liu Huiquan from the factory on the other side of the complex gives you a call. Would you have capacity for handling some jeans? They need to be sandblasted to make them look preworn. She has the equipment, but not enough workers to get the order completed in time. If you provide 7 workers, you will make a hefty profit; you could immediately start to support the local labour-rights organisation that your factory-floor supervisor has recommended.

Ask to see the sandblasting equipment before agreeing to provide workers: you have heard it can be dangerous.

▶ **296**

Provide the workers; it is better not to know more. You need the income, and your workers will not be exposed to sandblasting particles for long; it is only a temporary arrangement.

▶ **301**

379 ◀ WORLD FACTORY

Lush Fabric supply the organic-cotton fabric. The cotton itself is sourced from Kerala in South India, and the yarn is spun and fabric is woven in Bangladesh. Plantlife are pleased with the result, and place an order for a second run. You take the order although you only just broke even on the previous one. You need to keep your workers in work, and Marvellous have just cancelled their order for suit jackets even though you were already in the middle of making them.

Have the suit-jacket order incinerated: this is standard for unwanted branded goods.

 398

Sell the garments on to a textile reseller who has outlets in inland China.

Receive 15,000.

 82

380 ◀ WORLD FACTORY

Your new workers are very fast: they are desperate to earn enough to repay the Snakehead gang that brought them across the border into China. Ku Fang calls. He asks you if you have come across the Rainbow Plan for improving workers' pay; your factory does not have a Union, belonging to the All-China Federation of Trade Unions. It is imperative you set one up. He reassures you that you will have a say in appointing the Union committee. The next day another official, Chen Jianlin, arrives to monitor the first meeting.

Send your illegal Vietnamese workers out the back while the party official is presiding over your first Union meeting.

 27

Give your illegal Vietnamese workers the day off to ensure they are not discovered by the party official.

 46

Morale is high. Despite a steady stream of visitors, you complete a number of orders and after chasing late payments, you make a profit. Liu Huiquan from the factory on the other side of the complex gives you a call. Would you have capacity for handling some jeans? They need to be sandblasted to make them look preworn. She has the equipment, but not enough workers to get the order completed in time. If you provide 7 workers, you will make a hefty profit: much more than your usual profit from a single order.

Ask to see the sandblasting equipment before agreeing to provide workers: you have heard it can be dangerous.

Receive 25,000.

 296

Provide the workers. It is better not to know details; you need the income, and they will not be exposed to sandblasting particles for long, as it is only a temporary arrangement.

Receive 25,000.

 301

Yuan Bao writes you a letter claiming that the working conditions in the factory are responsible for the 3 miscarriages that she has had. She has only been working for your factory for a couple of years, but she started in the industry as a child, and when you read up on it, you discover that there are adverse reproductive effects associated with inhalation of synthetic fibres. As Yaun Bao is a migrant worker, gaining access to health care in the city is extremely expensive for her.

Extend your sympathies to Yuan Bao, offer her 5,000 towards getting medical help and tell her she can have her job back if she would like it.

Spend 5,000.

 288

Extend your sympathies to Yuan Bao but point out that it is her previous employment history and not your factory that is the cause of her present troubles.

 338

383

A few days later Li Pengjian asks you whether you will trial a method that your neighbouring factory manager, Madame Wang, has adopted. Rather than each making a single part of a garment, they would like to make whole garments. That way the fastest will not be held up by those who are slower, and it will vary the work. You consult with Madame Wang who recommends it, although she does admit the quality of the garments is sometimes lower. You agree to a short-term trial.

Ku Fang calls you: factories in the vicinity are letting workers make key operative decisions outside the Union; he reminds you that independent collectivisation is illegal.

> **51** IF taught workers English
> **38** IF did not teach English

384

Li Pengjian tells you Yuan Bao has just suffered a third miscarriage and has been told she will probably never have a child. She has only been working for your factory for a couple of years, but started in the industry as a child, and when you read up on it, you discover that there are adverse reproductive effects associated with inhalation of synthetic fibres. As Yaun Bao is a migrant worker, gaining access to health care in the city is extremely expensive for her.

Extend your sympathies to Yuan Bao, and offer her 5,000 towards getting medical help.

Spend 5,000.

> **288**

Extend your sympathies to Yuan Bao but point out that it is her previous employment history and not your factory that is the cause of her present troubles.

> **338**

Huang Jiao tells you that, as well as a small pay increase, they would like to alter the working method so that they each make whole garments rather than just a single part of a garment. This will vary the work and mean that the fastest ones will not be slowed down by the slowest not finishing their part of the garment as quickly. You consult with fellow factory managers including Madame Wang and find that she has already made this change, at the request of her workers. You agree to trial it.

Ku Fang calls you: factories in the vicinity are letting workers make key operative decisions outside the Union; he reminds you that independent collectivisation is illegal.

> **51** IF taught workers English
> **38** IF did not teach English

You discover that sourcing organic cotton is more expensive than you thought and email Run Rabbit with a higher price. Ku Fang calls: they would like you to appoint a workers' rep for consultation between the union and management on pay levels. He recommends Zhu Qing. You think she will be a good source of information regarding the situation of the workers. You have dinner with Madame Wang from ZhengXing Clothing Co. You discuss the current police crackdown on illegal immigrants.

The conversation later turns to rumours of strikes in other provinces: there isn't much information in the official news, but Madame Wang is concerned about unrest spreading.

 17

387

You receive an order of grey polo shirts from Sydney Workwear. Morale is strong: the workers appreciate your loyalty in re-employing your former workers, despite the cost to business, and many have taken up the offer of English lessons. Liang Qiang mentions you to a local NGO he is involved with, who put your name on a list of 'ethical' factories. You hear from fashion line Garb, who are bringing out an 'ethical' range; they will place an order if you comply with a number of international directives, including providing air conditioning.

Install air conditioning and make a thorough check to ensure you comply with international standards for working conditions. Take the order.

Spend 15,000.

 337

Ask Li Pengjian to find out whether the workers are likely to appreciate the installation of air conditioning.

252

388

You complete the workshirt order for Workers Comfort. Your workers are not happy at the idea of not going home and may not accept your offer: it is their only chance to see their families. Your accountant Wang Lin has done the accounts and you find you have made a reasonable profit. However, she is worried about the factory's productivity, as your workers have varying levels of skills.

Spend part of your profit on training workers.

Receive 15,000.

 159

Keep the profit. Your income is too precarious to risk additional outlay at the moment; you have not had any complaints about the quality of the garments.

Receive 30,000.

 169

Your workers are not happy about the docked pay – and you do not have much work for them as you have lost several orders due to the strikes. Liu Huiquan from the factory on the other side of the complex gives you a call. Would you have capacity for handling some jeans? They need to be sandblasted to make them look preworn. She has the equipment, but not enough workers to get the order completed in time. If you provide 7 workers, you will make a hefty profit.

Ask to see the sandblasting equipment before agreeing to provide workers: you have heard it can be dangerous.

▶ **296**

Provide the workers. It is better not to know; you need the income, and they will not be exposed to sandblasting particles for long, as it is only a temporary arrangement.

▶ **301**

You complete the waterproof trousers and receive new orders: organic-cotton sports T-shirts from Run Rabbit and orange gilets from Sportex. You are pleased to be receiving multiple orders, but are in danger of missing your deadlines. A former worker, Qiu Lian, has set up her own small factory in a makeshift extension on the roof of a nearby building. You admire her entrepreneurial spirit, and you know her work is of a high quality.

Outsource to Qiu Lian; you can pay for the work she does from your running costs, without touching your capital.

▶ **106** IF accepted heating grant
▶ **98** IF declined heating grant

Hire 4 new workers, which will mean having to dig into your capital this month to pay the additional cost. Outsourcing is out of the question.

Spend 12,000. Gain 4 workers.

▶ **216** IF accepted heating grant
▶ **405** IF declined heating grant

391 WORLD FACTORY

You get an order from Sydney Workwear for waterproof trousers. You hear rumours of dissatisfaction about the continued low pay. Your factory-floor supervisor, Li Pengjian, tells you that other local factories have started to provide free tuition in computing and English for their workers, and that your workers would like this opportunity too. Carol Zhang has been telling them about the night school she went to, to learn English, which helped her fulfil her dream of a desk job.

Tell Li Pengjian that you will only invest in training workers in skills that are useful to the factory.
It is not your role to direct the education of the workers.

Spend 3,000.

 126

Offer free extra tuition to your workers at the end of their working day, as well as improving their sewing skills.

Spend 6,000.

 392

392 WORLD FACTORY

Almost all of your younger workers take up the offer of English lessons. It takes valuable time to train your new workers in textile skills. Ku Fang calls. He wants your factory to set up a Union, belonging to the All-China Federation of Trade Unions. He reassures you that you will have some say in appointing the Union committee. Liang Qiang immediately makes a formal request that you implement the Rainbow Plan for improving workers' pay.

Tell Liang Qiang you hear him, but the Rainbow Plan is for the long term: pay will go up when your revenue goes up.

 107

Put the pay up in accordance with the Union long-term plan, although you will have to pay part of this month's pay from your capital.

Spend 12,000.

 150

WORLD FACTORY

A compliance company arrive without warning to inspect your factory on behalf of Run Rabbit. Their report lists key points that require immediate action. You must pay for fire extinguishers, ventilation fans, and the compliance-inspection fee. If you comply, then you will receive Worldwide Responsible Apparel Production (WRAP) certification, which should help you get orders from international companies in the future.

Turn the compliance company away and tell Run Rabbit you cannot afford the order.

》 208

Pay for improvements to the factory to meet the standards required.

Spend 25,000.

》 206

WORLD FACTORY

Marvellous call you: they have not received the suit jackets. Your shipping company tell you the order has got stuck at the port and that customs report that it is in a queue for checking, and it could take months. You ring Ku Fang in the municipal authorities business department to see if he can help but he is somewhat cool with you on the phone.

Ku Fang is clear that if he is to help, you must use a local cotton mill he recommends, and make a significant contribution to his Factory Development Fund.

Spend 30,000.

》 189

Marvellous call you: they have not received the suit jackets. Your shipping company tells you the order has got stuck in customs at the port; it could take months to clear. You ring Ku Fang in the municipal authorities business department to see if he can help. Ku Fang says he will see what he can do, and gives you a strong recommendation for a local fabric factory: if you mention his name, they will give you an excellent price.

You place an order with the fabric factory immediately; by the end of the day you get a call from customs to say the clothes have been cleared for shipping.

▶ 189

After investigating various options for outsourcing, you decide to outsource to Vietnam, which immediately increases your profit margins: the low labour costs makes it ideal. The first order goes well, with the factory in Vietnam producing excellent quality. The only problem is that the part of the order made in your factory is slightly different in terms of detailing on the garment.

Your client do not notice the discrepancy and you make a significant profit on that order alone.

Receive 30,000.

▶ 403

Having turned down Garb, you need to strengthen your ties with clients not in the fast-fashion industry. Ethical brand Geosync place an order for kaftans. Wang Lin advises you to move to piecework, a different financial model for paying your workers. Workers are paid per item they complete, incentivising them to work faster. Apparently skilled workers like it, as it means they can earn more to send home. Your financial situation is currently highly precarious.

Change to piecework. From now on you will pay workers according to how many garments they make, rather than paying a fixed monthly wage.

 299

Enquire as to the attitudes of your workers by asking your factory-floor supervisor, Li Pengjian, before you change your pay structure.

94

The municipal authorities are cutting down on smog by clamping down on local incinerators: you are fined 5,000 for using one. You complete the vest tops, and receive more orders for organic items, including baby clothes. You hear a report on the radio about major fabric dyeing factories (including the one recommended by Ku Fang) using cotton mills in Bangladesh that employ and house homeless children, who they have rescued from the streets.

Do nothing. The order is underway now, and anyway you applaud attempts to improve children's lives.

Spend 5,000.

 100

Remake the order with non-organic cotton; they will not be able to tell. You cannot deal with a factory employing young children under any circumstances.

Spend 5,000.

 68

399

A few days later Li Pengjian asks you whether you will trial a method that your neighbouring factory manager, Madame Wang, has adopted. Rather than each making a single part of a garment, they would like to make whole garments. That way the fastest will not be held up by those who are slower, and it will vary the work. You consult with Madame Wang who recommends it, although she does admit the quality of the garments is sometimes lower. You agree to a short-term trial.

Ku Fang calls you: factories in the vicinity are letting workers make key operative decisions outside the Union; he reminds you that independent collectivisation is illegal.

 153

400

Your workers are grateful for you enabling them to access health care, although the doctor immediately advises them against continuing working under those conditions. You receive the balance of payment on the order from Liu Huiquan. She would like to continue the collaboration: she still needs some additional workers to handle the sandblasting, but also wonders if she can outsource some of the sewing to you.

Provide workers and take on the jeans for sewing on Liu Huiquan's behalf.

Receive 40,000.

 288

Take on the jeans for sewing on Liu Huiquan's behalf, but tell Liu Huiquan she will have to find workers herself, as you will no longer provide them, given the health issues.

Receive 20,000.

 338

Lush Fabric supply the organic-cotton fabric. The cotton itself is picked in Kerala in South India, and the yarn is spun and fabric is woven in Bangladesh. You need to get more orders in so that you can really start making a profit; setting up a sales office in another city will make you stand out from the competition and lead to orders in new markets. Carol Zhang, your most successful salesperson, will run the new office.

Set up a sales office in Milan; rental costs are on a par with Beijing. You'll benefit from the city's association with high-quality clothing in attracting European clients.

▶ 401a

Set up a sales office in Beijing to participate in the burgeoning Chinese market for high-street fashion, as well as attract lucrative government orders.

▶ 33

BIGGER FASTER CHEAPER MORE

401a WORLD FACTORY

Are you a member of the All-China Union?

YES — Did you move to piecework?
- YES → **259**
- NO → **324**

NO — Did you pay a regular wage?
- YES → **194**
- NO → **193**

WORLD FACTORY

You complete and ship the hoodies for Run Rabbit. A workers' rights group approach you to ask if they can convert one of the factory storerooms into a small 'museum' for garment workers to counteract the negative image portrayed in the media. Lingerie company, Meow, place a small order for lace bodysuits.

Allow the workers' rights group to set up a museum to value the contribution that garment workers make to society.

 118

Say no to the museum; it will distract the workers and the emphasis on workers' rights may draw unwelcome attention from the authorities.

▶ 223

WORLD FACTORY

You place more orders from Garb and Zina with the Vietnamese factory. When you put the phone down, you hear a radio report that most factories in Vietnam pay well under a living wage, with labour conditions more precarious than those in China. A compliance inspector visits. She does not enquire as to whether you outsource orders but notes that your electrics are out of date and you should get them checked.

Get the electrics checked immediately.

Spend 3,000.

▶ 149

Leave the electrics for now: there have never been any problems before, and you do not want to disrupt the work.

 239

WORLD FACTORY

It turns out Yang Lin had lost her phone and her parents' numbers. They are delighted to be reunited. You are introduced to Jenny Rivers from Knitdare, a Manchester-based knitwear supplier, by Wu Fenfang, who owns a knitwear factory downstairs. Kanye West has been seen wearing a mock-collar sewn into a jumper, and would you be able to do some collar inserts for a run of jumpers they are looking at doing? There isn't much profit in it, but you are happy to oblige.

Despite producing several samples, the order never materialises; you later find out that the knitwear factory has gone bust.

▶ 45

WORLD FACTORY

You complete the school-uniform dresses and the orange gilets on time. You are introduced to Jenny Rivers from Knitdare, a Manchester-based knitwear supplier, by Wu Fenfang, who owns a knitwear factory downstairs. Kanye West has been seen wearing a mock-collar sewn into a jumper, and they wonder whether you would be able to do some collar inserts for a run of jumpers they are looking at doing? There isn't much profit in it, but you are happy to oblige.

Despite producing several samples, the order never materialises; you later find out that the knitwear factory has gone bust.

▶ 401

406 WORLD FACTORY

Thanks to the efforts of Carol Zhang in the Milan office, Marvellous, a classic brand from the UK, give you a medium order for women's suit jackets. Workers Comfort return with a very large repeat order of workshirts. They want the order completed very quickly in response to their rival's collection so you name a high price – which they accept. You do not have enough workers to complete the orders.

Hire 10 workers to manage the workload.

Gain 10 workers.

 406a

Tell your workers they will have to take on overnight shifts in order to finish the order.

> **22**

EFFICIENCY IS LIFE

406a WORLD FACTORY

Are you a member of the
All-China Union?

YES   NO

Did you move to piecework?   Did you pay a regular wage?

YES   NO   YES   NO

250   **180**

     323   **179**

WORLD FACTORY

Machinist Liang Qiang comes to see you: they were willing to put up with the low pay level while you were starting up. But he and the other workers would now like the wages to be put back up to 3,000 a month. Currently, Liang Qiang points out, they have barely enough to cover food bills, and certainly can't save anything to send home.

Put the wages back up. Source cheaper fabric to balance the books.

 274

Do not put up the wages as you cannot afford it.

 276

WORLD FACTORY

Li Pengjian, your factory-floor supervisor, tells you morale is high among the workers, thanks to your willingness to hear their perspective. You have made a profit this month, but discover that sourcing organic cotton is more expensive than you thought. You email Run Rabbit with a higher price. You have dinner with Madame Wang from ZhengXing Clothing Co. Ltd and your friend, the merchandiser Gloria Yeung. The major topic of conversation is a new police crackdown on illegal immigrants.

The conversation later turns to rumours of strikes in other provinces, although there is no information in the official news.

Receive 20,000.

 17

Zina call to thank you for getting the clothing out of customs and pay the balance; you make a small profit. You need to get more orders in to increase production and your profit; setting up a sales office in another city will make you stand out from the competition and lead to orders in new markets. Carol Zhang, your most successful salesperson, will run the new office.

Set up a sales office in Milan; rental costs are on a par with Beijing. You'll benefit from the city's association with high-quality clothing in attracting European clients.

Receive 10,000.

 135

Set up a sales office in Beijing to focus on the Chinese fashion market and lucrative government orders; relocation costs are less than moving abroad.

Receive 15,000.

 144

MAXIMUM DESIGN WOW AT MINIMUM COST

Did a compliance inspector ask to see ID for all your workers?

YES   NO

135

Did you allow Lu Qingmin to keep working despite her looking very young?

YES   NO

124   137

You complete the waterproof trousers. Your factory-floor supervisor, Li Pengjian, tells you that other local factories have started to provide free tuition in subjects such as computing and English for their workers, and that the workers would like this opportunity as well. Carol Zhang has been telling them about the night school she went to, to learn English, which helped her fulfil her dream of a desk job.

Offer free extra tuition to your workers at the end of their working day, as well as improving their sewing skills.

Spend 7,000.

 387

Tell Li Pengjian that you will only invest in training workers in skills that are useful to the factory. It is not your role to direct the education of the workers.

▶ 334

You discover that sourcing organic cotton is more expensive than you thought and email Run Rabbit with a higher price. Ku Fang calls: they would like you to appoint a workers' rep for consultation between the Union and management on pay levels. He recommends Zhu Qing. You think she will be a good source of information regarding the situation of the workers. You have dinner with Madame Wang from ZhengXing Clothing Co. You discuss the current police crackdown on illegal immigrants.

The conversation later turns to rumours of strikes in other provinces: there isn't much information in the official news, but Madame Wang is concerned about unrest spreading.

▶ 17

◀ WORLD FACTORY

Morale on the factory floor feels stronger as a result of your expressed willingness to engage with the workers. An ethical brand, Plantlife, call to say they are interested in placing an order. Unlike Garb, who are behind the ethical brand Geosync, they visit you at the factory before committing to the order. They are impressed by what they see, but they want you to reveal your labour costs.

Be honest and tell Plantlife what you pay.

 29

Tell Plantlife you pay more than you actually do: you do not want to lose the order.

▶ **200** IF accepted heating grant
▶ **201** IF declined heating grant

◀ WORLD FACTORY

You have dinner with merchandiser Gloria Yeung and neighbouring factory owner, Madame Wang. The conversation turns to rumours of strikes in other provinces: there is nothing in the official news. Your newly unionised workers form a committee for implementing the government-sponsored Rainbow Plan, for raising wages in the long term. Ethical brand, Plantlife, would like to place an order. Unlike Garb, they visit you at the factory before committing. They want you to reveal your labour costs.

Be scrupulously honest and tell Plantlife what you pay.

▶ **29**

Give Plantlife the impression you pay more than you do so that you do not lose the order; you pay at reasonable level for the industry, although still a little under a living wage.

▶ **200** IF accepted heating grant
▶ **201** IF declined heating grant

Ku Fang calls. He asks you if you have come across the Rainbow Plan for improving workers' pay. It has been brought to his attention that your factory does not have a Union, belonging to the All-China Federation of Trade Unions. It is imperative you set one up. He reassures you that you will have some say in appointing the Union committee.

Another official, Chen Jianlin, turns up the next day to monitor the first meeting. He has useful suggestions for increasing productivity.

▶ 23

Liang Qiang immediately comes to see you to say that the workers have voted unanimously for the pay to be returned at least to its previous level. The other workers selected Liang Qiang to be their spokesperson, and he wishes to represent their needs. You have other concerns on your mind. Of 15 free samples you have sewn for fast-fashion clients in recent weeks, only 2 placed an order.

Put the pay up as requested, although to start with it will have to come from your capital.

Spend 10,000.

▶ 131

Tell Liang Qiang you hear him, but your hand cannot be forced. Pay levels will go up when your revenue goes up.

 23

You invite Yan Rong, Yao Lin and Zhu Qing, along with Li Pengjian, the supervisor, into your office. They tell you that the move to piecework has divided the workforce, as it discriminates against those who are highly skilled but older and therefore a little slower. They tell you that life is precarious enough without the uncertainty each month of not knowing how much they will earn. They would like to be able to monitor the situation and meet with you again to discuss it.

Help your workers set up a legal Union under government auspices.

 413

Agree to the workers' request for regular consultation, although it will be unofficial as independent unionisation is illegal.

 97

"Who guarantees that willingness to work shall suffice to obtain work, that uprightness, industry, and thrift, are really the road to happiness? No one. He knows that every breeze that blows, every whim of his employer, every bad turn of trade may hurl him back into the fierce whirlpool from which he has temporarily saved himself. He knows that, though he may have the means of living today, it is very uncertain whether he shall tomorrow."

Friedrich Engels, The Condition of the Working Class in England, *1844*

EXPLORING THE WORLD FACTORY FURTHER

Your shift in the *World Factory* is now over. The game has stopped, but the phenomenon of *World Factory* in the real world continues relentlessly (a quick search of online wholesalers will indicate the scale of the phenomenon). For you, it is now time to count your money and your workers, and consider which garment best reflects your factory's ethos.

Options for how to continue:

- If you would like to explore *World Factory*'s scenarios like a choose-your-own-adventure book, turn to page 249 for instructions.

- If you would like to explore how to play *World Factory* in more detail, bringing you closer to the way the *World Factory* performances worked, turn to page 253 for instructions on how to play *World Factory* with a 'dealer'.

- If you would like to see what happened next in performances of *World Factory*, turn to page 285.

- If you would like to read about some of the real-world issues that lie behind the conundrums and stories on the *World Factory* cards, turn to the essays starting on page 303.

- If you have been playing in a group (whether as one factory or more), you might want to compare notes on your route through the *World Factory*, and the discussions it provoked. Below are some suggestions for discussion.

Questions relating to how you played the game that you might want to explore:

- How far were you driven by the desire to make a profit and how did this affect your decisions?

- What other kinds of motivation inspired your decisions?

- Did your decisions about what to do always reflect what you would have *liked* to do (if you didn't have financial or other constraints)?

- What frustrated or surprised you, and why?

- How many cards did you play – and did you play fast or slow, and why was that?

- What kinds of garments did you make, and what does that suggest about your factory?

- Were there any decisions that split the group and how did you resolve them?

- What was your attitude to your workers and was it consistent?

- Every seam on every garment you are wearing right now was sewn by someone. Does anyone know where, and under what conditions, the clothes they are wearing were made?

HOW TO READ MULTIPLE ROUTES

You can read *World Factory* like a choose-your-own-adventure book, by going back and reading multiple branches, taking you down different pathways. The map of card routes on page 263 will demonstrate how the routes not only diverge, but reconverge throughout the game.

This mode of reading will give you the greatest overview of the stories of the *World Factory*. However, it differs in one significant way from both the experience of the performance and the real-world situation the game sets out to imagine: in the real world, you can never go back. The relentless drive of the factory system means that there is never time to change your mind – as Shanghai factory owner Madame Wang says, you must 'Keep going forward.'

Bearing that in mind, reading in this way will nevertheless bring you in to contact with a wider range of the conundrums posed by the contemporary textile industry (specifically) and consumer capitalism (structurally). Please note that rather than always being divergent, like a decision tree (or a traditional 'Choose Your Own Adventure' book), the *World Factory* routes diverge and reconverge depending on your decisions (how they do this can be seen on the map). Sometimes a storyline will only deviate briefly and then reconverge – the effect of the decision in this case will largely have been to slow or speed up the pace of the development of your factory, often including gaining or losing capital or workers. Once you have tried a few routes, you will notice that several storylines are repeated. In fact, the game is constructed to ensure that certain key stories happen whichever route is taken (although you might be looking at different cards).

One way of reading multiple routes is to download a larger scale version of the card route map on page 263, and to use this to keep track of the route(s) that you have taken. You can then subsequently choose pathways that clearly diverge from your previous choices. As there are more than 100 million mathematically different routes through the game, it will never be possible to cover every minor variation. However, if you would like to encounter a full range of the divergent topics explored in *World Factory*, please see below some indications of routes you could follow to take you to different storylines.

Routes Through the Game

These routes are to be followed only once you have selected for yourself several other individual routes throughout the game. Although they will take you through specific storylines, they make you the external observer of a situation rather than an active participant in the ethical conundrums posed, leading to a different relationship with the cards. Rather than focusing attention on how decisions get made, this style of reading highlights a variety of challenges and consequences of *World Factory*. Keeping track of the number of workers and how much money you have as you move through the stories will give you insight into the consequences for scale/staff turnover and finances that the decisions in that particular path involve. The data regarding workers and capital is not directly described on the cards, but is nevertheless directly part of the scenario – your experience of the stories will only be partial without it.

Each route will start in similar ways, and then diverge (usually around 7–10 cards in) to explore different themes. These routes also demonstrate varying outcomes for the questions that are written into the majority of pathways; e.g. child labour; the practice of copying designs; the relationship to officials and corruption; perceptions of worker productivity in relation to payment methods. At the end almost all routes on the cards reconverge to the same story leading to the end cards.

ROUTE A: *To explore fast fashion, international outsourcing and questions of transparency:*

1 ► 2 ► 4 ► 254 ► 311 ► 11 ► 99 ► 109 ► 275 ► 53 ► 111 ► 290 ► 282 ► 281 ► 234 ► 386 ► 17 ► 17a ► 322 ► 349 ► 55 ► 55a ► 156 ► 70 ► 162 ► 89 ► 149 ► 61 ► 110 ► 239 ► 148 ► 133 ► 191 ► 296 ► 317 ► 303 ► 382 ► 338

ROUTE B: *To explore issues with sourcing organic cotton, follow the route above until CARD 17 (in italics below), then branch off:*

1 ► 2 ► 4 ► 254 ► 311 ► 11 ► 99 ► 109 ► 275 ► 53 ► 111 ► 290 ► 282 ► 281 ► 234 ► 386 ► 17 ► 49 ► 401 ► 401a ► 324 ► 324a ► 113 ► 166 ► 175 ► 168 ► 41 ► 100 ► 151 ► 102 ► 296 ► 317 ► 303 ► 384 ► 288

ROUTE C: *To explore pursuing profit, fast fashion and the Chinese market:*

1 ► 3 ► 6 ► 256 ► 314 ► 14 ► 273 ► 333 ► 284 ► 307 ► 339 ► 362 ► 138 ► 183 ► 58 ► 30 ► 144 ► 144a ► 242 ► 265 ► 62 ► 269 ► 75 ► 103 ► 95 ► 211 ► 223 ► 301 ► 319 ► 320 ► 288

ROUTE D: *To explore pursuing profit, workers' strikes, factory expansion and land grab, follow the route above until CARD 30 (in italics below), then branch off:*

1 ► 3 ► 6 ► 256 ► 314 ► 14 ► 273 ► 333 ► 284 ► 307 ► 339 ► 362 ► 138 ► 183 ► 58 ► 30 ► 30a ► 137 ► 137a ► 249 ► 38 ► 44 ► 63 ► 69 ► 210 ► 139 ► 244 ► 132 ► 143 ► 155 ► 178 ► 186 ► 199 ► 288

ROUTE E: *To explore workwear, compliance, and local outsourcing:*

1 ► 3 ► 5 ► 257 ► 10 ► 19 ► 274 ► 117 ► 159 ► 21 ► 337 ► 299 ► 304 ► 361 ► 66 ► 185 ► 404 ► 45 ► 64 ► 402 ► 118 ► 119 ► 122 ► 378 ► 296 ► 317 ► 303 ► 384 ► 288

ROUTE F: To explore attempts to improve working/living conditions, encountering issues of compliance, the challenges of supply-chain transparency and scaling-up ethical production:

1 ▶ 2 ▶ 4 ▶ 300 ▶ 13 ▶ 9 ▶ 271 ▶ 18 ▶ 410 ▶ 387 ▶ 252 ▶ 397 ▶ 94 ▶ 15 ▶ 412 ▶ 29 ▶ 201 ▶ 190 ▶ 190a ▶ 192 ▶ 196 ▶ 222 ▶ 205 ▶ 295 ▶ 246 ▶ 253 ▶ 233 ▶ 296 ▶ 340 ▶ 384 ▶ 288

ROUTE G: To explore challenges of raising workers' pay above standard levels, follow the route above until CARD 29 (in italics below), then branch off:

1 ▶ 2 ▶ 4 ▶ 300 ▶ 13 ▶ 9 ▶ 271 ▶ 18 ▶ 410 ▶ 387 ▶ 252 ▶ 397 ▶ 94 ▶ 15 ▶ 412 ▶ 29 ▶ 105 ▶ 105a ▶ 174 ▶ 153 ▶ 43 ▶ 112 ▶ 73 ▶ 79 ▶ 134 ▶ 145 ▶ 213 ▶ 296 ▶ 340 ▶ 384 ▶ 288

This list is not exhaustive – but it is designed to give a flavour of different scenarios across the game, and how particular stories reappear, modified by their different contexts. The stories on the cards are not, however, the whole story. Key to the performances of *World Factory* was the relationship between players and the dealers of the cards, played by performers. What follows will give a flavour of how that worked in the performances, as well as some indications for how playing with a dealer can enrich the game.

HOW TO PLAY WITH A DEALER

Playing with a dealer is best done with a larger group, where you can form several 'factories' (ideally in groups of between 3 and 6 players). Each factory needs their own copy of the book. Playing in this way will require you to do some initial preparation of the materials before playing the game.

Preparation

Either download from **www.nickhernbooks.co.uk/worldfactory,** *or copy the following from the book:*

- Money.

- Worker ID Cards.

- Lists of workers.

- Wild Cards.

- Worker Biography Cards.

- Sample chart for keeping track of money and workers.

In addition, you will find online:

- Further details about the scenarios on the cards and the garments you are making.

- Map of the card routes (at a larger scale for ease of reference).

You will need to as many copies of the Worker ID Cards as there are factories playing. You will need to make 4 copies of each of the money sheets per factory playing (for environmental reasons, you might want to use representative tokens instead, e.g. red and white poker chips, or raisins and peanuts). You will need to cut out the money, the Worker ID Cards, the Wild Cards and the Biography Cards.

Dealers

Before you begin, select 1 or more people to be dealers (there should be at least 1 dealer for every 3 factories). The dealers do not belong to a factory, but can work together with other dealers to deal money and workers to 1 or more factories. The dealers are responsible for dealing the money and the workers – that is, they provide the money and workers (or take them away) as specified on each card – they are not, however, responsible for what happens on the cards. The dealers can interact with the game in other ways, as specified in the following Dealer Briefing. These instructions should be provided to the dealers only. Dealers are also responsible for starting the game – and if multiple factories are playing, ensuring that they all start at the same time.

The dealer will need:

- The dealers' instructions.

- A 'bank' of money.

- Four pages of Worker ID Cards (in addition to the 24 each factory has at the start).

- Wild Cards.

- Biography Cards.

- Scissors.

- A pen.

- Paper.

- A timer.

At the start of the game, each factory should receive:

- 24 Worker ID Cards.

- 8 x 10,000 bank notes and 20 x 1,000 bank notes to make up their 100,000 in capital.

- A chart for keeping track of money and workers.

Once all the materials have been distributed and everyone is ready, the dealer should set the timer to 50 minutes and invite the players to turn to Card 1 to start playing.

Dealer Briefing

If preparing to play the game, this section is for the eyes of the dealer only. What follows is a range of possibilities, taken from the performances of *World Factory*, for how the dealer – or dealers – might interact with players. The person nominated to be the dealer can 'play' the role, taking on a persona, or simply carry out the practical tasks outlines below.

The Role of the Dealer

The dealer is a kind of cross between a croupier and a games master – the role requires you not only to manage money and workers, but to take on a kind of persona. Over the course of the game, you may change in your attitude to the game players, replicating different kinds of social relationships that are common in corporate structures. For example, you might take on the professionally friendly but distant persona of an air steward, or the slightly grumpy manner of a retail assistant. You might decide to mimic the overfriendly intimacy of an Apple Store employee, or you might take on a professional manner that makes it clear that your clients are almost beneath your notice. Your warmth or coolness (or sudden switch of attitude) bears no relation to the decisions being made by a factory in relation to the cards, although players might interpret it that way. You are not interested in the ordinary day-to-day decisions your factories are making.

Dealing the Cards

At the start of the game, the group should be allowed to take as long as they need to respond to the first question. If they ask you for advice on how to play, reply only with a slogan, or a phrase such as:

- 'It is up to you what it means to win.'

- 'It is down to you to organise your factory.'

- 'There are only ever two pathways offered at each fork in the road of the *World Factory*.'

Once play is established, you can use the slogans dotted in between the *World Factory* cards to 'advise' or 'encourage' the factories, and to put them under You will find slogans that your can use interspersed throughout the cards.

Dealing the Money

You will generally be taking money and providing it according to the instructions on the card. However, in addition to following these instructions, you might occasionally want to bribe or short-change the factories. This is best done in later parts of the game once play is established, and is a technique that is stronger when used sparingly. If caught out, you should always deny knowledge of whatever problem there is, then charmingly pay off the complainant.

It is possible that, over the course of the game, a factory will run out of money. As dealer, you can make any financial arrangement you wish with this factory. You may decide that a proportion of all future profits from the factory should come to you, or to charge extortionate interest rates. You may be generous and subsidise them unconditionally, although please be aware that unconditional lending does not reflect the real world.

Payday

After 6 minutes of game play, as dealer you may call 'Payday'. This only happens once – for the rest of the game the workers' pay comes out of running costs, unless specified otherwise on the cards.

> DEALER. Factories, your attention please. It's Payday. You do not
> have enough money to pay the workers' wages from your
> running costs this month. You will have to pay from your capital.
> *Xiexie (Pronounced 'syeh syeh' – 'thank you').*

If on CARD 1 the factory chose to lower wages, the wage bill will be 2,000 x 24 workers: 48,000.

If on CARD 1 the factory chose to sack half the workers, the wage will be 3,000 x 12 workers: 36,000.

If the factory hasn't yet decided what option to choose on CARD 1, the wage bill will be 72,000.

Corporate Hospitality

After around 12 minutes of game play, dealers may 'bribe' factories with 20,000. You may choose to single out a player to receive the cash, or give it to the factory collectively. You may slip it to them discreetly or ostentatiously count out more cash than is owed. If the factory resists receiving 'black' money, tell them it is a grant. If they ask what it is for, you might suddenly find they are busy doing something else, or respond with a slogan such as 'Time is money' or 'Work hard so your children won't have to.' Never explain, never excuse.

Wild Cards

At any point in the game after the 'corporate hospitality' stage, dealers may deploy one of the Wild Cards on pages 281–2 to intervene in the dynamic between the players, or change the speed of play.

Spring Festival

After 30 minutes of game play, dealers may call 'Spring Festival'.

Spring Festival is the annual two-week holiday for Chinese New Year, when China's 281 million migrant workers, who make up the factory workforce in the cities, will travel thousands of miles to their rural homes to meet up with family and friends. Without city registration, migrant workers cannot access health care or education for their families. Therefore, for many workers it is the only time they see their children who usually remain at home, looked after by their grandparents.

Before announcing Spring Festival, you may discreetly ask each factory for the amount of capital they currently have. You can write this up on a board, or announce the figures to the room:

> DEALER. Here are your Spring Festival accounts…

List how much capital each factory has, starting with the factory with the least and finishing with the factory with the most money (your attitude should be: the more money, the more distasteful). It is then time to announce the start of the Chinese Spring Festival:

> DEALER. Happy New Year! It is Spring Festival. All the factories are closing for two weeks and the workers are going home. If you would like to give a little cash present to your workers to see them on their way, hand it to your dealer now. *Xiexie*.

Gather the cash presents, expressing with a look or other body language your approval (or otherwise) of the amount provided by the factory. Then ask each factory to feedback on their decision as to whether to keep workers in the city for Spring Festival or to subsidise their travel home:

DEALER. Did you decide to hire a minibus to take your workers home for the Spring Festival, or did you offer the workers a bonus for staying behind in the city?

If the factory opted to hire a minibus, then ask them for 8,000 to pay the minibus driver.

If they opted to offer to pay the workers to stay, then point out that only 2 workers have decided to stay behind, costing them 4,000, so their factory has to close anyway.

Set a timer for 3 minutes, then take these book(s) from the players:

DEALER. Please make a note of what card you are on and hand me your book. You can't work, as your workers are still on holiday.

The dealers might hum a little pop tune or look at their phones to pass the time. They might flick through the book to see where the factories are at. They might gossip quietly about their factories with the other dealer. When the timer goes, hand the books back to your factories and allow them to resume play.

After Spring Festival, your attitude to your factories should become more capricious, less predictable: undermining the relationships built with each factory up until now in the game. Play is more serious now. The factories shouldn't be able to relax.

As dealer, you might want to:

- Imply that that a factory might need to worry about competition, or speed up their decision-making.

- Switch from friendly to cool. And vice versa. Arbitrarily.

- If dealers are responsible for more than 1 factory, make 1 a favourite for a bit, then switch favourites.

- Throw down money or worker cards in contempt, anger or overt boredom.

- Increase the use of slogans, e.g. 'Time is money'; 'Work hard, dream harder'; 'Uncertainty means progress'; 'Efficiency is life'.

Endgame

After 50 minutes, the timer will go off, and you must stop all players from continuing. This can be brutal. No more workers or money can be handed out or accepted.

> DEALER. Your shift as a manager in the *World Factory* is now over. Please count your money and your workers, and select a garment that best represents the ethos of your factory.

If desired, the dealer can then chair a conversation around the game play using the questions on page 248 as prompts.

WORLD FACTORY: PLAYING MATERIALS

The materials on the following pages are samples from the *World Factory* performances, reprinted here to help you create a more immersive, game-like environment for playing. All of them can be downloaded for printing or photocopying at www.nickhernbooks.co.uk/worldfactory, where you can find further materials to supplement your experience of the cards. Details of how you might use these materials can be found on page 253.

MAP OF CARD ROUTES

This map shows how all the cards in the *World Factory* game connect. Circles in grey demonstrate cards on which the decision you make will affect your route at a later point. Generally, these are scenarios that appear in every route, and may affect levels of workers and capital, as well as later cards. More than two lines emerging from a card indicates that an earlier decision will affect where you are now directed. A larger-scale version of this map can be downloaded at **www.nickhernbooks.co.uk/worldfactory**.

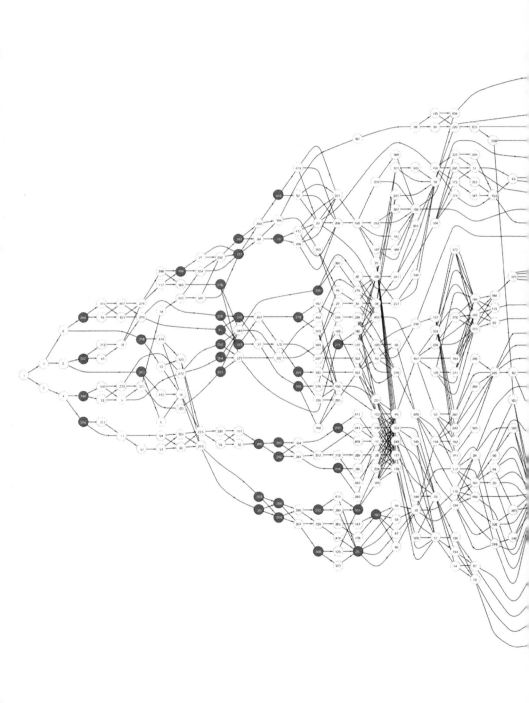

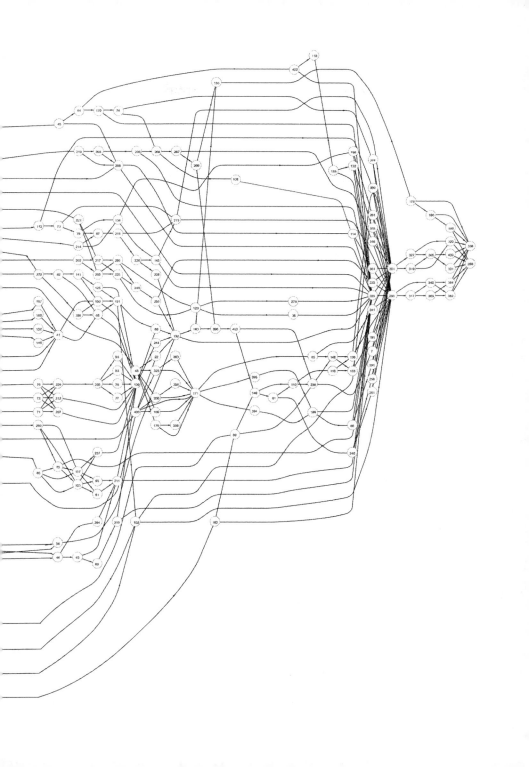

PLAYING CHART

This is a sample chart that can be used for keeping track of how much money and how many workers you have, as well as any other details you wish to note down. It is necessary for when the game is played without the paper representations of money and workers (which are reproduced on the following pages).

Card	Capital	Workers	Wage level	Garment orders	Notes
1	100,000	24	3,000		

CAPITAL

You begin the game with 100,000. This is your capital. This is the money that you have after covering the day-to-day running costs of your factory. Your starting capital is made up of 8 bank notes worth 10,000 each and 20 bank notes worth 1,000 each. *World Factory* uses an invented currency. However, the ratio between different levels of value expressed in the game are based on the real world – but without the distortions of currency fluctuation that would occur when using an actual currency.

時間就是金錢　　　　　　　　　　10,000

10,000

TEN THOUSAND

10,000　　　　　　　　Time is money, efficiency is life

時間就是金錢　　　　　　　　　　10,000

10,000

TEN THOUSAND

10,000　　　　　　　　Time is money, efficiency is life

時間就是金錢　　　　　　　　　　10,000

10,000

TEN THOUSAND

10,000　　　　　　　　Time is money, efficiency is life

WORKER ID CARDS

Each factory starts with 24 workers. Please find here sample ID cards for the first 12 workers, as they have particular significance in the game. You can find more detailed biography cards for each in the next section. You can download additional ID cards at **www.nickhernbooks.co.uk/worldfactory**, as well as lists of workers' names. These lists can be used if your factory expands such that it is impractical to engage with each worker's details individually. Thus the growth of your factory will reproduce the impression of ever greater distance from your workers.

Tian Jianying

附上照片
ATTACH PHOTO

出生日期/D.O.B.: 10/02/1987
性别/GENDER: Female
職位/POSITION: Sewing Machinist
省市/PROVINCE: Sichuan

#18000

Huang Jiao

附上照片
ATTACH PHOTO

出生日期/D.O.B.: 25/02/1993
性别/GENDER: Female
職位/POSITION: Sewing Machinist
省市/PROVINCE: Sichuan

#110000

Li Pengjian

附上照片
ATTACH PHOTO

出生日期/D.O.B.: 02/01/1975
性别/GENDER: Male
職位/POSITION: Floor Supervisor
省市/PROVINCE: Hunan

#14000

Yang Lin

附上照片
ATTACH PHOTO

出生日期/D.O.B.:
性别/GENDER: Female
職位/POSITION: Clothing Packer
省市/PROVINCE: Sichuan

#19000

Yan Rong

附上照片
ATTACH PHOTO

出生日期/D.O.B.: 03/12/1965
性別/GENDER: Male
職位/POSITION: Clothing presser
省市/PROVINCE: Sichuan

#I5000

Zhu Qing

附上照片
ATTACH PHOTO

出生日期/D.O.B.: 10/04/1985
性別/GENDER: Female
職位/POSITION: Sewing Machinist
省市/PROVINCE: Chongqing

#I7000

Liu Chengtian

附上照片
ATTACH PHOTO

出生日期/D.O.B.: 30/07/1989
性別/GENDER: Male
職位/POSITION: Pattern-Cutter
省市/PROVINCE: Chongqing

#I11000

Liang Qiang

附上照片
ATTACH PHOTO

出生日期/D.O.B.: 13/07/1989
性別/GENDER: Male
職位/POSITION: Sewing Machinist
省市/PROVINCE: Sichuan

#I3000

Yao Lin

```
附上照片
ATTACH PHOTO
```

出生日期/D.O.B.: 07/03/1960
性別/GENDER: Female
職位/POSITION: Sewing Machinist
省市/PROVINCE: Chongqing

#16000

Deng Weiqing

```
附上照片
ATTACH PHOTO
```

出生日期/D.O.B.: 20/02/1989
性別/GENDER: Female
職位/POSITION: Sewing Machinist
省市/PROVINCE: Chongqing

#11000

Yuan Bao

```
附上照片
ATTACH PHOTO
```

出生日期/D.O.B.: 25/03/1980
性別/GENDER: Female
職位/POSITION: Sewing Machinist
省市/PROVINCE: Sichuan

#112000

Lu Qingmin

```
附上照片
ATTACH PHOTO
```

出生日期/D.O.B.:
性別/GENDER: Female
職位/POSITION: Workshop Assistant
省市/PROVINCE: Chongqing

#12000

WORKER BIOGRAPHY CARDS

These cards are arranged in alphabetical order by name. Each gives a small amount of further detail about one of the workers at your factory. These biographies are fictionalised versions of interviews with workers at the Zhengxing Clothing Co. factory, in Jiading District, north of Shanghai, where the *World Factory* shirt was manufactured.

Deng Weiqing

From Chongqing; went out to the factories to work at the age of 17 after her father died. Started working in a clothing factory in Fujian, before moving to Zhenjiang, Jiangsu, where she met her husband. Her mother has taken care of the children back in Chongqing province since the youngest was a year old. When she is not working, which is 'rare', she likes to 'browse shops, sleep'.

Huang Jiao

Has worked as a machinist in 3 other factories, all in different cities. In 2011 she went to Shenzhen and worked there for less than a year, then went back to Fujian. Brother works in an electronics factory. She is keen to take charge of her own destiny, and believes strongly in self-improvement. She takes night classes whenever she does not have to do overtime.

Liang Qiang

From Bazhong, Sichuan Province. Has always worked in textiles; used to work in denim. Has links with local labour-rights organisations promoting workers' rights. Having previously worked in very large factories where there have been serious safety violations, he has chosen to work in a smaller factory where there is closer contact between management and the workers. Has a son aged 2 and a daughter aged 4. Both are looked after by his wife's parents in Hunan Province.

Li Pengjian

From Changsha, Hunan Province. Active with a local labour-rights organisation, which arranges cultural activities for workers' emancipation and self-improvement. He has worked in the industry for 24 years, in the role of factory-floor supervisor for the past five. His wife currently works in a textile factory in Jiangsu Province; his son, aged 19, works in an electronics factory in Dongguan.

Liu Chengtian

Has been a machinist, made samples, also done ironing and cutting, a bit of everything, but trained in tailoring back home and has been a pattern-cutter for 5 years here in this factory; worked before that in 4 other factories. He has cut workwear, fashion, domestic and international orders. Likes cutting menswear, jackets and coats. 'Sometimes I make samples. Sometimes there are lots of orders. Basically, if there's work, I'll do it. After all, it's a group, if there's work, we'll do it together.'

Lu Qingmin

Assists the machinists by cutting off edges, ironing collar pieces, preparing pocket flaps, etc. Has been working at this factory for 2 years. Parents work in southern China; she lives with her aunt here in the city. Likes the outdoors. She is saving money to go to night school.

Tian Jianying

Has worked at 5 other factories previously. Makes her own clothes when she has a chance. Comes from rural Sichuan; has a little boy aged three, who is looked after by her 3 back home. Her motto is 'work hard for a better life'.

Yang Lin

Parents live in Anhui, only sees them at Spring Festival; but 2 elder sisters live in the city as well, also working in garment factories. They see each other quite a lot, she can get there by bus on her day off. Her sisters work for a big textile company but has never been there as wasn't allowed in, there's about 70–80 workers there. Likes to 'watch TV, Chinese and Korean TV drama, and to go online, chat with friends. Pop music, I downloaded lots. Internet singers.'

Yan Rong

From Lishan District, Sichuan. Previously worked in Wuxi, in a larger factory with 70–80 people, which manufactured and sold their own fashion to the Chinese market. Married but with no children; his wife works in a button factory. Their parents are still alive and they send money home to support them; they see them at Spring Festival. Has he seen much change in the industry? 'Not much, it's more or less the same: don't know and can't explain. If there's work, then we work.'

Yao Lin

Has worked in the industry for 26 years. Husband is also a machinist (at another factory) and has recently been involved in strikes for better pay. Her children also now work in the city; her daughter is pregnant. She will probably give up work to look after her first grandchild back home in Chongqing Province where they can access health care, while her daughter stays in the city to work.

Yuan Bao

When she first arrived here she worked in electronics for a year. Before that worked in textiles, after graduating from school as a teenager. Prefers working in a smaller factory. In 1997 went out to work in Dongguan, Guangdong: 'They're all fashion factories, hundreds to thousands of employees.'

Zhu Qing

Has done a lot of different things, including working in an embroidery factory, telesales, running her own business selling clothes, in Baotou. Lived in Quanzhou, Fujian, where she made Nike skateboard shoes. Originally came out 16 years ago to earn money and had planned to go back home after a few years, but there's no one left back in the rural area she came from, and the land was bought up by developers.

WILD CARDS

These cards either invite players to undertake a task, or change the way decision-making works among the players. The cards can be used to speed up or slow down game-play, or to reorganise interpersonal relationships, particularly with regard to status. The aim is to provoke players to think about their assumptions around the process of making decisions. The use of these cards is completely discretionary, but it is recommended that not more than one of each type of card is handed to each factory over the course of the game, and in the case of playing with multiple factories, that no single card is used with more than two factories.

Manufacturing anomalies are often known in the retail business as 'unique design features', where you can see that the work is done by human hand rather than a machine. Such mistakes come about when workers are under pressure to complete the work fast or are inexperienced. Examine your garments for anomalies, mistakes and discrepancies.

3 people have been found dead in a containerload of fabric from North Korea, including fabric destined for your factory (you bought it from a Chinese company and did not realise it was produced there). The authorities have detained your accountant Wang Lin for taking payments in return for organising the smuggling of 'illegal economic migrants' across the border into China. You may be charged with manslaughter unless you immediately write and issue a public apology.

Property prices are rising rapidly, and developers have bought the factory complex in which your factory is housed. They want to convert it into an arts centre with a gallery and bookshop. They nevertheless want to keep the atmosphere of an industrial working space, and therefore will not close down all of the factories. Submit a claim detailing why your factory should be one of the ones that is housed in the new complex.

Write the voice-over for a video advert for your factory for foreign clients, to play over panning shots of your factory floor, whilst your machinists are hard at work. When finished, the video will be presented on your page on Chinese factory and wholesaler marketing websites such as Made-in-China.com and Alibaba.com, which reach millions of potential retail business customers globally.

905 ◀ WORLD FACTORY

Management Structure Change: Appoint a CEO. For the next 3 cards, the CEO will have the final say in each choice. The rest of the management team may advise the CEO, but the decision rests with her or him.

906 ◀ WORLD FACTORY

Management Structure Change: Nominate 2 people to act as workers' representatives. From now on they will be responsible for putting the case for the rights of your workers, while you decide on which option to take.

907 ◀ WORLD FACTORY

Management Structure Change: Appoint 2 financial advisers from amongst your team. Your current capital is all that stands between you and oblivion. The appointed advisers must advise on a financial strategy to enable your factory to survive, and devise a plan for how to attract further investment in your factory.

908 ◀ WORLD FACTORY

Management Structure Change: Devise a system for voting by secret ballot, using the paper provided in your box. For the next 3 cards, use the method of voting you have devised to make decisions.

THE RECKONING

In performances of *World Factory*, the scenario cards are played for around one hour – audiences are brought sharply out of the game at that point, to give the impression that while their 'shift' is now over, the world of the *World Factory* continues. That is, there is no 'end' to the stories explored. Having asked the audience to give back everything except their capital, the dealers invite them to count the money and choose a garment from their rail that 'best represents their factory'. The dealers then briefly leave the space, and video screens then show the dealers having a low-key, slightly exhausted cup of tea in their dressing room, highlighting the theatrical labour within the performance.

Throughout the course of the game, the *World Factory* computers produced data from the decisions made by the 16 different 'factories' playing the game. In the next part of the performance, called The Reckoning, this data was revealed to the audience in a format that was part game show, part award ceremony. Each night, the data was calculated afresh from the decisions made in the game. The next pages reproduce the script of The Reckoning, showing the data that was calculated on one particular night's performance (6th June 2015 at the Young Vic). Suspended above the *World Factory* performance space, there were 4 large video screens, 2.2 metres tall by 5.5 metres long – one screen on each side of the space. The facing screens displayed the same information as each other, in pairs.

ON SCREENS: THE RECKONING / 清算

The DEALERS *enter at 150% high-octane energy, as though it is a TV studio. The vibe is City of London, to 'Money Honey' by Lady Gaga. The* DEALERS *are now dressed in clothes 'made' over the course of the game by the 'factories'.* HEATHER *runs up onto the podium and clicks her fingers.*

BEEP [the 'BEEP' throughout this sequence is the sound of a shop barcode scanner].

VOICE-OVER (*in Chinese, then English*). 清算 / The Reckoning.

> *Music changes to electronic muzak. Total change of energy. The* DEALERS *wait, looking coolly round the room, gently bobbing a hip to the music. Surveying everyone. Subtitle comes up before* HEATHER *speaks, like the subtitle is cuing her. Ditto with* JAMIE.

JAMIE/HEATHER. Hello, *World Factory.* / 大家好，世界工廠.

HEATHER (*in Chinese, with English subtitles on screen*).
我們今天非常高興的來看一看你們這一年的收獲。

ON SCREENS: We are delighted to be back to report on your year in the life of the *World Factory*.

JAMIE (*in English, with Chinese subtitles on screen*). So the question is: what did we get up to?

ON SCREENS: 現在來看一看你們成果吧？

HEATHER (*in Chinese, with English subtitles on screen*). 你好，Lucy.

ON SCREENS: Hello, Lucy.

LUCY. *Ni hao.*

HEATHER (*in Chinese, with English subtitles on screen*). 謝謝 Lucy，　她會和我們看一看今年的數據，
而這些數據是由世界工廠的超級電腦演算而成。

ON SCREENS: Thank you. Lucy will be taking us through the statistics that we generated tonight with the help of the *World Factory* supercomputer.

JAMIE (*in English, with Chinese subtitles on screen*). Whilst Naomi will be giving us the low-down on our garments – say hi, Naomi.

ON SCREENS: Naomi 會跟大家講解一下我們所製作的衣服 — 和大家打個招呼吧 Naomi

NAOMI. Hello, everyone.

BEEP.

VOICE-OVER (*in Chinese, then English*). 選擇 / Choice.

ON SCREENS: CHOICE / 選擇

During the following sequence, NAOMI starts working her way around the tables, and comments on garments every now and then: she is the resident expert on clothing, and she's sharing with us the details of what we made tonight. Assessing the clothes that each factory has selected (two per cluster). Pick up garment off a table – comment on seam/stitch details. Find label, have a look. Comment on probable price. If workwear: 'workwear chic…' If fast fashion: comment on colour or fabric: 'Does what it needs to.' Finish with 'It's so…' She collects all the items she'll need for the demonstrations during The Reckoning, and takes them with her.

JAMIE (*in English, with Chinese subtitles on screen*). It is all about the choices you made. Some of you might ask, what choice did you really have?

ON SCREENS: 這全是因為你們所做的選擇。 你可能會問，我們真的有選擇權嗎？

HEATHER (*in Chinese, with English subtitles on screen*). 但是我們知道在世界工廠，你生存下來就是一個贏家了。和我們說一說吧 Lucy。

ON SCREENS: But as we all know in the *World Factory*, surviving is winning. Over to you, Lucy.

HEATHER *comes down off the podium.*

LUCY. So how many choices did you make, together, tonight?

LUCY *clicks her fingers. Beat.*

SCREEN 1: YOU HAVE MADE 273 DECISIONS

SCREEN 2: 16 ROUTES THROUGH THE 5 MILLION+ PATHWAYS OF THE WORLD FACTORY

LUCY. 273 decisions: each a step along a road, over 100 million possible pathways through the game. So far two-thirds of those who have entered the *World Factory* overall, not just tonight, at the first fork in the road chose to lower wages – this mirrors the current UK labour market where, in real terms, wages have got lower, thanks to a rise in temporary work and zero-hours contracts –

JAMIE (*interrupting*). Thank you, Lucy. (*Clicks his fingers.*)

BEEP.

VOICE-OVER (*in Chinese then English*). 材料 / Stuff.

ON SCREENS: STUFF / 材料

LUCY. Thank you, Jamie. Let's take a look, *World Factory*, at the number of garments you have made.

She clicks her fingers, a beat, then –

SCREEN 1: YOU HAVE MADE 337,460 GARMENTS

SCREEN 2: THIS IS EQUIVALENT TO 2,234 x THE AVERAGE WARDROBE

LUCY. Well, you made more tonight than they did last night [*or week, etc.*]. This reflects the high street, where we see an insatiable demand for new clothes. Last year, globally, 150 billion garments were manufactured. Over to you, Naomi.

NAOMI. Looking around, I see a lot of workwear, but a lot of you found yourselves however in fashion, whether you wanted it or not. Because that's where we are seeing the demand. So an item like this – (*Holding up a black skirt.*) I'd say would usually retail at £7.99 in the UK, that's about €7.99 in Europe and $7.99 in the States. It can easily be dressed up with a statement necklace, black crop top and leather ankle boots.

LUCY. Thank you, Naomi.

Which factory proved itself able to meet that demand? (*Clicks her fingers.*)

SCREEN 1: (*a graph entitled:*) WHICH FACTORY MADE THE MOST GARMENTS?

SCREEN 2: (*scrolls through all the garments that are manufactured during the performance, and details their retail price*)

LUCY. Factory O.

HEATHER *finds that factory and tells us their Chinese name.*

[*In the original game, every factory was invited to select a Chinese name 'to bring good fortune'.*]

Bigger, Faster, Cheaper, More...

NAOMI (*holding up the blue-gold chain top*). Of course, it isn't always about quantity. Sometimes it's about quality. Although, with something like this – (*Holding up the American-flag summer vest.*) it really is more about getting that volume piece out there. It'll be worn once, twice at most, so the fabric isn't too important. Thank you, Lucy.

LUCY. Let's take a look at fabric. You have used – (*Clicks her fingers.*)

SCREEN 1: YOU USED 32,700 KG OF COTTON

SCREEN 2: WHICH TOOK 654,000,000 LITRES OF WATER

LUCY. Those big numbers really are big.

NAOMI (*holding up something cotton – blue T-shirt*). Organic cotton is really in at the moment, and this looks like something someone might really love, so they're going to wear it a lot. If it's lucky, your consumer might pass it on to a charity, and 8 out of 10 times it won't get sold in the shop, it will get sold on to a textile recycling plant.

So it might go to South Asia for sorting and then get shredded down for shoddy and maybe even end up as an aid blanket!

LUCY. Thank you. (*Clicks her fingers.*)

SCREEN 1: YOU USED 66,900 KG OF SYNTHETIC FABRIC

SCREEN 2: WHICH TOOK 100,350 KG OF OIL

LUCY. Oil-based fabrics: acrylic, nylon, polyester, Lycra, Spandex, Naomi.

NAOMI. Lucy. And something like this – (*Holds up something – not workwear.*) might end up being sorted offshore in a special economic zone, like in Dubai or India and sent into East Africa, and from there it might get smuggled to southern Africa for resale... It is then on to the black market there – illegally, because the market for second-hand clothes simply wipes out the local textile industry.

LUCY. Thank you, Naomi. (*Clicks her fingers.*)

ON SCREENS: WHICH IS EQUIVALENT TO 3,010 AVERAGE CAR JOURNEYS FROM LONDON TO MANCHESTER

LUCY. Manchester: the 'northern powerhouse' where this whole journey began.

NAOMI. Classic copies like this – (*Holds up leather jacket.*) are big business at the moment for resale in Lithuania for the Russian market. But workwear – (*Holds up some workwear.*) there's not so much of a resale market for it. It's straight to landfill. Thank you, Jamie.

JAMIE *clicks his fingers.*

BEEP.

VOICE-OVER (*in Chinese, then English*). 資產 / Assets.

ON SCREENS: ASSETS / 資產

LUCY. Your workers are your greatest asset. How did you treat them? How did they fare? (*Clicks her fingers.*)

SCREEN 1:

WHICH FACTORY IMPROVED CONDITONS MOST?

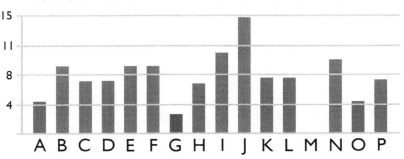

SCREEN 2: (*scrolls through the different things factories could do to improve working conditions, and how we rated them*)

LUCY. Factory J.

> HEATHER *finds factory and gestures.* LUCY *clocks which factory it is, and prioritises them later when asking for money for a workers' collective.*

> Let's take a look at the bottom of the chart. Factory M and G – where are you?

> HEATHER *finds the factories and gestures to them.*

> You really stitched your workers up there, didn't you? Didn't give a –

JAMIE. Thank you, Lucy. (*Clicks his fingers.*)

> *BEEP.*

VOICE-OVER (*in Chinese then English*). 發展 / Growth.

ON SCREENS: GROWTH / 發展

LUCY. Did you increase the size of your workforce? Did you grow? Did you choose to grow? (*Clicks her fingers.*)

ON SCREENS: (*a graph entitled:*) WHICH FACTORY EXPANDED THE MOST?

LUCY *gestures to which factories were the largest.*

LUCY. Factory H expanded the most. So how many workers did you have? (*Goes over to the factory who expanded the most; whispers to the factory.*) It's on the graph – (*Repeat how many workers they have.*) That's a big responsibility. But is it always about growth? And who helped you to grow?

JAMIE. Thank you, Lucy. (*Clicks his fingers.*)

ON SCREENS: 62% PARTNERED WITH A PARTY OFFICIAL FOR BUSINESS EFFICIENCY

DEALERS *all gesture to a screen each. A moment's pause.*

When everyone has read the screen, JAMIE *clicks his fingers.*

BEEP.

VOICE-OVER (*in Chinese then English*). 金錢 / Money.

ON SCREENS: MONEY / 金錢

HEATHER (*in Chinese, with subtitles*). Speaking of money – last but not least, the data that you may or may not have thought mattered most – Lucy.

LUCY. So let's have a look at your end-of-year profit. (*Clicks her fingers.*)

ON SCREENS: 1,482,000 END-OF-YEAR PROFIT

LUCY *reads total amount off the screen.*

JAMIE. Although that's not the whole story, is it? Some of you have more in your pockets than you've got on the books –

LUCY (*interrupting*). Okay. (*Clicks her fingers.*)

ON SCREENS: (*a graph entitled:*) WHICH FACTORY MADE THE MOST MONEY?

LUCY. Factory K.

HEATHER (*i.e. gives its Chinese name*). Factory K.

LUCY. Let's take a look at this other statistic here. You were all asked this question.

**ON SCREENS: 50% Factories that paid a regular wage /
50% Factories that moved to piecework**

LUCY. Did you work them hard? Did you? Look at that stat – this is who you are, *World Factory*, tonight. What did you pay per piece, I wonder? For a collar?

NAOMI. 20 cents.

LUCY. Cuff?

NAOMI. 15 cents.

LUCY. Button?

NAOMI. 10 cents.

LUCY. Seam?

NAOMI. 5 cents.

Flashes up briefly:

ON SCREENS: KEEP GOING FORWARD

Then follow on to:

VOICE-OVER (*in Chinese then English*). 未來 / The Future?

ON SCREENS: THE FUTURE? / 未來

VOICE-OVER. The *World Factory* is on the move again. Where will it end up?

In China, labour costs are rising, and workers are increasingly organised – in spite of government restrictions.

It is now time for your dealers to offer you four different possible futures for your factories.

You must decide which future to invest your capital in. Your dealers now have 45 seconds each to recommend a course of action. *Xiexie.*

BEEP.

NAOMI *dashes up onto the stand. She has 45 seconds to get her pitch across.*

ON SCREENS: TEXTILE-WASTE PROCESSING

NAOMI. I love fashion. And I love clothes. But how many of us have thrown away clothes because we no longer wear them? And where does it all end up? In the UK, for example, over 50% of clothing ends up in landfill. With China's burgeoning consumer culture, textile waste is a rapidly growing issue. You could change that; set up a textile-waste processing plant. Collect China's unwanted clothes.

Exploit fast fashion – don't let it exploit you!

Resell China's unwanted clothes in Africa and South Asia.

Help international relief efforts by turning them into aid blankets.

VOICE-OVER. You have 15 seconds left.

NAOMI. The potential is global: and completely unfettered by regulation. It is maximum design wow, for minimum cost!

Don't make the planet a fashion victim. Make money by making it better!

After 45 seconds, regardless of whether they have finished, they have to stop when they hear the BEEP, which also triggers the next pitch.

LUCY *dashes up onto the stand. She has 45 seconds to get her pitch across.*

ON SCREENS: SET UP A WORKERS' COLLECTIVE

LUCY. End exploitation.

Better wages!

Better conditions!

World Factory – our workers are organising!

The independent labour movement is gaining pace in China, against the most incredible odds.

It is time for us to work in a way that champions people and our planet; that protects, trains, empowers and retains your best asset – the people who make your clothes. Your factory can set up an advice centre to support each and every worker, young and old. You can set yourself up as a non-governmental organisation – link up to local groups; protect your workers' safety and their rights.

Until now, as owners, you have passed the risk on to your workers. Choose a fairtrade future and allow your workers to collectivise!

VOICE-OVER. You have 15 seconds left.

LUCY. Share your profits with them!

Hand over the keys to decision-making to the collective voice. Form alliances within and beyond China; pool your resources!

Yes this is risky – but every single future presented here involves risk. A fairtrade future is the only way to protect people and end exploitation.

WORKERS' RIGHTS ARE HUMAN RIGHTS!

After 45 seconds, regardless of whether they have finished, they have to stop when they hear the BEEP, which also triggers the next pitch.

HEATHER *dashes up onto the stand. She has 45 seconds to get her pitch across.*

ON SCREENS: RELOCATE TO AFRICA

HEATHER. Africa is the new land of dreams.

Are you fed up with the rising labour costs in China?

Are you fed up with the government interfering with all your decision-making?

Do you want to help people get jobs?

If you are, Africa is the place for you!

(*Aside.*) Forget about China selling to the US…

Set up in Africa!

Not only do many African countries welcome Chinese investment, you can also get support from the China-Africa Development Fund. Geographically it is at the heart of the world.

Africa is very close to the Europe and Middle-Eastern markets.

This means a very short supply time for garments – which can be transported in as little as a week to wherever they need to go.

And don't forget: labour costs are much lower than China. You will be able to provide work for hundreds of local people, pulling them out of poverty.

VOICE-OVER. You have 15 seconds left.

HEATHER. Just think of the potential when you can promise the retailers a turnaround from design to consumer purchase in just 7 weeks!

Most important of all, you will save time, and time is money!

After 45 seconds, regardless of whether they have finished, they have to stop when they hear the BEEP, which also triggers the next pitch.

JAMIE dashes up onto the stand. He has 45 seconds to get his pitch across.

ON SCREENS: RELOCATE TO UK

JAMIE. Come home. Bring back our *textile* industry – back where the factory system began – back where it belongs – in Britain. Great Britain.

The UK is *now* one of the cheapest *manufacturing* locations in the whole of the Western Hemisphere. Consumers increasingly want to support local industries. They want to feel a connection with their clothes.

Bringing garment factories back to Britain is a win-win situation: if we want to bring down carbon emissions, reducing the amount of clothing we import can only be a positive – it will also benefit consumers, with shorter supply times and lower transportation costs.

VOICE-OVER. You have 15 seconds left.

JAMIE. A return home would mean homegrown jobs and sustainable growth. Reducing the UK's reliance on free-trade deals, it will serve the desire of *consumers* to purchase labels that say '*Made in the UK*'.

Our bright *future* can be lit by our bright *past*. Make Britain great again!

BEEP.

VOICE-OVER. You now have 45 seconds to choose which you would like to invest your capital in. Please choose your future.

BEEP.

During this 45 seconds, the audience discuss their options for how to use the money they have left over from the game, while the DEALERS hover anxiously, waiting to see who will back 'their' future.

After 30 seconds:

VOICE-OVER. You have 15 seconds left.

BEEP.

VOICE-OVER. Please now take your capital and hand it to whichever future you would like to venture on.

BEEP.

DEALERS (*to tables nearest to them, if they don't give the cash to them immediately*). You can split your capital.

DEALERS run around collecting cash, persuading anyone who is unsure. Once all the money is collected, each DEALER takes what they have received to their console and puts it through the money-counter, to work out how much money they have got.

JAMIE. Relocation to the UK: 272,000.

HEATHER. Set up in Africa: 280,000.

LUCY. Workers' collective: 347,000.

NAOMI. Textile recycling: 982,000.

NAOMI, as the DEALER who received the most money, repeats the amount.

DEALERS wait for everyone to be finished counting the money, then read out their Future and their amount in this order: JAMIE, HEATHER, LUCY, NAOMI. The DEALER who received the most money repeats their Future and winnings.

DEALERS turn money-counters off.

Audio cuts in – the sound of applause seguing into the sound of industrial textile-waste processing.

DEALERS *bow and generally respond to the canned applause –* *but as though they were responding to a global broadcast audience* *rather than the people in the room.* JAMIE *starts to take garments* *from the floor and the rails and throw them at* NAOMI's *stand. All* DEALERS *dump clothes on* NAOMI's *stand,* NAOMI *climbs up* *amongst them.* NAOMI *judges the clothes as they pile up around* *her.* LUCY *up on platform reaches the top, just as –*

BEEP.

David Paul Jones' music, 'Hidden Seams', plays.

On the SCREENS, *film in black and white of scenes of factories,* *textile mills, trashed garments. Throughout the sequence, statistics* *are occasionally projected, the numbers reflecting live the decisions* *made that night:*

ON SCREENS: YOU USED 69,130 KG OF MIXED FIBRES

BEEP (Round One).

JAMIE (*as 'Andy'*). I think the retailers have got a lot to answer for. I think everything's done now to a price to suit the retailers. And the quality for me isn't there any more. I mean, you can get a quality piece of fabric woven in the Far East, but you'll pay through the nose for it. And you'll probably be able to get that same piece of fabric manufactured in the UK, cheaper. But then you've got the cost of having the garment made.

BEEP.

ON SCREENS: YOU MADE 1,150 COPIES

NAOMI (*as 'Jenny'*). I just think if people were conscious and saw how garments were made – like, the whole process – 'I've seen a worker working 8 hours picking cotton', and then how that's then spun and then sewn and – You know, you go to a shop and you just buy this and this and this… people just think that these clothes magically appear on clothes racks in shops. I don't know where it can go, because I think products have got so cheap that they cannot possibly get any cheaper.

BEEP.

SCREEN 1: YOU INCINERATED 0 GARMENTS

SCREEN 2: Jeremy Hunt, Conservative Party Conference Autumn 2015

LUCY. There's a pretty difficult question that we have to answer, which is essentially: are we, the British, going to be a country which is prepared to work hard in the way that the Chinese are prepared to work hard, in the way that Americans are prepared to work hard? And that is about creating a culture where work is at the heart of our success.

ON SCREENS: 57% FACTORIES THAT CONSULTED WITH THEIR WORKERS

HEATHER *improvises in Chinese, in the manner of a TV presenter. Her attitude implies: 'Everything is brilliant, the show must go on!'*

BEEP (Round Two).

JAMIE. People don't buy clothes that are going to last. They just buy them for one particular occasion. And then throw them away, which is sad for the world. Which is why we're using so much oil.

BEEP.

NAOMI. I would love to see things that are sold in the UK made in the UK – but unless there was – some kind of a government intervention or some kind of regulation which said, I don't know –

BEEP.

SCREEN 1: 56 CHILDREN WERE EMPLOYED

SCREEN 2: Liam Fox, Conservative Party Conference, 2016

LUCY. As a newly independent World Trade Organisation member outside the EU, we will continue to fight for deregulation. Adam Smith argued that it is a moral right for people to buy whatever they want from those who sell it the cheapest. It really can be win-win, it is not a zero-sum game.

ON SCREENS: YOU CONCEALED THE TRUTH 39 TIMES

BEEP.

HEATHER *improvises in Chinese in the same manner.*

BEEP (Round Three).

JAMIE. What people don't realise, polyester, viscose, it's all oil-based. If we didn't do that, if we used the natural resources, such as wool, that gets manufactured by grass, we'd be a lot more ecological.

BEEP.

ON SCREENS: YOU MADE 2,500 MILITARY UNIFORMS

NAOMI. Designers know that this stuff goes on, but we all kind of think, 'Well, we can't do anything about it,' and everybody feels that they've got no kind of choice or effect or decision, and –

BEEP.

LUCY. The global influence Britain enjoys today is largely down to our proud trading history. We were once the workshop of the world.

BEEP.

ON SCREENS: WORKERS INJURED 4

HEATHER *improvises in Chinese again.*

BEEP (Round Four).

JAMIE. People aren't aware of the history. People don't care either. If you talk about fabrics to anybody, you're talking a foreign language.

BEEP.

ON SCREENS: GARMENTS MADE 337,460

NAOMI. It's like – 'Well, I've been exposed to it, and I know about it, but I'm not choosing to do anything about it.'

BEEP.

ON SCREENS: KEEP GOING FORWARD

As the music swells, the table lights go out one by one, to blackout, apart from the film on the screens.

BEEP.

All voices rise again, intermingling, chattering, repeating sequences from earlier. The chattering resolves into the music, David Paul Jones' vocals:

Hands working hands
Breakneck speed
All these dreams
Hidden seams.

The music and video end with a turning textile-mill wheel slowing to a halt. Beat.

Receipt printers start to print receipts detailing each factory's decisions throughout the show. Lights up. Applause. DEALERS stay around to give out receipts, chat to the audience and answer questions. As well as recording the decisions made by their factory, the receipt displays the aggregate of cotton, synthetics, non-recyclable mixed fibres, and water used to produce the fabric for the garments their factory 'manufactured' in the game.

Audience members are allowed to stay in the space as long as they wish to. Meanwhile, the theatrical labour continues. Stage management start to refold and pack up the garments 'made' and handed out over the course of the evening. Sometimes audience members help out.

WORLD FACTORY: THE CONTEXT

Throughout the research for *World Factory* we have engaged with a wide variety of experts, touching on many interlinked issues. Here, we gather thoughts from a selection of those researchers, critics and thinkers, to provide some context for the situation we are exploring through the game – and to offer some thoughts as to potential alternative futures for consumption and production.

WHY WE NEED A FASHION REVOLUTION

Orsola da Castro

Clothes are our chosen skin. They are a reflection of ourselves and of what we stand for, and matching our clothing to our beliefs is a fundamental and powerful form of political self-expression. Karl Marx said that religion is the opiate of the masses. To bring this to a contemporary context, consumerism is our crack cocaine. The implication that the quantity of goods that are available to us somehow represents a form of freedom has left us with a massive debt towards the people who produce those goods – and towards the planet we inhabit.

The fashion industry directly employs a staggering number of people: at least 75 million people with more than double that indirectly dependent on the sector – an estimated 80 million in China alone. Yet fashion hasn't necessarily extended the benefits of its increasing profits to its extensive workforce in developing countries. Rather, it has continued the long-held practice of keeping workers in conditions of semi-captivity and exploitation. In the process, it has had catastrophic effects on our environment and the people who inhabit it, impoverishing rather than enriching our global culture.

To put it into context, in order to produce over 100bn garments annually, we produce 400bn square metres of cloth, 60bn of which are wasted on the cutting-room floor. And that doesn't even take into consideration accessories such as handbags, shoes, jewellery and hair clips, which are often made from dangerous and environmentally unsound materials, such as plastic and polluting metals. Further, the environmental impact of fashion extends beyond such materials and into the water supply. For example, it takes 2,720 litres of water to produce one T-shirt. Not surprisingly, the Aral Sea, which provides water for cotton irrigation in Uzbekistan, one of the world's largest cotton producers, is now almost completely dry. Furthermore, up to 20% of China's industrial water pollution comes from chemical textile waste discharge in rivers.

All of this environmental destruction adds up: the fashion industry is one of the most polluting industries in the world, right behind oil. And while it has been corrupting our environment, it has also been selling a dream of aspiration and glamour. The 'It' bag, craved as a status symbol, is in fact mass-produced by underpaid workers. They have, in turn, taken the place of skilled artisans who once made high-quality products but have since lost their livelihood. Fast fashion has been labeled a democratisation – but it is hard to see how something made in such exploitative conditions could possibly be democratic. For something to be democratic, or aspirational, it should advance everyone involved in its production, not merely function as a status symbol for its end users. Lack of transparency and the inability to trace the provenance of a garment and its raw materials make for all sorts of murky waters in between.

Where Do We Go from Here?

Yet the power of a carefully chosen, sustainably made garment has never been more relevant. We are living in a time of monumental changes and cultural shifts: the technological age of information implies that, as people, we can make our voices heard through a variety of different channels in many ways. Awareness of social and environmental issues has never been more wide-reaching. This isn't to say that saving the planet and having a social conscience are new concepts: they were alive and well last century, culminating in the 1960s 'peace and love' ethos. Fashion was a major part of that movement's aesthetic and messaging. Take the example of blue jeans: an outspoken canvas of painted and embroidered slogans and personal opinions, they were a symbol of protest, of anti-conformism, the look of a generation who wanted an end to the Vietnam War, or nuclear power. In that same era, consider the miniskirt, and how it became a shocking symbol of emancipation and freedom for young women.

But something happened as we went from the Age of Aquarius to the era of Reagan and beyond. Stupefied and spoiled by a sea of choices – of things to buy, of opportunities and stuff – we forgot about the planet for a few decades. We forgot about the people who make our clothes. The industry decamped to developing countries that offered cheap labour and the opportunity to bypass regulations that ensured decent wages, the right to unionise and the controlled disposal of waste. Lower cost and lower regulation, in turn, paved the way for fast fashion, mass-production of luxury goods and hyperconsumerism.

Today, aware of the shift in attitude of their consumers, big brands, whether high-street or high-end, are redesigning themselves to become sustainable. But instead of blazing new trails, they're following the lead of small, pioneering innovators, designers and individuals for whom doing things right has never gone out of fashion. In the process, they're exposing their own ethical inadequacies. Fashion should be about trailblazing trends, but the fashion industry as we know it is out of touch, incapable of harnessing the power and gaining the respect of a younger generation of both fashion designers and fashion consumers that are looking for a different aesthetic and different aspirations. While the fashion industry explores its future, what can consumers do to become a part of the solution? The answer is simple: they can buy garments that are made to last by people who are paid well for their work, and demand quality, not just in the products we buy, but in the lives of the people who make them.

Orsola Da Castro is the co-founder of Fashion Revolution, an organisation and project to challenge the fashion industry to become transparent and environmentally sustainable. The aim of Fashion Revolution is to create connections throughout the fashion supply chain, to tell stories and ask questions, activating designers, brands, students, garment workers, citizens, media, parliamentarians, cotton farmers and celebrities; to create a global movement for positive change, respect and honesty.

THREADING THE GLOBAL COTTON SUPPLY CHAIN

Mark Sumner

Paarth is a cotton grower in a small village near Bhuj, six hours from Ahmedabad in North West India. His family has been growing cotton for generations. During the Indian green revolution of the 1960s, cotton farmers were encouraged to use synthetic fertilisers, pesticides, herbicides and irrigation to maximise yields and profits. But after years of growing cotton like this, Paarth has decided he wants to revert to a more traditional, organic way of growing cotton; he's been told by a local cotton trader in Bhuj he could make more money by growing organic cotton. As Paarth doesn't want his children to be farmers, he wants to make as much money as possible from his small holding; he's hoping to send his daughter to university to become an engineer.

4,000 miles away in a shopping mall in the UK, an educated twenty-something needs a new vest top. She has heard somewhere that cotton, although a natural fibre, is associated with all sorts of sustainability issues mainly to do with child labour and chemical use. She believes that organic cotton is okay and doesn't have these problems, but the only organic vest top she can find costs £8. The standard cotton vest top she is looking at right now is only £2.50 and she can't decide if the extra £5.50 for organic cotton is worth it. If the shopper could see Paarth, would she be encouraged to pay the extra to help him and his family?

'If' is such a big word in the context of the cotton and fashion industry. The distance between Paarth and the consumer who wears his fibre is huge, not just in terms of distance, but also in terms of transparency and human connections.

From Production to Consumption

Most of the 22 million tonnes of cotton grown each year across the globe is used for clothing; clothing which is sold by the brands we see every day on our local high streets and on the web. But these brands do not buy a single kilogram of cotton, they don't know Paarth, and Paarth doesn't know them. Yet they are connected by his cotton through a global chain of transactions, and these brands are totally dependent on the supply of this fibre. Very few brands know who has grown the cotton they use, how it was grown, what pesticides have been used, whether there was any child labour involved, whether a fair price was paid for the cotton and whether the farmer used any slave labour to produce the cotton. Yet what most clothing brands do know is that the single biggest impact they have on the environment is associated with the materials they use in their products. Depending on where the cotton is grown, it can take up 27,000 litres of water to grow just one kilogram of cotton; that's enough cotton for just a couple of vest tops. For Paarth, that means using irrigation water that has been diverted from rivers fed by the glaciers of the Himalaya. This lack of visibility in the supply of cotton for a number of responsible brands is not through a lack of trying; many leading brands are trying to establish a connection with farmers and their production processes, but the dynamics of the cotton market, as it is currently structured, refuses to allow the connections to be established.

The cotton supply chain is complex. From Paarth's farm, the cotton could take many paths on its way to becoming a vest top in the shopping mall. Paarth will harvest his cotton in October and November, ready to sell it at the local market in January. He'll probably use an agent to collect the cotton from his farm, who will sell it on his behalf to another agent acting for a local ginner. The ginner's job is to separate the cotton fibre from the seed and bale the cotton. He will then sell the bales of cotton to a trader who will collect cotton from other ginners and farmers ready for sale to a spinner. The spinner will mix cotton from many different bales to get the best yarn at the right price for his customer, the knitting mill. At this point it is impossible to identify where Paarth's cotton is in the mix of white fibres from a multitude of farmers, traders and ginners that now makes up a 5-tonne order of cotton yarn. At the knitter, some of the yarn may be allocated to an order for white fabric for his customer, the garment maker, but the knitter doesn't know what the fabric is going to be used for. At the garment maker, the fabric is allocated to a number of product lines to make T-shirts, underwear and our vest tops. The vest tops are made, packed and shipped to the brand for a July delivery. During this process, the cotton may have travelled from Bhuj, to Coimbatore in South India, to Sri Lanka and to Vietnam before making its way to the UK via container ship and 5 weeks on the water.

Consumer Behaviour

Imagine standing in the shopping mall and asking the brand to trace back all these exchanges to identify a single farmer who grew the cotton used in the vest top that cost £2.50, cotton that was harvested nine months before, and was mixed with cotton from other farmers at the ginner and spinner, and passed through multiple hands on its way to the garment maker and on to the shipping container. Imagine the challenge of asking for this information when the hands involved in the process only know their immediate supplier and immediate customer. And imagine the challenge when these hands speak a multitude of languages. Most intriguingly, imagine trying to get this information when some of these hands don't want you to find out where the cotton came from; because if you did find out where it came from you'd find children were used to pick the cotton, or that slaves were forced to work in factories, or that toxic chemicals were used in the production processes. These are real issues those involved in sustainable cotton are faced with, and brands have spent millions to try to unpick this tangled cotton chain.

But even if they could trace the cotton used in their product to the farmer who grew it, would this help our consumer consider a more sustainable choice when shopping for clothes? Would our shopper in the mall actually pay the extra for the organic cotton, or would they just pay £2.50 because understanding sustainability is just too complicated? Even though the data from almost all the current market research on consumer attitudes to sustainable clothing suggests most of us want 'greener' clothing, the actions we see on the high street do not reflect this intention. The reality of market research is that the research measures our intention is to be green, but it does not provide an accurate measure of our actual purchasing behaviour. Analysis of the hard data of actual consumer behaviour shows consumers are more interested in the styling, colour, fit, comfort and quality of their clothes at the time of purchase than they are with how environmentally friendly the garment is or where the cotton came from. So even if we could connect Paarth with the shopper, she may simply decide that she prefers the colour and style of the cheaper vest top and buy that instead of the top made from Paarth's cotton.

Meanwhile, Paarth is still trying to find ways to earn enough money to get his children to university so they can work in the city and get away from farming cotton. He has become disheartened with growing organic cotton. It is hard work following the organic model and his yield has decreased; without the use of intensive farming techniques he is not able to grow as much cotton as he used to. The cost of irrigated water is increasing; changing weather patterns mean there is less snow in the Himalayas and therefore less water in the rivers and irrigation canals. Meanwhile, it appears that the market for sustainable cotton is faltering. Indeed, research by NGOs has found that of the annual production of 2.1 million tonnes of sustainably grown cotton (around just under 10% of total world production of cotton) less than 400,000 tonnes is actually sold as sustainable cotton. After all the effort from farmers such as Paarth, their sustainable cotton is often treated like any other conventionally grown cotton.

Paarth moans to the cotton trader in Bhuj who suggested growing organic cotton in the first place that he is not making enough money. Over a cup of chai, the trader suggests he could help Paarth for a small fee. The trader knows how to get hold of counterfeit transaction certificates that are used to trace organic cotton. He tells Paarth he could grow conventional cotton, with all the benefits of higher yields and less effort, and then sell the cotton at the organic rate by using these transaction certificates. It is illegal and does nothing to help protect the environment or reduce the impacts of cotton growing on water consumption, pesticide use and the protection of local flora and fauna. But Paarth wants his children to work in the city and not be poor cotton farmers at the end of a long and complex supply chain.

Does the way we value our clothes in the 'developed' world help farmers like Paarth resolve the dilemmas they are facing? Could, or should our shopping habits have more consequences associated with the purchase choices we make? Ultimately where does the responsibility lie for making the right choice: with the farmer, the supply chain, the brands, governments or with us, the consumers?

Dr Mark Sumner is a Lecturer in Sustainability, Retail and Fashion, in the School of Design at the University of Leeds. He used to work as the sustainability specialist for the UK's largest clothing retailer.

CLOTHING IN CIRCULATION:
The Hidden Global Trail of Second-Hand Garments

Lucy Norris

'Everyone says that the clothes come over because there's a water shortage in the West. Water is just as expensive as clothes are for these people, that's why they wear their clothes a couple of times, then throw them away. That's what everyone says, and what we always hear... I wouldn't know why else they come... who knows, maybe they just don't like washing their clothes!'

Unravel, documentary, dir. Meghna Gupta, 2012

These are the comments of low-paid women workers taking a break as they sort through mountains of imported cast-offs in a Special Economic Zone on the west coast of India. They are trying to imagine the privileged lives of Western women that they see on the Discovery Channel while picking through the unfamiliar clothing that those women discard. How can the sorters make sense of an alien value system that results in over US$4 billion worth of used clothing discarded from the world's richer nations circulating the globe annually? Their job is to slash garments to make them unwearable, and thereby prevent them from being sold for reuse in the Indian black market; India's indigenous textile industry is protected by high tariffs on imported second-hand clothing. These mutilated clothes will be downcycled into reclaimed fibres, regenerated into yarn, and woven into one-season 'shoddy' blankets, using technologies developed in Yorkshire over 200 years ago, and now embedded in India's cheap informal economy. These blankets are sold to the poor across Asia, but international charities are also major buyers, stockpiling them ready to be distributed to disaster victims worldwide.

Global Secondary Markets

Ironically, many of these garments will originally have been donated to charities in the world's richest countries, which sell them in bulk to textile recyclers. The recyclers finely hand-sort these piles of random donations into hundreds of categories and find buyers in highly networked second-hand markets. Their profits depend upon keeping the labour costs of sorting extremely low (often employing workers who are 'far from the labour market', a euphemism for immigrants and the chronically disadvantaged), and finding niche buyers for exceptionally high-value garments, such as vintage and retro styles, and collectible T-shirts. Less than one fifth of used clothing is resold within the wealthier nations in which it is collected; the bulk, around three fifths, is exported to poorer economies across the globe, where it is sold to end users via networks of local dealers. The top grades, or 'creamy layer', of nearly new, high-quality brands are sent to Eastern Europe, good-quality summer clothing is in demand in Africa, while the lowest grades are shipped to Pakistan. The remaining fifth is recycled into wiping cloths and reclaimed fibres, for example in north India.

Having started as a free 'gift', used clothing appears to magically make money for everyone along the value chain, from Western charity to petty sub-Saharan dealer, and this is often described as a 'win-win system'. However, those brokers running huge sorting operations at the beginning of the chain are able to profit far more through high volumes of cheaply obtained stock than a small dealer in a developing rural market who can't afford to invest much at a time. Her livelihood is far more vulnerable to the vagaries of quality in the unopened bale she has bought. And, of course, it is the end buyer who eventually pays for the Western charity's cut, the textile recycler's profits, the importer's fee and the local dealer's margins.

The structural inequalities of the global second-hand clothing economy mirrors those characterising the economics of global fast fashion, where, as with many global commodities, wastes are externalised and reprocessing is hidden in less developed countries, out of sight from consumers. Garment production is concentrated in low-wage economies, exported to consumers in wealthier nations, who then simply burn or bury their cast-offs as rubbish, or re-export them back to poorer countries. The effects of exporting used clothing to countries that have, or used to have, an indigenous textile industry is also highly contentious, and many developing countries have imposed high tariffs or outright bans. However, banning imports but turning a blind eye to smuggling simply increases the profits for all. Therefore many regional import/export hubs are located near to countries that have imposed protective bans on imports, in order to facilitate cross-border smuggling.

This unwillingness to fully consider the fundamental injustice of this global economic system is reflected in the environmental and target-orientated focus of current waste policies in wealthier nations. In UK policy, for example, many of the concerns expressed about post-consumer clothing are framed around reducing carbon, water and waste impacts, and improving collection rates in the light of the EU Landfill Directive's 2020 deadlines. In 2016, WRAP estimated in its *Value of Clothing* report that about 1.13 million tonnes of unwanted clothing are generated in the UK every year. About 48% are reused (70% of which are exported overseas with little or no traceability), 14% are recycled, 7% are incinerated, but 31% simply end up in landfill every year. The environmental impacts of reuse over recycling are expressed through carbon savings: for every tonne of T-shirts reused, 12 tonnes of CO2e is saved, compared with less than 1 tonne CO2e if they were recycled.

Capitalism Embraces Closed-loop Systems

Initiatives to encourage people to stop throwing clothes away have been focused on strategies to make us value our clothing for longer. Clothing sustainability experts and designers exhort us to invest in more durable, sustainable clothing, while community projects encourage the growth of clothes swapping as social events, and fashion hacktivists promote confidence in our own capacity to re-imagine and re-skill ourselves so that we can upcycle, alter and repair our clothing as radical anti-capitalist engagement. But at the same time, the emerging service economy model is capitalising on these ideas, integrating itself into previously non-marketised, thrifty practices, from providing alteration and repair services to developing profit-based exchange platforms. New business models for leasing clothing, clothing take-back schemes and clothing lending libraries are all being trialled at local levels.

However, all of these sustainable strategies are now being subsumed under a new conceptual umbrella, the 'circular economy', promoted most vocally by supranational institutions such as the Ellen MacArthur Foundation and the World Economic Forum, and adopted as a policy objective by the European Union and many national governments. Circular-economy models are explained at this level as a business-led solution to problems of resource security and global sustainability. Fostering economic growth without resource depletion is a key tenet, and their goal is to live as a global society within planetary boundaries. Waste is seen as a loss of material and technological resources; these are 'externalities' that could be profitably brought within a closed-loop system, or could instead become useful to a series of related industries, with one using the by-products of another.

With growing pressure on the availability of resources such as water, energy and chemicals required to produce both natural and synthetic oil-based fibres, fashion brands are beginning to sign up to the circular economy, and to find ways to recapture the value of pre- and post-consumer waste through investment in new technologies, such as automatic sorting and chemical-fibre recycling, to guarantee control over resources. In order to keep valuable materials in circulation and achieve their goal of 'eliminating waste', these fashion brands are now turning their attention to understanding their customers' attitudes and beliefs, in order to encourage people to return their unwanted clothing and help the company recoup these precious materials, thereby 'closing the loop'. This involves trying to understand how cultural concepts are expressed through everyday habits and routines in order to 'change mindsets'. In the terminology of the growing service economy, consumers are being framed as users, and international brands appear to see these users as weak points in emerging systems of control.

Alternative and Open Economies

Despite its solid foundations in concepts of sustainability, such as industrial symbiosis and industrial ecology, cradle-to-cradle principles, bio-mimicry and the service (performance) economy, the mainstream circular-economy model is essentially a global capitalist construct that continues to promote economic growth as a fundamental objective, and has paid little attention to issues around social justice and equality. Key questions are how emerging models of the circular economy might deal with the democratic control of resources, and at what scale these systems will operate. Alternative economic models are being developed by locally-based design activists and fashion hacktivists who work with concepts, such as open-source design and materials, transparency in supply chains, and collaborative manufacture, to experiment with different framings of value, and in particular to understand how these framings shape alternative visions of society. Critically, how will these emerging sustainable urban and regional economies interact with global capital that is so heavily invested in an unequal world?

Dr Lucy Norris is an anthropologist whose current research interests include design practice, material culture and alternative economies. She is currently Guest Professor of Design Research and Material Culture at Weißensee Kunsthochschule Berlin, Visiting Fellow at the Centre for Circular Transitions, University of the Arts, London, and Honorary Fellow at University College London. She is the author of Recycling Indian Clothing: Global Contexts of Reuse and Value (*Indiana University Press, 2010*). *Her work can be found at www.lucynorris.co.uk.*

GROWTH, THY NAME IS SUFFERING: The Workers of the Workshop of the World

Jenny Chan, Mark Selden and Ngai Pun

Outside the lab, there is no high-tech, only implementation
   of discipline.
Execution is the integration of speed, accuracy, and precision.
Value efficiency every minute, every second.
Achieve goals or the sun will no longer rise.
The devil is in the details.
Growth, thy name is suffering.

Terry Gou, CEO of Foxconn

In 2010, 18 young workers committed suicide at Taiwanese-owned Foxconn Technology group, China's largest industrial employer with 1.4 million employees. One of their main contractors, Apple, has since shifted part of its orders to other suppliers to minimise the reputational risks and intensify pressure on Foxconn, but has failed to address the fundamental problem in its supply chains. The relentless demands Apple imposes on its manufacturing subcontractors for low prices and high productivity continue to jeopardise workers' health and well-being. With a shift in manufacturing from the developed countries of North America, Europe, and East Asia to China and other developing countries, China has not only become 'the workshop of the world', but signs show that it is also becoming the epicentre of world labour unrest in the wake of privatisation, global outsourcing, and transnational manufacturing. The Foxconn suicides can be understood as an extreme form of labour protest to expose an inhumane workplace. But many more workers are standing up to defend their rights and interests in other ways. Text messaging and online group discussion services have facilitated faster organising and more face-to-face meetings in factory dormitories and other private spaces. In past years, work slowdown, strikes, riots, massive suicide threats, and lawsuits were staged among angry workers, calling for reform of enterprise-level trade unions.

China's Migrant Workers

'Birds, don't be silly, no one cares whether you're tired from flying, people only care how high you fly,' mused a nineteen-year-old migrant working girl from central China's Hubei Province. Working for Foxconn, she hoped to secure a better life for her mother and herself in Greater Shanghai. With China's accelerated economic reforms in the 1980s and 1990s, privatisation, marketisation, migration, urbanisation, and globalisation became hallmarks of Deng Xiaoping's modernisation project. High-speed growth spurred dreams of success, and in 2016, there were more than 281 million migrant workers, who travelled thousands of miles to find employment in global factories in the coastal areas and the cities, only returning once a year, for Spring Festival. Nevertheless, the Chinese state defines and registers rural migrant workers as rural citizens in perpetuity. This includes those who were born, and even have spent their entire lives, in cities. The village-allocated subsistence plot of land and the entitlement of rights to cultivate it as a birthright remain intact, arguably as a form of insurance in the event of layoffs or return to the village, but they are of little interest to most of those who were born and grew up in the coastal areas and the cities.

The children of post-Mao China have grown up with new and different hopes and expectations than their parents. Large enterprises help shape rosy dreams for working-class youth. A Foxconn recruitment slogan reads: 'There's no choosing your birth, but here you will reach your destiny. Here you need only dream, and you will soar!' A colourful poster exults, 'Pool the whole country's talent, paint splendid prospects.' A 2007 survey conducted in Beijing and other major cities found that 70% of the 4,637 rural migrant worker respondents working in manufacturing, services, and extractive and construction industries aspired to 'receive technical training,' viewing it as the key toward fulfilling their dream of rising within the system, making a career, and developing their capabilities. The contrast is clear with first-generation migrants who were born in the 1960s and described their primary concern as 'making money' before returning to the countryside.

'Hand in hand, heart to heart, Foxconn and I grow together,' reads a bright red banner above the production line. Foxconn management – facing a young cohort of workers with higher education and greater mobility – has sought new ways to motivate its workers, while imposing ever-more demanding quotas. It presents a caring image through various kinds of employee activities, such as day trips, picnics, hiking, fishing, singing contests, pop concerts, dance shows, basketball tournaments, and annual partner-matching parties on Valentine's Day. These activities have increased notably since the string of employee suicides in spring 2010. But sports and entertainment programmes aside, many workers voice frustration with boring repetitive work, long hours of compulsory overtime, and above all the inability to rise above the workshop floor through development of skills.

At Foxconn, and, of course, not only there, every second counts toward profit. Posters on the Foxconn workshop walls intone: 'Value efficiency every minute, every second.' 'Achieve goals or the sun will no longer rise.' 'The devil is in the details.' On the production line, protracted twelve-hour work days, six or seven days a week during peak seasons, break the endurance and health of even the strongest. 'I soon found a job at Foxconn,' a 22-year-old new graduate recalled, 'only to learn that what the company valued most was discipline and obedience, not the leadership and interpersonal communication skills I had acquired in college.' It is the high aspirations of the young rural migrants that make the reality of work on the assembly line at Foxconn and other factories so frustrating. Further, to cut housing costs, she and many of her co-workers 'chose' to move to the collective factory dormitory, where social space is incorporated in the production system to facilitate just-in-time production. The fulfillment of personal and familial needs in either the shared dorm room (usually 6–12 men or women) or the private rental market is very challenging for low-income workers.

Student 'Internships'

One of the biggest concerns that has emerged about Foxconn's labour practices is its 'internship' programme for teenage students. Overall, Foxconn used the labour of 150,000 student interns – 15% of its entire Chinese workforce – during the summer of 2010. It continues to hire new interns as cheap and flexible labour today. The training is supposed to be related to students' field of study and working over 8 hours a day is strictly prohibited. However, interviews with 38 interns from 8 schools revealed that local governments and Foxconn collude in evading these rules. 16-year-old Cao Wang (the names of all interviewees are aliases), who was studying textiles and fashion, was required to do nothing but tighten screws for 12 hours a day throughout her internship; Chen Hui, a 16-year-old construction student, polished iPad casings; Yu Yanying, 17, studying petro-chemistry, stuck labels on iPad boxes. From day one, students did the same jobs as workers in the factory for up to one year, but were paid less for their labour (interns remained as 'students' and were *not* entitled to government-administered social insurance as co-workers under Chinese law). In this way Foxconn saves money and gets access to a disposable labour force that could be 'sent back to the school' when peak production periods had passed.

Labour Unrest and Trade Unionisation

The right of the workforce to strike was recognised in China's constitution in 1975 and 1978, then revoked in 1982 and in subsequent constitutions. But this legislative change has not stopped workers from going on strike. In times of crisis, workers have repeatedly taken multiple forms of collective action to secure their rights and interests. Labour and social unrest has been growing, fuelled in part by a younger and better-educated cohort of migrant workers, who are less tolerant of injustice and highly motivated to demand higher wages and better benefits. In April 2014, over 40,000 workers from all departments and branches at the world's largest footwear supplier, Taiwanese-owned Yue Yuen in Dongguan, Guangdong Province, demanded the social insurance to which they are legally entitled. Halting production for 12 days, they compelled the municipal human resources and social security officials to mediate. On 1 May, senior management promised to provide insurance premiums in accordance with workers' actual wages. They refused, however, to pay the 'historical debts', that is, unpaid welfare benefits owed to employees. While striking workers frequently succeed in gaining victories at a single factory, they have faced formidable difficulties in extending successes throughout an industry or a municipality, still less in establishing worker-responsive unions.

Responding to worker actions, some local governments have created grassroots unions, each a member of the All-China Federation of Trade Unions. By December 2009, unions had been set up in 92% of the Fortune 500 companies operating in China, including the million-worker-strong Foxconn, and this trend has continued since. The official slogan of the All-China Federation of Trade Unions is, 'When there's trouble, seek the trade union.' But worker activists again and again found both official and company unions unresponsive to their plight and have turned to strikes and other protest actions. Our multi-year ethnographic research revealed no evidence that Guangdong union federation officials have restructured the Foxconn union, China's largest, to make it more accountable to workers. Public-relations responses aside, there is still no evidence of meaningful worker–management dialogue. There has, however, been growing criticism from below of Foxconn management and its control over the trade union. In September 2012, amid a factory riot (at the Taiyuan plant in Shanxi), a 21-year-old Foxconn migrant worker called on senior management and the company union to act responsibly toward workers:

> Please remember, from now on, to treat your subordinates as humans, and require that they treat their subordinates, and their subordinates, and their subordinates, as humans.

The Future?

As the backbone of the nation's industrial development, young workers today have higher expectations than the first wave of rural migrants. They aspire to develop technical skills, earn living wages, enjoy comprehensive welfare, and hold the full range of citizenship rights in the towns and cities they inhabit. 'Realise the great Chinese dream, build a harmonious society,' reads a government banner. To realise individual and national dreams, however, workers will have to secure justice and dignity, which in turn will require the institutionalisation of worker power. In globally connected production, a new generation of migrant workers could shape Chinese and world labour politics.

Here
The foam lining highlights the perfection of Apple
But not our tomorrow
The scanner repeatedly announces 'OK'
But not the 'FAIL' in our hearts
24 hours a day, the blinding lamps illuminate the iPhones
Scrambling our days and nights
Thousands of repeated movements accomplish impeccable work
Testing the limits of our painful, numb shoulders
Each screw turns diligently
But they can't turn around our future.

A Foxconn worker's poem

Adapted from 'China's Rural Migrant Workers, the State and Labour Politics, by Jenny Chan and Mark Selden, Critical Asian Studies, 46:4, 599–620 (2014), and 'Dying for an iPhone: The Lives of Chinese Workers', Jenny Chan, Ngai Pun and Mark Selden, Chinadialogue (April 2016).

WORLD FACTORY

YOU ARE NEVER SECURE:
UK Workers in the Era of 'Flexibility'

Brendan Burchell and Alex Wood

'You're never secure; you're never secure in your hours'

Interview with a UK supermarket worker

Zero-hour contracts have become a hot topic in the British media during recent years. It is argued that the declining unemployment of recent years, is in fact largely due to people accepting the low-quality jobs which have proliferated since the financial crash of 2008. For many in the UK, the precarious nature of much of this work is epitomised by so called 'zero-hours contracts'. The UK government's Department for Business, Innovation & Skills (now Department for Business, Energy & Industrial Strategy) understands 'zero-hours employment' to be employment 'in which the employer does not guarantee the individual any work, and the individual is not obliged to accept any work offered.' This implies that both employers and employees have equal and reciprocal rights. In practice, though, low-end workers with little bargaining power and few employment alternatives often have no choice but to accept the diktats of their employer. Despite working whenever their employer demands, they have no guarantee of future work, meaning their income is unpredictable and insecure.

What has propelled this issue into the headlines is the insecurity, anxiety and stress which people experience when their working time is unpredictable and determined by their employer. Yet these experiences are not only characteristic of zero-hours employment. They are actually common to other far more prevalent forms of employer-driven so-called 'flexible employment'. In fact, the Fifth European Working Conditions Survey (2012) found that in Europe, around 35% of workers reported facing changes in their work schedule and almost 20% only knew of these changes on the same day or the day before they were due to work.

The uncertainty caused by changes to the number of working hours and timing of shifts has serious consequences, especially for low-paid workers, such as those working in UK and US supermarkets. Having unpredictable hours also makes it difficult for people to take on other jobs or to study, even if they are only working part time, as they are concerned they cannot avoid potential clashes with their current job. Perhaps most concerning is how detrimental changes to hours and schedules can be for people's ability to care for their children, grandchildren and parents. In our research we heard harrowing accounts of the lengths some employees had to go to find childcare if they were offered additional shifts at short notice. Changes to schedules can therefore also damage precious family relationships and make it difficult to have a normal family life, as employees are worried that if they cannot work when they are offered several hours by their employers, then they will be offered less work over subsequent weeks. Social relationships also suffer as people are unable to commit to recreational activities, whether it's playing sport or meeting up with friends. Parents can face difficulty in planning quality time with their children, even for special occasions such as birthday parties. For spouses and partners it can be hard just finding time to see each other. Managers should not only be concerned about these issues from an ethical perspective but also from a business one. Similar experiences of job-related insecurity, stress, anxiety and depression have repeatedly been shown to reduce employee performance and productivity.

Yet at present, management has an imbalance of power which is prone to abuse – one high-profile company, it was noted, routinely dismisses staff after 12 weeks so they will not be eligible to statutory benefits. Firms that employ zero-hours workers at times of high demand often resemble 'sweatshops' in the pace of work, which creates health risks, such as repetitive strain injuries. There is not just a problem with too few hours for such workers – there can also be the problem of excessive hours in sectors like logistics. The absence of sick pay leads to workers going in to work when unwell, which increases the possibility of accidents and an exacerbation of health problems.

Zero- and short-hours contracts are becoming widespread in professional-type jobs, even including starter pilots in airline companies, and also in the public sector as an adjustment to government spending cuts. This has included social-care workers, hospital staff, and education workers. Each of these has created unfair conditions for workers: social-care workers, for example, are often only paid if they cross the threshold into a home, and are unpaid for 'doorstep' support, while teachers might work one shift in the morning and one more at the end of day, requiring them to remain at an institution for the intervening and uncompensated period of time. Workers on such contracts are often ineligible for basic rights, such as statutory sick pay and redundancy, as their hours are too few to qualify.

What Can Be Done?

There has been much talk about how zero-hours contracts might be better regulated, or even banned. But in addition to legal regulation, our research suggests that employee well-being could also be improved through a better understanding of the problems associated with flexible scheduling. Firstly, managers need to recognise how difficult flexible scheduling can be for employees. Managers generally accept their duty of care in relation to workplace hazards, such as dangerous machines, toxic chemicals, lifting heavy objects, bullying, discrimination and so on. The problems caused by flexible scheduling also need to be considered by managers as part of their duty of care towards employees, particularly vulnerable workers. Managers must also take on greater responsibility for ensuring that, as much as possible, scheduling is predictable and meets the needs of employees.

The most obvious way in which these problems can be reduced is by eliminating zero-hour contracts and other forms of flexible scheduling where possible. There are some companies where these forms of employment can easily be justified from a business perspective, but such contracts are increasingly used where the demand for labour is actually quite predictable. If more attention is paid to rostering, employees should not need to have their hours of work varied in a chaotic way from week to week. Secondly, research suggests that the involvement of employees or employee representatives in planning work schedules leads to schedules that are less disruptive to employees' lives, reducing stress and anxiety. Mitigating the misery that can be caused by insecure scheduling should be an integral part of management training. Managers who have never had unpredictable schedules imposed upon them, and who have little understanding of the lives of their employees outside the workplace, are in a poor position to make decisions about more humane scheduling. Therefore, health and safety forums, policies and procedures (such as those carried out by union health and safety reps), should be widened to include scheduling issues.

Nevertheless, until the problem of insecurity caused by such contracts is formally recognised and dealt with, Engels' characterisation of the precarity of English working conditions is likely to become as pertinent to the twenty-first century as it was to the nineteenth:

> Who guarantees that willingness to work shall suffice to obtain work, that uprightness, industry, thrift, and the rest of the virtues recommended by the bourgeoisie, are really [the working-man's] road to happiness? No one. He knows that he has something today and that it does not depend upon himself whether he shall have something tomorrow. He knows that every breeze that blows, every whim of his employer, every bad turn of trade may hurl him back into the fierce whirlpool from which he has temporarily saved himself, and in which it is hard and often impossible to keep his head above water. He knows that, though he may have the means of living today, it is very uncertain whether he shall tomorrow.

Engels, *Condition of the Working Class in England* (1845)

Dr Brendan Burchell is Reader and Head of the Department of Sociology, University of Cambridge. Dr Alex Wood is a researcher with the Oxford Internet Institute, University of Oxford. This article was adapted from: 'Beyond Zero Hours: reducing the misery of insecure hours', The British Safety Council (September 2014) and the policy research report, 'From Zero Hours to Zero Stress: Making Flexible Scheduling Work' (University of Cambridge, February 2016).

WELCOME TO THE AGE
OF IRRESPONSIBILITY

Ha-Joon Chang

It is a great time to be a top manager in the corporate world, especially in the US and Britain. Not only do they give you a good salary and handsome bonus, but they are really understanding when you fail to live up to expectations. If they want to show you the door in the middle of your term, they will give you millions of dollars, even tens of millions, in 'termination payment'. Even if you have totally screwed up, the worst that can happen is that they take away your knighthood or make you give up, say, a third of your multimillion-pound pension pot. Even better, the buck never stops at your desk. It usually stops at the lowest guy in the food chain – a rogue trader or the owner of a clothing factory in Bangladesh. Occasionally you may have to blame your main supplier, but rarely your own company, and never yourself.

Welcome to the age of irresponsibility. The largest companies today are so complex that top managers are not even expected to know fully what is really going on in them. These companies have also increasingly outsourced activities to multiple layers of subcontractors in supply chains criss-crossing the globe. Increasing complexity not only lowers the quality of decisions, as it creates an information overload, but makes it more difficult to pin down responsibilities. The multiple suicides of workers in Foxconn factories in

China have revealed Victorian labour conditions down the supply chains for the most futuristic Apple products. But the top managers of Apple escaped blame because these deaths happened in factories in another country (China) owned by a company from yet another country (Hon Hai, the Taiwanese multinational).

The problem is even more serious in the financial sector, which these days deals in assets that involve households (in the case of mortgages), companies and governments all over the world. On top of that, these financial assets are combined, sliced and diced many times over, to produce highly complicated 'derivative' products. The result is an exponential increase in complexity. Andy Haldane, executive director of financial stability at the Bank of England, once pointed out that in order to fully understand a 'Collateralised Debt Obligation Squared' or CDO2 – one of the more complicated financial derivatives – a prospective investor needs to absorb more than a billion pages of information. Given this level of complexity, financial companies have come to rely heavily on countless others – stock analysts, financial journalists, credit-rating agencies, you name it – for information and, more importantly, making judgements. This means that when something goes wrong, they can always blame others: poor people in Florida who bought houses they cannot afford; 'irresponsible' foreign governments; misleading foreign stock analysts; and, yes, incompetent credit-rating agencies.

The result is an economic system in which no one in 'responsible' positions takes any serious responsibility. The first thing we need is to modernise our sense of crime and punishment. Most of us still instinctively subscribe to the primeval notion of crime as a direct physical act – killing someone, stealing silver. But in the modern economy, with a complex division of labour, indirect non-physical acts can also seriously harm people. If misbehaving financiers and incompetent regulators cause an economic crisis, they can indirectly kill people by subjecting them to unemployment-related stress and by reducing public-health expenditure. An adequate regulatory framework would hold to account those in the financial sector who commit such 'long-distance crimes'.

More importantly, we need to simplify our economic system so that responsibilities are easier to determine. This is not to say we have to go back to the days of small workshops owned by a single capitalist: increased complexity is inevitable if we are to increase productivity. However, much of the recent rise in complexity has been designed to make money for certain people, at the cost of social productivity. Such socially unproductive complexity needs to be reduced. Financial derivatives are the most obvious examples. If we are really serious about preventing another crisis like the 2008 meltdown, we should simply ban complex financial instruments, unless they can be unambiguously shown to benefit society *in the long run*. We do this all the time with other products – think about the safety standards for food, drugs, automobiles and aeroplanes. What would result is an approval process whereby the impact of each financial instrument, concocted by 'rocket scientists' within financial firms, is assessed in terms of risks and rewards to our system as a whole in the long run, and not just in terms of short-term profits for those firms.

Indeed, by glorifying the pursuit of material self-interest by individuals and corporations, we have created a world where material enrichment absolves individuals and corporations of other responsibilities to society. In the process, we have allowed our bankers and fund managers, directly and indirectly, to destroy jobs, shut down factories, damage the environment and ruin the financial system itself in the pursuit of individual enrichment. The financial system needs to be reformed to reduce the influence of short-term shareholders so that companies can afford to pursue goals other than short-term profit maximisation. We should reward behaviour with public benefits (e.g. reducing energy consumption, investment in training), not simply through government subsidies but also by bestowing it with a higher social status.

This is not just a moral argument. It is also an appeal to enlightened self-interest. Without measures to simplify the system and recalibrate our sense of crime and punishment, the age of irresponsibility will destroy us all.

Extracted from 'In today's corporations the buck never stops. Welcome to the age of irresponsibility', (Guardian, *9 July 2013), and* 23 Things They Don't Tell You About Capitalism (*Penguin, 2011*).

HOW CAN WE MAKE THINGS BETTER?

Joe Smith and Renata Tyszczuk

'A... bee puts to shame many an architect in the construction of her cells. But what distinguishes the worst architect from the best of bees is this, that the architect raises his structure in imagination before he erects it in reality. At the end of every labour-process, we get a result that already existed in the imagination of the labourer at its commencement. He not only effects a change of form in the material on which he works, but he also realises a purpose of his own that gives the law to his modus operandi, and to which he must subordinate his will.'

Karl Marx, *Capital: A Critique of Political Economy* (1859)

When capitalist economies produce and consume things they 'realise a purpose of their own'. However, there is a well-established tendency for current discussion of economies of production and consumption to assume that the rules of the game have long been set in stone. That is: we are participating in a global race for productivity, efficiency and innovation. In its crudest expression this is a global and ceaseless pursuit of lower wages and taxes, higher productivity, cheaper processes and the generation of new products and markets. Protectionist measures tend to change the number of competitors in, rather than the rules of, this contest.

But for all the advantages of the architect over the bee, the latter doesn't need to be told about the physical limits that surround their constructions. Human builders, propelled by their active imagination, proceed as if nothing can get in their way. In the last few decades they – we – have had to learn the hard way about constraints upon the way people make and use things. Climate change, resource depletion and the loss of species and habitats, and the increasingly evident human costs of these, all introduce profound doubt. They appear to constrain the imagination. Can an entrepreneur or a factory owner – the architects of capitalism – afford such doubt if they are to be effective players?

The Future

Is it possible to imagine a future form for the factory system that is environmentally, socially and economically viable? In truth, this isn't a question: it is an obligation. In 2016, the International Monetary Fund pronounced that the world economy must decarbonise within decades. The statement assumes a far-reaching transformation of the capitalist political economy of energy, and by implication, changes in the functioning of economic, social and political systems. This was a remarkable event: a statement by a keystone institution of globalisation that imagined a future of self-imposed restraint. It is more than a footnote to observe that this was not the first of its kind. The event needs to be placed within the context of a string of fifty years of pronouncements by senior business and political figures about the unsustainability of advanced capitalism. A prominent early example was the 1972 Club of Rome's Report Limits to Growth, chaired by banker Aurelio Peccei.

Most responses to the notion of limits have resulted in a dogged pursuit of conceptual 'silver bullets', including notions such as steady state economics, sustainable development, and the circular economy. These tend to suggest that there is a magic terminological wand within reach that will allow us to carry on more or less as we are but with a good dose more efficiency. However, the Paris Agreement on climate change commits governments to do things they don't know how to do, with tools they don't yet have, in a very short space of time.

To achieve the Paris goals while satisfying our central needs and wants, the nature of what we make, how we care for it, and how long we live with stuff, let alone how much stuff we actually have, will all have to change.

This moves to centre-stage the question: 'How can we make things better?' The English industrial region that includes the Don and Derwent valleys is a powerful place to consider this. John Smedley's cotton millstarted as a water-powered mill, and is today debating how and when it should replace the mucky and inefficient oil boilers that have for decades provided heat for the buildings and production processes. The Gripple company is on the lookout for ideas that cut their bills and impacts, but also constantly casts around for product ideas that could help others do the same. These companies want to produce quality goods, and 'make things better' in both senses of the phrase. They are concerned to offer satisfying, secure work that brings out the full potential of their teams and their products. However, they, unlike Marx's account of the architect, aren't free to imagine and build their constructions unimpeded: they are constrained by wider economic and policy frameworks. Nevertheless they have both, throughout their short and long histories, been testing what is possible to imagine and do differently with factories – in other words, they both demonstrate that a factory is itself a permanent prototype.

Working with a body of factories old and new, and simultaneously studying the past, present and possible futures of those wider frameworks, has led us to some general conclusions about how every factory in the world could come to make things better. Above all, we conclude that producers, consumers and policy-makers must closely attend to, and refresh, the concept of quality. 'Quality' can mean demanding good things that are produced through good work, by consuming less but better, caring for these things more, sharing when possible, and ideally finding new lives for the material upon disposal. There are clear ecological reasons why humanity, above all its richest members, needs to significantly reduce the quantity of material goods it consumes. However, this message has seen environmentalists dismissed by many as a mournful lot, pleading for a denials and reductions that seem at odds with the dominant cultural trends of advanced capitalism.

Yet there is within easy reach an equal and opposite argument: that is that the great carbon bonfire of the twentieth century gave us a bad deal in the form of, above all, poor-quality goods and life experiences. It has fuelled junk-food consumption and associated public-health crises. It has driven the explosive growth of disposable fashion, resulting in badly paid and often hazardous jobs, and huge environmental costs. Cheap oil has stoked massive increases in car production, use and disposal, and brought into being transport systems that have locked most people into many millions of hours of unpaid labour behind the wheel of a car. The pursuit of quality can make reduction both economically and culturally viable. Hence connecting the notion of 'lifestyle' to a much fuller sense of 'quality' in goods and services can ensure that good lives don't have to cost the earth. We all inhabit the World Factory, and should not underestimate our capacity to apply it in these ways to 'purposes of our own'.

Joe Smith, Professor of Environment and Society, Department of Geography, The Open University and Dr Renata Tyszczuk, School of Architecture, University of Sheffield; this essay draws on their work with the Arts and Humanities Research Council (AHRC)-funded Stories of Change project, which explores energy and community in the past, present and future. John Smedley Ltd, Lea Mills, Derbyshire, and Gripple Ltd, Sheffield, are two of the factory partners in the Future Works strand of the project. Future Works focuses on energy transitions and industrial making (storiesofchange.ac.uk).

CREDITS

The game was conceived and designed by Zoë Svendsen and Simon Daw as part of their theatre production *World Factory*, and written by Zoë Svendsen, with Simon Daw, Brian Walters, Hilary Seaward, Kate O'Connor, Lucy Wray and Lucy Ellinson.

Editorial assistance was provided by David Isaacs, Graham Riach, Claire Wilkinson and Jack Belolli.

The game is based on research undertaken with many experts, in consultation with Zhao Chuan, Wu Meng, and Mark Sumner.

The original production of *World Factory* was created and produced by METIS in co-production with the New Wolsey Theatre, Young Vic and Company of Angels and first performed at the New Wolsey Theatre and Young Vic in 2015.

The 2016 tour of *World Factory* was produced by Artsadmin with Cat Harrison as lead producer, and was performed at Cambridge Junction, Attenborough Centre for the Contemporary Arts (Brighton) and HOME (Manchester).

In 2017 *World Factory* was commissioned and presented at Brierfield Mill, a derelict textile factory near Burnley, as part of the Super Slow Way Fabrications Festival. It was produced by Artsadmin with Cat Harrison as lead producer and Alex Legge as assistant producer.

World Factory was shortlisted for the Berlin Theatertreffen International Stückemarkt 2016.

Cast and Creative Team

(original production / tour / Brierfield Mill)

DIRECTION/DESIGN   Zoë Svendsen and Simon Daw
GAME   Zoë Svendsen, Simon Daw, Brian Walters, Hilary Seaward, Kate O'Connor, Lucy Wray and Lucy Ellinson
COLLABORATORS IN CHINA   Zhao Chuan, Wu Meng & Grass Stage
PERFORMERS   Heather Lai, Jamie Martin, Lucy Ellinson / Lucy Wray, Naomi Christie / Jennifer Lim
LIGHTING DESIGN   Guy Hoare
SOUND DESIGN   Matthias Kispert
ADDITIONAL COMPOSITION   David Paul Jones
ASSOCIATE DIRECTION   Kate O'Connor and Lucy Wray
PRODUCTION MANAGER   Tom Albu / Mike Ager / Steve Wald
TECHNICAL STAGE MANAGER   Anthony Hannah / Nick Slater / Peter Scandrett
STAGE MANAGER   Catherine Lewis / Katy Farlie / Alec Reece
COMPANY STAGE MANAGER   Lucy Wray / Hannah Moore
SOFTWARE DEVELOPMENT   Dan Williams
RESEARCH CONSULTANT   Mark Sumner
EDITORIAL ASSISTANT   David Isaacs
VIDEO PROGRAMMER   Lanz
CHOREOGRAPHIC CONSULTANT   Imogen Knight / Vicki Manderson
RELIGHTS   Chris Swain
ASSOCIATE LIGHTING DESIGNER (Brierfield)   Jeremy Duncan
COSTUME SUPERVISOR   Clio Alphas / Holly Henshaw
PR (tour)   Natalie Reiss
METIS ADMINISTRATOR   Alison Cooke
PRODUCER   Rachel Parslew for METIS / Cat Harrison for Artsadmin
ASSISTANT PRODUCER (Brierfield)   Alex Legge for Artsadmin

The 2016 tour of *World Factory* was subsidised by public funding through an Arts Council England National Lottery grant in addition to financial support from University of Cambridge Cambridge Humanities Research Grant and ESRC Impact Acceleration Account funds, Cambridge Festival of Ideas, Cambridge Junction, Attenborough Centre for the Creative Arts Brighton and HOME Manchester. The original production was created from a period of research supported by funds from the National Lottery through Arts Council England, Cambridge Humanities Research Grants Scheme, Max Planck Institute for the History of Science in Berlin and the Sino-British Fellowship Trust, as well as with the support of the New Wolsey Theatre, Ipswich; Young Vic; Company of Angels; Free Word; Centre For Chinese Contemporary Art (CFCCA); CSV Media Clubhouse, Ipswich; Birkbeck Centre for Contemporary Theatre; National Theatre Studio; Grass Stage; and the MPhil in Public Policy, Digital Humanities Network, CRASSH, Judith E Wilson Fund and the English Faculty, all University of Cambridge. BICC (the British Inter-University Chinese Centre funded by the AHRC) has supported research for events in Manchester and Shanghai. The University of Leeds provided expert advice. The digital quilt and app technology for the shirt was provided by theFusionWorks.

METIS is a Cambridge-based performing arts company/network that creates interdisciplinary performance projects created through rigorous research. A fascination with maps, space, technology, travel and history drives our work in a range of media. metisarts.co.uk

Research

World Factory was conceived and created as performance research. It is featured in *Dark Mountain Issue 8: Techne* (October 2015); *Performance Research: On Game Structures* (September 2016); *Contemporary Theatre Review: Interventions* (October 2015); and *Exeunt Magazine* (June 2015).

The Shirt

World Factory was researched by having a shirt manufactured in a Chinese factory. Part research method, part art object, The Shirt is a specifically designed consumer item, manufactured in a Chinese factory, which uses bespoke digital technology to make visible all the people and processes behind its production. The Shirt has barcodes on it, and when you put your smartphone over the barcode, using a bespoke app, it will trigger digital content that reveals the very people and processes involved in making the actual shirt in your hands. The Shirt can be purchased online through METIS.

The *World Factory* shirt was made in the Zhengxing Clothing Co. factory, in Jiading district north of Shanghai; the shirt labels were also produced in Shanghai. The workers who sewed the shirt mainly come from two areas; from Ma'anshan in Anhui province, and from around Fuzhou in Jiangxi province, which is 13–14 hours from Shanghai by train, then up to 4–5 hours by bus. The buttons on the shirt come from Jiashang. Between Shanghai and Jiashang the industrial zone of small and large-scale factories is almost continuous. The people who work at this factory come partly from the local area and partly from the mountainous area surrounding Chongching. The threads on the shirt come from Zhejiang Lishui. The fabric was woven at Jinsuo Textile Company in Zhonghan. The cotton comes from three main cotton-growing areas in China, including Xinjiang.

The Digital Quilt

Further research was undertaken using a method of 'research-in-public', consulting with experts from across the global textile industry, through informal conversation events in galleries and cafés. Online, we developed the 'digital quilt', which links the game fictions with real-world events: at the end of each performance, audiences receive receipts detailing the decisions they made with links to the online research. The Shirt app and the Digital Quilt were created with Cambridge-based design and software innovators, TheFusionWorks. digitalquilt.info

The Pattern

World Factory: The Pattern is an educational resource pack created by METIS during the research process for the show. Aimed at KS3–GCSE, it explores the global textile industry focusing particularly on the relationship between China and the UK. It provides resources for the teaching of the National Curriculum across a range of subjects including Geography, History, Business Studies and Design Technology. Its tools bring the topic of globalisation to life for students of a wide range of abilities, developed with direct input from teachers, education professionals and students. metisarts.co.uk/the-pattern

www.nickhernbooks.co.uk

facebook.com/nickhernbooks

twitter.com/nickhernbooks